Lecture Notes in Computer Science   12529

Founding Editors

Gerhard Goos
   Karlsruhe Institute of Technology, Karlsruhe, Germany
Juris Hartmanis
   Cornell University, Ithaca, NY, USA

Editorial Board Members

Elisa Bertino
   Purdue University, West Lafayette, IN, USA
Wen Gao
   Peking University, Beijing, China
Bernhard Steffen
   TU Dortmund University, Dortmund, Germany
Gerhard Woeginger
   RWTH Aachen, Aachen, Germany
Moti Yung
   Columbia University, New York, NY, USA

More information about this subseries at http://www.springer.com/series/7410

Thyla van der Merwe · Chris Mitchell ·
Maryam Mehrnezhad (Eds.)

Security
Standardisation
Research

6th International Conference, SSR 2020
London, UK, November 30 – December 1, 2020
Proceedings

 Springer

Editors
Thyla van der Merwe (iD)
Mozilla
London, UK

Maryam Mehrnezhad (iD)
School of Computing
Newcastle University
Newcastle upon Tyne, UK

Chris Mitchell (iD)
Information Security Department
Royal Holloway, University of London
Egham, UK

ISSN 0302-9743 ISSN 1611-3349 (electronic)
Lecture Notes in Computer Science
ISBN 978-3-030-64356-0 ISBN 978-3-030-64357-7 (eBook)
https://doi.org/10.1007/978-3-030-64357-7

LNCS Sublibrary: SL4 – Security and Cryptology

This Springer imprint is published by the registered company Springer Nature Switzerland AG
The registered company address is: Gewerbestrasse 11, 6330 Cham, Switzerland

Preface

The 6th Conference on Security Standardisation Research (SSR 2020) was held as an online conference during November 30 – December 1, 2020. The main purpose of this conference was to discuss the many research problems deriving from studies of existing standards, the development of revisions to existing standards, and the exploration of completely new areas of standardization. Additionally, as in previous years, SSR 2020 aimed to be a platform for exchanging knowledge between academia and industry, with the goal of improving the security of standardized systems.

Overall, there were 20 submissions to SSR 2020, of which 7 were accepted. Apart from a couple of papers rejected because they did not obey the submission instructions, all submissions were reviewed by at least three Program Committee members. The accepted papers cover a range of topics in the field of security standardization research, including analysis, evaluation, and comparison of standards and their implementations, standards development, improving existing standards, and potential future areas of standardization.

As an innovation, this year we encouraged submissions in the area of legal aspects of data protection and privacy. The focus on privacy was reflected in a number of our submissions and accepted papers. In addition to regular research papers, we also encouraged the submission of Systematization of Knowledge (SoK) papers relating to security standardization as well as Vision papers. The vision track was intended to report on work in progress or concrete ideas for work that has yet to begin. The diversity in types of submissions was well received by the authors. The set of accepted papers is made up of five research papers, one SoK paper, and one vision paper.

The SSR 2020 program included two invited keynote addresses to shed light on security standardization from both industrial and academic perspectives.

- Professor Liqun Chen, University of Surrey, UK
- Nick Sullivan, Cloudflare, USA

We would like to thank all the people who contributed to the success of SSR 2020. First, we thank the authors for submitting their work to our conference. We heartily thank the Program Committee for their careful and thorough reviews. Thanks must also go to the shepherds for their expert guidance and helpful advice on improving papers. We are grateful to all the people at Mozilla, who supported hosting SSR 2020 as a virtual conference. Finally, we thank all the attendees of SSR 2020.

October 2020
Maryam Mehrnezhad
Thyla van der Merwe
Chris Mitchell

Organization

General Chair

Thyla van der Merwe   Mozilla, UK

Program Committee Chairs

Chris Mitchell   Royal Holloway, University of London, UK
Maryam Mehrnezhad   Newcastle University, UK

Steering Committee

Liqun Chen   University of Surrey, UK
Shin'ichiro Matsuo   Georgetown University, USA
Thyla van der Merwe   Mozilla, UK
Chris Mitchell   Royal Holloway, University of London, UK
Bart Preneel   Katholieke Universiteit Leuven, Belgium

Program Committee

Steve Babbage   Vodafone, UK
Richard Barnes   Cisco, USA
Benjamin Beurdouche   Mozilla, France
Lily Lidong Chen   NIST, USA
Liqun Chen   University of Surrey, UK
Zhaohui Cheng   Olym Information Security Technology Ltd., China
Benjamin Dowling   ETH Zürich, Switzerland
Felix Günther   ETH Zürich, Switzerland
Feng Hao   University of Warwick, UK
Matt Henricksen   Huawei, Singapore
Jonathan Hoyland   Cloudflare, UK
Saqib A. Kakvi   Bergische Universität Wuppertal, Germany
Mohsin Khan   University of Helsinki, Finland
Markulf Kohlweiss   The University of Edinburgh and IOHK, UK
Stephan Krenn   AIT, Austrian Institute of Technology, Austria
Thalia Laing   HP, UK
Wanpeng Li   University of Aberdeen, UK
Catherine Meadows   Naval Research Laboratory, USA
David Naccache   ENS Paris, France
Kenny Paterson   ETH Zürich, Switzerland
Christopher Patton   Cloudflare, USA
Andrew Paverd   Microsoft Research Cambridge, UK

Gaëtan Pradel	INCERT, Luxembourg
Raphael Spreitzer	SGS Digital Trust Services GmbH, Austria
Ehsan Toreini	Durham University, UK
Christopher Wood	Cloudflare, USA
Joanne Woodage	Microsoft Research Cambridge, UK
Kazuki Yoneyama	Ibaraki University, Japan

External Reviewers

Dustin Moody	NIST, USA
Ray Perlner	NIST, USA

Contents

On the Memory Fault Resilience
of TLS 1.3

Lukas Brandstetter, Marc Fischlin[⊠], Robin Leander Schröder,
and Michael Yonli

Technische Universität Darmstadt, Darmstadt, Germany
marc.fischlin@cryptoplexity.de

Abstract. Recently, Aranha et al. (Eurocrypt 2020) as well as Fischlin and Günther (CT-RSA 2020) investigated the possibility to model
memory fault attacks like Rowhammer in security games, and to deduce
statements about the (in)security of schemes against such attacks. They
looked into the fault-resistance of signature and AEAD schemes. Here,
we extend the approach to the TLS 1.3 key exchange protocol.

Our results give a mixed picture about the fault resistance of TLS 1.3.
Full fault attacks on the handshake protocol, where the adversary can
modify the content of variables arbitrarily, render the protocol completely insecure. On the positive side we argue that differential faults,
where the adversary can flip selected memory cells, do not seem to
be harmful to key derivation in the pre-shared-key mode for the handshake. The weaker random fault attacks, where some bits in memory are
flipped randomly, still enable successful attacks against the record layer.
We therefore present a slight modification for the nonce generation in
TLS 1.3 which withstands such attacks.

Keywords: Memory faults · TLS 1.3 · Protocol · Security model

1 Introduction

The advent of Rowhammer [21], an attack enabling memory faults at run time,
not only poses threats to computer security as a whole, but also to cryptographic
protocols in particular. The applicability of fault attacks against cryptographic
primitives has been successfully demonstrated against derandomized signature
schemes like EdDSA in [25] (using Rowhammer specifically) and in [31] (with
other techniques). Yet, attacks on cryptographic primitives under memory faults
have been treated earlier, attracting a first bigger attention with the work by
Boneh et al. [6] and timely follow-up works like [4,20]. Rowhammer in this
regard is one additional technical mean to introduce faults in the cryptographic
computations, on a hardware level.

The question in how far faults in cryptographic computations influence the
security, and in particular the security models and statements, has been investigated in several aspects. The most prominent areas are hedging against bad

ⓒ Springer Nature Switzerland AG 2020
T. van der Merwe et al. (Eds.): SSR 2020, LNCS 12529, pp. 1–22, 2020.
https://doi.org/10.1007/978-3-030-64357-7_1

randomness [2], related-key security [3], and tamper resilience [15]. Recently, incited by the attacks on derandomized signature schemes, Aranha et al. [1] as well as Fischlin and Günther [13] aimed to model memory faults abstractly in security games, specifically for signature schemes and authenticated encryption. They also provide extensive overviews about other related work and discussions about limitations of the model, e.g., with respect to control-flow attacks.

While being slightly different in the details, both works [1,13] are similar in spirit. They model the signing process abstractly as a sequence of algorithmic steps and the adversary can choose to alter the content of variables between steps, depending on the type of fault attack by flipping or setting bits at chosen or random positions. The goal of the adversary is now to forge a signature with the advanced capabilities.

1.1   Fault Attacks on TLS 1.3

So far, another important cryptographic protocol suite has not undergone a more thorough treatment with respect to fault attacks and a modelling as in [1,13]: secure communication based on key exchange and channel protocols. We are especially interested in the new TLS 1.3 [28] standard, as it is, or at least, will be used to protect much of today's web traffic. Unlike its previous versions, TLS 1.3 has seen much more scrutiny of the academic cryptography community in the design process.

Despite the existence of realistic attack scenarios and improved variants of Rowhammer [26,32], resistance to memory faults was not part of the formal treatment of TLS 1.3. At least not explicitly. By this we mean that the TLS 1.3 protocol is composed of several cryptographic sub protocols, e.g., a Diffie-Hellman key exchange (possibly combined with a pre-shared-key) in the handshake protocol, or an authenticated encryption with associated data (AEAD) scheme to protect the payload on the record layer. These primitives may have been treated to some extend in the presence of fault attacks, but not in the domain of the TLS 1.3 protocol suite.

The effect of faults on AEAD schemes, for example, have been considered before. One of the most prominent attack is the *forbidden attack* on AES-GCM described by Joux [19]. This attack shows that if the nonce for AES-GCM repeats then an attacker can derive the secret authentication key and forge ciphertexts. The practicality of this attack in the context of TLS (1.2) has been demonstrated by Böck et al. [5].

The nonce-misuse problem in AEAD schemes has also lead researchers and practitioners to design robust schemes, such as AES-GCM-SIV [16–18]. Here, SIV stands for *synthetic* IV [30] and describes a method to ensure non-repeating initialization vectors. The approach is usually to apply a pseudorandom function (for an additional key or a key derived from the main key) on a given nonce, associated data, and message to derive a value IV. This value IV is then used to encrypt the message in counter mode. The value IV also serves as an authentication tag[1].

Fischlin and Günther [13] show that such SIV-AEAD schemes are not resilient against random fault attacks. In such fault attacks some bits of the nonce may flip randomly, whereas in differential faults the adversary can control where to flip bits, and in full fault attacks the adversary can overwrite the values. The reason for the vulnerability of SIV-AEAD schemes against the weak form of random faults is that such schemes still compute the same ciphertext when run on the same data, breaking confidentiality because an adversary can now see if the same message has been encrypted twice. This weakness shows the fundamental limitations of nonce-misuse-resistance for AEAD schemes: While this is a nice-to-have feature, acting as another line of defense, it is arguably looking at the wrong layer. Providing replay or reordering protection is something one would expect from a (stateful) cryptographic channel where multiple messages are transmitted and one has a notion of an order of these messages; the primary goal of AEAD schemes is to encrypt and authenticate individual messages. To draw an analogy, no one would expect a block cipher to return different values for repeating inputs, yet (probabilistic) encryption schemes should hide the fact if the same message is encrypted twice or not.

Indeed, Fischlin and Günther [13] show how to "re-randomize" the deterministic AEAD schemes withstanding differential faults for all variables. Their solution is to prepend a random message block before calling the SIV-AEAD scheme. One can think of this solution as a compound nonce consisting of the SIV and the random value. This, nonetheless, works once more on the AEAD layer and does not also ensure unique nonces on the channel level.

1.2   Our Contribution

Our goal here is to tackle fault attacks on the TLS 1.3 protocol. We do not aim to give a comprehensive analysis for the compound handshake and record layer protocol as secure connection under fault attacks, since such proofs turn out to be very tedious even in the standard attack model without faults. Another reason is that we can often show that fault attacks are easy to execute and it suffices to expose insecurity even in an intuitive sense. Nonetheless, we argue that some attack strategies cannot lead to a break, or how one could adapt the protocol to harden against some attacks.

Record Layer. We start with the record layer: Can we ensure that nonces passed from the calling channel protocol to the AEAD scheme are unique? If we can guarantee this then, together with a fault-resilient AEAD scheme, we should get advanced security guarantees for the entire record layer. We consider this question with a strong focus on the TLS 1.3 protocol.

---

[1] The terms IV and nonce are often used interchangeably in the literature. In the context of TLS 1.3 we usually adopt the approach to let the nonce be derived from the IV value *write_iv* together with the sequence number.

We first discuss that channel protocols where the sending party only increments a sequence counter to ensure nonce uniqueness are doomed to fail against memory faults. That is, we argue that being able to introduce random faults enables the adversary to drop ciphertexts on the channel without the receiver noticing. In case of AES-GCM the forbidden attack even allows the adversary to forge new ciphertexts.

Observing that a pure sequence counter is insufficient we introduce the rolling IV method as a countermeasure, and especially how to embed it in the TLS 1.3 record layer. Recall that in this protocol the sending party holds a random $write\_iv$ value and the key, called $application\_traffic\_secret$. In addition, the sender holds a sequence counter seqno which is initialized with 0 and incremented with each transmission. The nonce for the AEAD scheme is computed as $write\_iv \oplus 0..0\|$seqno.

Clearly, the way TLS 1.3 computes the nonce succumbs to our general attack above, independently of the resistance of the AEAD scheme, i.e., even if a nonce-misuse-resistant scheme or a fault-resistant scheme is used. We therefore use the HKDF.Expand pseudorandom function, used in several places in the TLS 1.3 protocol, to update the IV value, too. That is, we let IV$\|$prenonce $\leftarrow$ HKDF.Expand(IV, "next nonce") and then derive the nonce value as nonce $\leftarrow$ prenonce $\oplus 0..0\|$seqno as before.

We show that the above approach yields a collision resistant nonce generation under differential faults. Some care must be taken with concrete parameter choices, though, because iterating the IV computation needs to take the birthday bound into account. We discuss this in more detail in the technical part.

Handshake Protocol. We also look into the fault resistance of the handshake protocol of TLS 1.3. We show that the protocol is completely insecure against full fault attacks where the adversary can overwrite memory arbitrarily. This should not be surprising because such attacks are very powerful.

We give some positive result for the pre-shared-key mode where the parties compute the session keys from a shared key PSK (and potentially adding a Diffie-Hellman step). According to the protocol one computes the early secret as $ES \leftarrow$ HKDF.Extract$(0, PSK)$. We show that differential fault attacks still yield randomly distributed early secrets assuming related-key security of the HKDF.Extract function.

In summary, our findings do not allow an ultimate statement about the security or insecurity of the TLS 1.3 protocols against memory fault attacks. Some attacks work, and this may not be expected in light of the strength of, say, full fault attacks. Yet, we also argue that some strategies are less promising. The latter also points to general countermeasures to impede such attacks.

2   Transport Layer Security

2.1   TLS 1.3 Handshake

The TLS 1.3 handshake protocol comes in three variants: Diffie-Hellman only ((EC)DHE), pre-shared key mode (PSK), or a combination of the two modes

(PSK+(EC)DHE). All three protocols share the common structure displayed in Fig. 1 where we use the presentation in [9,10]. The protocols differ only in the way how the (combination of the) two keys, the Diffie-Hellman key and the pre-shared secret, enter key derivation.

The client starts with the ClientHello message including a nonce r_c and for the DH mode also a key share g^x, and specifies identifiers for shared keys via the PreSharedKey message. We note that each PSK identity is accompanied by a *binder* value which is an HMAC over the binder key and the client hello and the list of identities (without the binder values); this step is omitted in the figure. Already at this point, if using a pre-shared key mode, the client may compute the early secret ES and derive further early keys. The server responds with the ServerHello message with a nonce r_s, the choice of key identifier in PreSharedKey and/or its Diffie-Hellman share g^y. The server can derive keys via HKDF on the pre-shared key PSK and/or the Diffie-Hellman value and the transcript hashes. The server may also include a certificate and a signature in CertificateVerify. The server also computes a finished message Finished which is an HMAC over the derived keys and the transcript hash. Upon receiving the server data, the client computes the keys, checks the HMAC value, and sends its finished message Finished. The client may also authenticate via a certificate-based signature, albeit this is seldomly used in classical applications like securing web communication.

Both parties once more use HKDF and transcript hashes to derive the shared session keys from the master secret MS. In particular, the client holds the *client_application_traffic_secret* secret for sending messages (abbreviated $CATS$ below) and the server holds *server_application_traffic_secret* (abbreviated $SATS$ below).

2.2   TLS 1.3 Record Layer

The record layer protection in TLS 1.3 is exclusively done with an authenticated encryption scheme with associated data [29]. For this the sending party derives a record layer key and an IV from its secret $CATS$ resp. $SATS$. This is again done via HKDF.Expand by

$$client\_write\_key \leftarrow \mathsf{HKDF.Expand}(CATS, \texttt{"key"}, \texttt{""}, key\_length),$$
$$client\_write\_iv \leftarrow \mathsf{HKDF.Expand}(CATS, \texttt{"iv"}, \texttt{""}, iv\_length)$$

and analogously for the server for *server_write_key* and *server_write_iv*. In addition, both parties initialize a number *client_seq_no* resp. *server_seq_no* of 64 bits with 0.

To protect of the payload via the AEAD scheme, the AEAD scheme expects a key key, a nonce N, associated data A, and the message m. The key for TLS is the client or server *write_key*, the associated data is the TLS record header, and the payload is given by the data to be sent. The nonce N is derived by adding the sequence number *seq_no* to the *write_iv* value, padded with 0-bits from the left. The ciphertext is then given as $C \leftarrow \mathsf{AEAD.Enc}(write\_key, N, A, m)$. Decryption on the other side is performed via $m \leftarrow$ AEAD.Dec($write\_key, N, A, C$), where the associated data is taken from the record header.

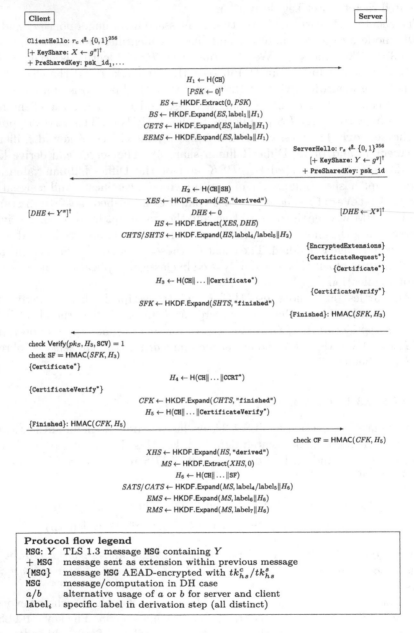

Fig. 1. The TLS 1.3 (EC)DHE/PSK/PSK+(EC)DHE handshake protocol.

3   Fault Attacks Against the TLS 1.3 Record Layer

We first argue that the TLS 1.3 record layer is not fault resistant against attacks aiming at the sequence counter. Similar attacks when nonces are reused have been described on earlier TLS versions. They are usually known under the term *forbidden attack* [19]. For example, Böck et al. [5] intercept HTTPS connection data and wait for a nonce reuse in the underlying AEAD scheme, say, caused by a bad pseudorandom number generator. In TLS 1.3 nonces are supposed to be unique because the protocol increments the sequence number with each cipher-text (and updates the keys or terminates the connection before a wrap-around would occur). This is where we use the possibility to fault the sequence number. We emphasize that our attack is on the channel layer and works independently of the strength of the AEAD scheme.

3.1   Outline of the Attack

We first present the general attack strategy against counter-based channel pro-tocols in Fig. 2. The idea is to reset the sequence number of the sender via a differential fault to obtain another ciphertext for the same nonce value. This either leads to an attack where the adversary can drop parts of the communi-cation, without the receiver noticing. This clearly violates security of a channel protocol and is independent of the question if the AEAD scheme is vulnera-ble against nonce misuse attacks or not. We also discuss below that for some of the AEAD schemes specified by TLS 1.3 such a second ciphertext with a reset sequence number allows not only to supress ciphertexts but to forge other ciphertexts.

We note that the attack may still work if one faults the sequence counter randomly. In the most simple case we can hope to flip the last bit from 1 to 0 in the counter to match the previous value again, applying the general attack as before. Otherwise we need to guess the number of ciphertexts till the random flips let the counter value appear again and suppress all ciphertexts in between. The success probability is of course lower than in the full-fault case. For the forbidden attack against AES-GCM we only need to find two ciphertexts created with the same nonce due to random faults. Because the used sequence numbers are not transmitted as part of the ciphertext in TLS 1.3, we may then need to try pairs of ciphertexts in order to recover the necessary authentication information.

Remarkably, TLS 1.3 may even be susceptible to fault attacks if the par-ties would try to prevent counter resets by updating the channel key via the KeyUpdate sub protocol *each time after having transmitted a single message*. This KeyUpdate step would renew the key, the IV value, and reset the sequence number to 0. However, the update request itself is also sent through the record layer protection, such that the attack (with C_2 being the update request) applies again. Only this time, the sender would expect some KeyUpdate response before continuing with the fresh key. Hence, this attack only works if we can forge a new ciphertext $\tilde{C}_3$ by recovering the authentication key of the AEAD scheme (as, for example, in AES-GCM).

Sender	Advrsry	Receiver
IV, key		IV, key
seqno ← 0		seqno ← 0

// message m_1 with associated data A_1

$C_1 \leftarrow$ AEAD.Enc(key, IV ⊕ $\underset{=0}{\text{seqno}}$, A_1, m_1) $\xrightarrow{\quad C_1 \quad}$ relay $\xrightarrow{\quad C_1 \quad}$

| seqno ← seqno + 1 | | seqno ← seqno + 1 |
| seqno ← 0 ⚡ | | |

// message m_2 with associated data A_2

$C_2 \leftarrow$ AEAD.Enc(key, IV ⊕ $\underset{=0}{\text{seqno}}$, A_2, m_2) $\xrightarrow{\quad C_2 \quad}$ drop

seqno ← seqno + 1

// message m_3 with associated data A_3

$C_3 \leftarrow$ AEAD.Enc(key, IV ⊕ $\underset{=1}{\text{seqno}}$, A_3, m_3) $\xrightarrow{\quad C_3 \quad}$ relay C_3 or forge $\tilde{C}_3$ $\xrightarrow{\quad C_3/\tilde{C}_3 \quad}$

Fig. 2. Overview over attack flow. Note that the attack where the adversary only drops C_2 cannot be prevented if one can fault the sequence counter. If we assume that creating two ciphertexts with the same sequence number allows to forge ciphertexts, then the adversary can even inject its own ciphertext $\tilde{C}_3$. Details are discussed in the text.

3.2 Attacks on the Symmetric Cipher Suites

TLS 1.3 defines the following cipher suites for encryption on the record layer: AES-GCM [12], AES-CCM [11] and ChaCha20-Poly1305 [33]. We briefly discuss, and to a large extend recall from previous work, that one can mount attacks against AES-GCM and ChaCha20-Poly1305, which allow us to forge tags by faulting a counter. These attacks recover a secret which is used during the generation of the tag and can be used to generate tags for arbitrary messages. The attack on AES-GCM allows us to recover a secret which can be used to tamper with messages until a re-keying occurs or the session ends. Our attack on ChaCha20-Poly1305 only allows us to recover a secret which can be used to tamper with the current message.

AES-CCM combines a CBC-MAC with a counter-based encryption [11], xoring the output of AES applied to the nonce and a block counter to the plaintext blocks. The mode is also known to show weaknesses under fault attacks [8] but this primarily concerns the confidentiality. We are not aware of fault attacks against integrity, similar to the attacks against the other schemes. Indeed, recovering the authentication key for AES-CCM would require a key-recovery fault attack on AES.

Fault Attack on AES-GCM. On a high level, AES-GCM may be subdivided into one algorithm concerned with encrypting the plaintext and another algorithm concerned with generating a MAC. The encryption algorithm relies on counter mode which encrypts counter blocks to generate a key stream. This keystream is then XORed with the plaintext. The encryption of AES-GCM starts with the second counter block since the first counter block is used for the generation of the tag [12]. A tag is generated by applying GHASH with its hash subkey H on the data that ought to be authenticated and then encrypting the output in counter mode with the first counter block [12]. It should be noted that GHASH on its own is not a secure cryptographic hashing function [12]. Knowing its image together with the ciphertext and the associated data is sufficient to mount an attack. This has been demonstrated by the forbidden attack [5].

There are some parallels between the forbidden attack and this attack, however while the forbidden attack relies on nonce reuse in order to decrypt a tag, we break the encryption by faulting the counter. Faulting the least significant bit of the second counter block results in the first plaintext block and GHASH image being encrypting with the same counter block. Knowing the first plaintext block thus allows us to recover the plaintext tag value and apply a root finding algorithm to recover the hash subkey H.

Fault Attack on ChaCha20-Poly1305. ChaCha20-Poly1305 combines the procedures ChaCha20 for encryption and Poly1305 for authentication [33]. Here, ChaCha20 is a stream cipher and generates blocks of keystreams, which are XORed with the data in order to encrypt it [33]. The encryption algorithm requires a key, a counter, a nonce, and the plaintext [33]. Poly1305 requires a message and a one time key in order to generate a tag [33]. In the case of ChaCha20-Poly1305 as used by TLS 1.3 the one time key are the first 32 keystream bytes of ChaCha20 with the counter value of 0 [28,33]. The first plaintext block however, is encrypted with a counter value of 1 [33]. We can forge a tag by faulting the counter for the encryption to 0 and obtaining the first 32 keystream bytes. This scenario is very similar to our previous one with the exception that the nonce is used to generate Poly1305 one time key. As a result, only the current message can be tampered with the obtained one time key.

Mitigating the Attacks. The attacks above affect the TLS 1.3 standard but are based on AEAD primitives defined outside of the RFC. As such, a mitigation on the AEAD level will leave the TLS standard untouched while requiring modifications of other standards. On the positive side we note that the usage of the AEAD scheme within the TLS 1.3 protocol adds some additional obstacles to our attacks: Violating the protocol may result in the end of the session, in which case our recovered secrets become useless.

4   Rolling IVs: Immunizing TLS 1.3 Record Layer

In this section we present a method to prevent the adversary from creating two identical nonces in the record layer protocol when faulting the memory. We note that Patton and Shrimpton [23] in their analysis of the TLS 1.3 channel protocol have already considered abstract nonce generation algorithms, but not in the memory fault model.

4.1 Security Definition

We focus here on the adversary's (in)ability to make the channel protocol insert the same nonce twice into the AEAD scheme. If we can prevent this, even in presence of faults, it follows that the AEAD scheme should provide the desired security if only called for distinct nonces. In particular, we investigate only the part about creating nonces, omitting the security of the channel protocol as a whole.

We consider an abstract game between the nonce generation part of the record layer and the memory-faulting adversary. Following [13] we mark variables x which can be faulted as $\llcorner x \lrcorner$, and when accessing a variable during the execution we write $\langle x \rangle$ to denote the fact that we run a callback with the adversary, where the adversary can decide to replace the value by some value (full faults, written $\langle x \rangle_{\text{full}}$), add an offset Δ bit-wise (differential faults, written $\langle x \rangle_\Delta$), flip at most N bits at random bit positions (random faults, written $\langle x \rangle_\$$), or leave the value unchanged (no faults). We do not consider bit-setting attacks as in [1] here. In all cases the adversary does not learn the actual value x but can only influence the content. Unless mentioned otherwise we also assume that memory faults are persistent, meaning that any changes by memory faults leave the variable in that state (unless the algorithm itself changes the value).

For an execution of algorithm A which accesses a faultable variable x multiple times, we denote by x_A all the different values occurring in the execution in correct order. This also includes the initial value if the variable (resp. its value) before it is modified. We usually write $x_A[1]$ for the first value in this vector, $x_A[2]$ the second value etc.

In the abstract nonce-misuse game between an adversary $\mathcal{A}$ and an update algorithm we assume that nonces are generated from an initial random value IV, corresponding to the *write_iv* value in TLS 1.3, and a deterministic value seqno initialized to some constant seqno_0, corresponding to the 0-initialized counter value in TLS 1.3. The deterministic algorithm nextNonce outputs a nonce nonce and also updates IV, seqno. The adversary can call all algorithms and fault their variables, but this is specified on an algorithmic level not for the abstract security game. The goal of the adversary is to generate colliding nonces in some of the calls.

Definition 1 (Nonce-Misuse Fault Resistance). *For a nonce-generation algorithm* nextNonce *define its nonce-misuse fault-resistance against algorithm* $\mathcal{A}$ *as*

$$\text{Adv}^{\text{FRNonceMu}}_{\text{nextNonce},\mathcal{A}} := \text{Prob}\left[\textbf{Exp}^{\text{FRNonceMu}}_{\text{nextNonce},\mathcal{A}}\right]$$

for the experiment in Fig. 3.

We note that the TLS 1.3 nonce generation is not secure against random fault attacks according to the above security game. For this the adversary calls

$\mathbf{Exp}_{\mathsf{NextNonce},\mathcal{A}}^{\mathsf{FRNonceMu}}$	ONextNonce()
1 : win $\leftarrow$ **false**	1 : $(\mathsf{IV}, \mathsf{seqno}, \mathsf{nonce}) \leftarrow \mathsf{nextNonce}(\mathsf{IV}, \mathsf{seqno})$
2 : $\mathcal{N} \leftarrow \emptyset$	2 : **if** nonce $\in \mathcal{N}$ **then** win $\leftarrow$ **true**
3 : IV $\xleftarrow{\$} \{0,1\}^{\mathtt{IV\_length}}$	3 : $\mathcal{N} \leftarrow \mathcal{N} \cup \{\mathsf{nonce}\}$
4 : seqno $\leftarrow$ seqno$_0$	4 : **return** nonce
5 : $\mathcal{A}^{\mathsf{ONextNonce}()}()$
6 :   **return** win

Fig. 3. Security of nonce updating algorithm

nextNonce(IV, seqno)
---
1 : $/\!/$ NxtNnc_length=IV_length+prenonce_length
2 : $\llcorner\mathsf{IV}\lrcorner\|\llcorner\mathsf{prenonce}\lrcorner \leftarrow \mathsf{HKDF.Expand}(\langle\mathsf{IV}\rangle_\Delta, \texttt{"next nonce"}, \mathtt{NxtNnc\_length})$
3 : $\llcorner\mathsf{nonce}\lrcorner \leftarrow \langle\mathsf{prenonce}\rangle_\Delta \oplus 0..0\|\langle\mathsf{seqno}\rangle_{\mathrm{full}}$
4 : $\llcorner\mathsf{seqno}\lrcorner \leftarrow \langle\mathsf{seqno}\rangle_{\mathrm{full}} + 1$
5 :   **return** $(\mathsf{IV}, \mathsf{seqno}, \mathsf{nonce})$

Fig. 4. Nonce updating algorithm for TLS 1.3 in rIV$_{\mathrm{TLS\ 1.3}}$

nextNonce for $2^t - 1$ times, $t \geq 1$ being small, without faulting any value. The counter is then of the binary form $0\ldots0\|1^t$. Then it makes another call to nextNonce but this time induces a random fault at a single bit position. Since the sequence counter is 64 bits the probability of flipping one of the lower t bits back to 0 is $t/64$, in which case the nonce would repeat.

4.2   Rolling IV in TLS 1.3: rIV$_{\mathrm{TLS\ 1.3}}$

We next describe our update algorithm the idea is to use the key derivation procedure HKDF.Expand to update the write_iv. The procedure are displayed in Fig. 4. Since we require pseudorandom outputs we opt for the already implemented HKDF.Expand function in TLS 1.3 which is assumed to be a pseudorandom function. We emphasize that we do not use the HKDF.Extract procedure for updating IV. This step in TLS 1.3 is typically used when mixing in new key material. We also remark that the update algorithm for the IV does not take advantage of seqno and merely iterates the Expand procedure on the current IV value. The update of the sequence number increments seqno, as in TLS 1.3.

The nonce is then defined as in TLS 1.3 as the exclusive or of the sequence counter (padded from left with 0's) and a random value. Whereas TLS 1.3 uses the current IV value we run the IV once more through the Expand procedure to update IV and generate a fresh (pre-)nonce prenonce (instead of using the updated IV directly to generate the nonce). This is necessary because in our model the adversary gets to learn the output nonce. One may argue if this appropriately captures attacks on TLS 1.3, where the nonce is not transmitted in clear. We take here a conservative approach for two reasons. First, the AEAD scheme may not hide the nonce perfectly (i.e., only provides IND-CPA instead of IND-$CPA in the terminology of [29]). While the TLS standard currently only specifies AEAD schemes which are believed to hide the nonce, this is not listed as an explicit property. Second, derivatives of TLS 1.3, e.g., when using unreliable transmissions, may decide to sent nonces in clear. Without the call to Expand the adversary may thus learn the current and future IV values, whereas our security proof relies on the values having sufficient entropy (Fig. 5).

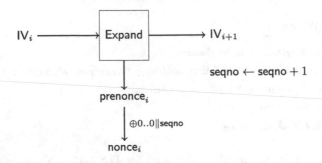

Fig. 5. Rolling IV algorithm rIV$_{\text{TLS 1.3}}$. Note that TLS 1.3 uses the identity function instead of Expand.

We remark that the sequence counter will not contribute to the security under faults, since it can be set arbitrarily. However, it may still be relevant if we consider security in the absence of faults, see Sect. 4.4. Also observe that sender and receiver in the original TLS 1.3 protocol need to locally synchronize seqno (which is not transmitted in clear), such that the synchronization for the IV values here does not require a significant change in this regard.

4.3   Security of rIV$_{\text{TLS 1.3}}$

We next argue security of our construction. Recall that we allow the adversary to mount differential faults on IV and nonce (before it is output), and full faults on the sequence counter. For the security proof we require that HKDF.Expand acts as a pseudorandom function when using a random key of length iv_length. That is, for algorithm $\mathcal{D}$ let

$$\text{Adv}^{\text{prf}}_{\text{HKDF.Expand},\mathcal{D}} := \left| \text{Prob}\left[\mathcal{D}^{\text{HKDF.Expand}(\text{key},\cdot)}() = 1 \right] - \text{Prob}\left[\mathcal{D}^{R()}() = 1 \right] \right|$$

be the distinguishing advantage of $\mathcal{D}$ when either communicating with oracle HKDF.Expand(key, ·) for key $\xleftarrow{\$} \{0,1\}^{\text{iv\_length}}$, or with a random function R with the same input-output length as HKDF.Expand.

As in previous works on fault resistance [1,13] we assume an "atomic" behavior of some steps where the adversary cannot tamper with the memory. In our case this refers to the HKDF.Expand evaluation, where the adversary can only modify the values before and after the execution.

Theorem 1. *The* rIV $_{TLS\ 1.3}$ *construction from Fig. 4 is* FRNonceMu-*secure under full faults on state variable* seqno *and differential faults on state variable* IV *and on the ephemeral values* nonce, *assuming pseudorandomness of* HKDF.Expand. *More precisely, for any adversary* $\mathcal{A}$ *making at most* q *oracle queries to* ONextNonce, *there exists an algorithm* $\mathcal{D}$ *against the pseudorandomness of* HKDF.Expand, *making at most one oracle call, such that*

$$\mathsf{Adv}^{\mathrm{FRNonceMu}}_{\mathsf{rIV}_{TLS\ 1.3},\mathcal{A}} \leq q \cdot \mathsf{Adv}^{prf}_{\mathsf{HKDF.Expand},\mathcal{D}} + 2 \cdot \binom{q}{2} \cdot 2^{-\min\{\mathtt{prenonce\_length},\mathtt{iv\_length}\}} \quad (1)$$

Proof. Consider an attacker $\mathcal{A}$ running experiment $\mathbf{Exp}^{\mathrm{FRNonceMu}}_{\mathrm{Nonce},\mathcal{A}}$, making at most q calls to the nonce-outputting oracle. Let IV_i be the value for IV when entering the ith oracle call. In particular IV_1 is the first (random) value chosen by the game, and IV_{q+1} is the last derived value. During the nonce generation the adversary may add a value Δ_i to IV_i immediately before calling HKDF.Expand. Similarly, let seqno_i be the sequence number when entering, seqno_i^1 be the value which the adversary picks for computing the nonce, and seqno_i^2 be the value when updating the sequence value. Finally, let $\mathsf{prenonce}_i$ be the output of HKDF.Expand and to which the adversary can add a value δ_i before the actual nonce value is computed (and which is then checked against the current nonce set $\mathcal{N}$).

We proceed by game hopping. Let Game$_0$ be the original attack as above. We make gradual changes in the following hops till we reach an easy-to-analyze setting.

Game$_1$. In game Game$_1$ we make a useful syntactical change in the game: When calling Expand for input $\mathsf{IV}_i \oplus \Delta_i$ for a previously seen input value, i.e., if $\mathsf{IV}_i \oplus \Delta_i = \mathsf{IV}_k \oplus \Delta_k$ for some $k < i$, then we immediately set the output to the replies before, IV_{k+1} and $\mathsf{prenonce}_k$, without evaluating the function. Note that the probability of $\mathcal{A}$ winning in game Game$_0$ is the same as in game Game$_1$ because the behavior of the scheme is identical.

Game$_2$. In game Game$_2$ we first perform a game hop in which we replace all values IV_{i+1} and $\mathsf{prenonce}_i$ for $i = 1, \ldots, q$ by truly random and independent values, *but uphold consistency:* If the input key $\mathsf{IV}_i \oplus \Delta_i$ to Expand has appeared before then we use the same reply as before. We say that the values IV_{i+1} and $\mathsf{prenonce}_i$ are picked randomly but consistently.

We show that this modification is indistinguishable from $\mathcal{A}$'s perspective by the pseudorandomness of HKDF.Expand. Consider the hybrids H_j for $j = 0, \ldots, q$ where we only replace the first j values $\mathsf{IV}_2, \ldots, \mathsf{IV}_{j+1}$ and $\mathsf{prenonce}_1, \ldots, \mathsf{prenonce}_j$ by random and consistent values (in the moment they are derived), and do not alter the other values for $i > j$. Then the hybrid H_0 corresponds to the original game (with IV_1 still being random and the other values computed via Expand), and H_q corresponds to the modified game where all values are random but consistent.

Furthermore, we can link the hybrids by an algorithm $\mathcal{D}$ against the pseudorandomness of HKDF.Expand. Algorithm $\mathcal{D}$ simulates an attack for $\mathcal{A}$. For this it picks j uniformly between 1 and q and mimics the game of hybrid H_j perfectly, using random and consistent values for $\mathsf{IV}_2, \ldots, \mathsf{IV}_j$ as well as for $\mathsf{prenonce}_1, \ldots, \mathsf{prenonce}_{j-1}$. Only for the computation for the values IV_{j+1} and nonce_j it either picks consistent values, or if the input $\mathsf{IV}_j \oplus \Delta_j$ is new, it calls its external oracle about ("next nonce", iv_length + prenonce_length). For the remaining rounds it obeys consistency resp. computes HKDF.Expand locally on the given values. Eventually $\mathcal{D}$ outputs 1 if $\mathcal{A}$ wins in the simulation.

Note that when $\mathcal{D}$ has access to HKDF.Expand(key, $\cdot$) then it (almost) simulates hybrid H_{j-1}. Here it is important to note that the adversary may fault IV_j in the jth call before the evaluation of HKDF.Expand. If the value $\mathsf{IV}_j \oplus \Delta_j$ has appeared before, then it is replaced consistently. Else, since IV_j is a uniformly random value and the adversary only adds an offset Δ_j independent of IV_j, the input is statistically close to a uniformly chosen key key. The only difference lies in the condition that $\mathsf{IV}_j \oplus \Delta_j$ is different from the previous $j-1$ values, such that the statistical distance to uniform is at most $(j-1) \cdot 2^{-\mathtt{iv\_length}}$. Hence, the resulting input key $\mathsf{IV}_j \oplus \Delta_j$ has the same distribution as key, up to a statistical error.

If, on the other hand, $\mathcal{D}$ has access to a random function then the response is either consistently set, or it is uniformly distributed because the output of the oracle is random. Hence, $\mathcal{D}$ perfectly simulates hybrid H_j in this setting, without statistical error.

By a standard analysis for the hybrid argument it follows that $\mathcal{D}$'s advantage is larger than a $1/q$ fraction of the absolute difference for $\mathcal{A}$'s success probabilities between Game_1 and Game_2, plus the sum of the collected statistical distances. The latter is at most $\sum_{j=1}^{q}(j-1) \cdot 2^{-\mathtt{iv\_length}} \leq \binom{q}{2} \cdot 2^{-\mathtt{iv\_length}}$.

In Game_2 all values $\mathsf{prenonce}_i$ are uniformly distributed. Next look at the step where our algorithm computes nonce. If the adversary adds a value δ_i to value $\mathsf{prenonce}_i$ via the callback, and chooses an arbitrary value for seqno_i^1, then the value $\mathsf{prenonce}_i$ at this point is unknown to $\mathcal{A}$. Hence, $\mathsf{nonce}_i = \mathsf{prenonce} \oplus \delta_i \oplus 0..0 \| \mathsf{seqno}_i^1$ is also uniformly distributed on the first prenonce_length bits. It follows that in the ith call the probability that this value matches any of the at most $i-1$ values in $\mathcal{N}$ is at most $(i-1) \cdot 2^{-\mathtt{prenonce\_length}}$. Summing over all at most q oracle queries yields the bound

$$\sum_{i=1}^{q}(i-1) \cdot 2^{-\mathtt{prenonce\_length}} \leq \binom{q}{2} \cdot 2^{-\mathtt{prenonce\_length}}$$

for the final game. This concludes the proof. □

4.4   On Selecting the IV and nonce Sizes

Note that the bound of the $\mathsf{rIV}_{\mathrm{TLS}\ 1.3}$ solution in Theorem 1 has a quadratic term $q^2 \cdot 2^{-\mathtt{prenonce\_length}}$, stemming from the birthday bound for collisions among the random prenonces. This means that we can expect the prenonces to repeat after roughly $2^{\mathtt{prenonce\_length}/2}$ encryptions, even if there is no fault attack. This is sharp contrast to TLS 1.3 where the nonce $write\_iv \oplus 0..0\|\mathsf{seqno}$ does not repeat (without faults): when a wrap-around of the counter is about to happen then the parties need to renew the traffic secrets or cease the connection.

Put differently, we pay for the additional security against faults with a stricter limit on the number of encryption steps—or with higher values for iv_length and prenonce_length. Unfortunately, TLS 1.3 is rather inflexible in this regard: All mentioned AEAD schemes mentioned in the TLS 1.3 standard [28] use 96-bit nonces [22,33]. An option may be thus to use only, say, 80-bit prenonces and 16-bit sequence numbers, such that the padded xor basically concatenates the prenonce and sequence number. Then one would obey to the common nonce limits and, as long as one merely encrypts less than 2^{16} message fragments, the likelihood of nonces repeating under fault attacks is roughly 2^{-48}, and nonces never repeat if the sequence number is not faulted at all. The bound of 2^{16} may be acceptable especially in scenarios where TLS is run on constraint hardware devices which are more susceptible to fault attacks.

We remark that TLS 1.3 is, in principle, not bound to 96-bits nonces. It supports any value between $\max\{8, \mathtt{N\_min}\}$ and N_max bytes, where the bounds N_min and N_max are determined by the AEAD scheme. If one, for instance, allowed for 256-bits nonces, then one could use 192 bits for random part and 64 bits for the sequence number.

5   Memory Fault Attacks on the Handshake Protocol

In this section we discuss fault attacks on the handshake step. While most results are negative, i.e., there are fault attacks, we can also argue that in the PSK mode *differential* (and therefore *random*) faults may not succeed.

5.1   Attacks

We first discuss how a full fault attack (in which the adversary can arbitrarily substitute a value by a different one) on the Diffie-Hellman exponent renders the TLS 1.3 handshake (EC)DHE protocol to be insecure, at least in theory. For the attack the adversary persistently changes the client's secret exponent x when it is going to be accessed for computing g^x by a value x^* which is known to the adversary. Then the adversary lets the client (using x^*) interact genuinely in a session with a server instance. Since the pre-shared key PSK is set to 0 in this variant, the only secret information entering key derivation is the Diffie-Hellman value Y^{x^*}. But this value is now known to the adversary such that the adversary can compute all session keys, too.

The attack can be mounted analogously on the server side, replacing y by an adversarial y^*. Yet, in either case it requires to change the value exactly at the right point in time and persistently. Assume for instance that the adversary changes x to x^* on the client side, between the sending of the key share with the ClientHello message (still with g^x) and the computation of the Diffie-Hellman key (then with Y^{x^*}). In this case client and server would derive different Diffie-Hellman keys.

Another potential attack is to run a memory fault attack against the underlying signature scheme. TLS 1.3 lists for example ECDSA and EdDSA as a potential signature algorithms. If one applies now the memory-fault attacks of Poddebniak et al. [25] to the (derandomized versions of these) signature schemes then an attacker can derive the party's signing key. Once it holds the key it can impersonate the party in another execution and thereby break the security of the key exchange protocol. Note that these attacks only requires random faults in order to succeed.

Finally, the Flip Feng Shui attack of Razavi et al. [26] on Diffie-Hellman over residue classes could be applied to TLS 1.3 in principle. The attack works for Diffie-Hellman protocols over $\mathbb{Z}_p^*$, where the parties use a subgroup in $\mathbb{Z}_p^*$ generated by g. By flipping bits in the prime p the parties then compute g^x mod p^* instead. The attack now works if g generates a small subgroup relative to p^*. In this case the adversary may be able to compute the Diffie-Hellman key of the parties.

5.2   Resistance Against Differential Faults on Pre-shared Keys

We discuss here briefly that some types of memory fault attacks on the pre-shared secret of TLS 1.3 are not very promising. But we first point out that if the adversary is able to fully fault pre-shared keys in a client and in a server session, both sessions possibly starting with different values PSK_C resp. PSK_S (but under the same identifier), then it can break authenticity of the handshake protocol. It can set both keys to the same value PSK^* in a full-fault attack and then let both parties execute a handshake for this shared secret. Then both parties would successfully connect, even when checking the binder values, although they should detect a mismatch for the original secrets PSK_C and PSK_S. If the parties run the handshake in PSK-only mode, without Diffie-Hellman, then the adversary can even compute the session keys with the help of PSK^* for that execution.

From now on we focus on differential fault attacks on PSK. We assume that PSK is uniformly over $|PSK|$ bits, i.e., if derived from previous connections. [2] We first observe that the value PSK is only used once in the handshake protocol, when computing the early secret $ES \leftarrow$ HKDF.Extract$(0, PSK)$. We can hence assume that the adversary faults PSK in a session at the beginning, before the early secret is derived. Instead of diving into fault-resistance of key exchange we focus on the fault-resistance of the extraction step.

The idea of the following definition is to let the adversary learn values $ES \leftarrow$ HKDF.Extract$(0, \langle PSK \rangle_\Delta)$ for random PSK for which the adversary can add an offset Δ. In the security game we demand that the outputs look random

---

[2] While the PSK can in principle be derived out-of-band, TLS 1.3 emphasizes that low-entropy and non-uniformly distributed secrets like passwords are susceptible to offline attacks.

$\mathbf{Exp}_{\mathsf{Extract},\mathcal{A}}^{\mathrm{FrRkPRF}}$	OExtract(id)
1: $b \xleftarrow{\$} \{0,1\}$	1: **if** $PSK[\mathrm{id}] = \bot$ **then** $PSK[\mathrm{id}] \xleftarrow{\$} \{0,1\}^{|PSK|}$
2: $PSK[] \leftarrow \bot$	2: $y \leftarrow \mathsf{Extract}(PSK[\mathrm{id}])$
3: $R \xleftarrow{\$}$ random function	3: **if** $b = 1$ **then** $y \leftarrow R(PSK[\mathrm{id}]_{\mathsf{Extract}})$
4: $a \xleftarrow{\$} \mathcal{A}^{\mathsf{OExtract}(\cdot)}()$	4: **return** y
5: **return** $a = b$	

Fig. 6. Security of fault-resistant related-key pseudorandom algorithm. Recall that $PSK[\mathrm{id}]_{\mathsf{Extract}}$ denotes the vector of values which the variable $PSK[\mathrm{id}]$ holds during the execution in fault attacks, in our case the original input value and the faulted value accessed once.

Extract($\llcorner PSK \lrcorner$)
1: **return** HKDF.Extract$(0, \langle PSK \rangle_\Delta)$

Fig. 7. Extraction step

(but repeat if the disturbed value has appeared before). To capture attacks in which the adversary manages to make $PSK \oplus \Delta = PSK' \oplus \Delta'$ for independently sampled PSK, PSK' collide, in which case two parties with different pre-shared keys would agree on the same key, we let the output of HKDF.Extract run against a random function which one applies to both values PSK and $PSK \oplus \Delta$, given as the vector $PSK_{\mathsf{HKDF.Extract}}$ according to our notation for fault attacks:

$$R(PSK, PSK \oplus \Delta) = R(PSK_{\mathsf{HKDF.Extract}}).$$

Doing so, if the adversary succeeds in creating collisions $PSK \oplus \Delta = PSK' \oplus \Delta'$, then HKDF.Extract would return the same value, yet the random function (which also takes $PSK \neq PSK'$ as input) would return independent values. This would allow the adversary to distinguish the two cases easily.

Definition 2 (Fault-Resistant Related-Key Pseudorandomness). *For a function* Extract *let the fault-resistant related-key pseudorandomness against algorithm* $\mathcal{A}$ *be the advantage*

$$\mathsf{Adv}_{\mathsf{Extract},\mathcal{A}}^{\mathrm{FrRkPRF}} := \mathrm{Prob}\left[\mathbf{Exp}_{\mathsf{Extract},\mathcal{A}}^{\mathrm{FrRkPRF}}\right]$$

for the experiment in Fig. 6.

To argue security we assume that HKDF.Extract is a related-key dual-PRF. This means that for algorithm $\mathcal{D}$ let

$$\mathsf{Adv}_{\mathsf{HKDF.Extract},\mathcal{D}}^{\mathrm{rk\text{-}prf}} := \left|\mathrm{Prob}\left[\mathcal{D}^{\mathsf{HKDF.Extract}(0,\mathsf{key}\oplus\cdot)}() = 1\right] - \mathrm{Prob}\left[\mathcal{D}^{R(\cdot)}() = 1\right]\right|$$

be the distinguishing advantage of $\mathcal{D}$ when communicating either with oracle HKDF.Extract$(0, \mathsf{key}\oplus\cdot)$ for key $\xleftarrow{\$} \{0,1\}^{|PSK|}$ for which the adversary can choose the offset Δ, or with a random function R with the same output length as HKDF.Extract.

Concerning the related-key pseudorandomness of HMAC, on which HKDF is based, one knows that HMAC used with a weak hash function like MD5 allows partial key recovery in related-key attacks [7, 14, 27]. For the strong hash function suggested by TLS 1.3, the best bounds are generic ones, shown by Peyrin et al. [24]. They show distinguishers based on related-key attacks of order $2^{n/2}$ for the output length n of HMAC, improving over the generic bound $2^{\ell/2}$ for the size ℓ of the inner state of the hash function.

Theorem 2. *The extraction construction from Fig. 7 is* FrRkPRF-*secure under differential faults on variable PSK, assuming related-key dual pseudorandomness of* HKDF.Extract. *More precisely, for any adversary $\mathcal{A}$ making at most q oracle queries to* OExtract, *there exists an algorithm $\mathcal{D}$ against the related-key dual pseudorandomness of* HKDF.Extract, *making at most q related-key queries, such that*

$$\mathsf{Adv}^{\mathrm{FrRkPRF}}_{\mathsf{HKDF.Extract},\mathcal{A}} \leq \mathsf{Adv}^{rk\text{-}prf}_{\mathsf{HKDF.Extract},\mathcal{D}} + \binom{q}{2} \cdot 2^{-|PSK|}. \tag{2}$$

Proof. Start with the FrRkPRF attack and assume that the challenge bit b is 0 such that the attacker only receives HKDF values. We assume that the adversary never uses the same offset Δ for the same id twice, because it can already compute the answer. We also assume for simplicity that faults are transient, such that the adversary picks a fresh fault Δ to the value $PSK[\mathrm{id}]$. We can easily simulate persistent faults by adding the previous fault value with the new change. Denote this attack as Game_0.

Game_1. We first show that we can simulate attacks for multiple keys $PSK[\mathrm{id}]$ and distinct id's by a single key PSK. To this end, for each newly created key for id and input Δ we can pick a random $\delta_{\mathrm{id}} \xleftarrow{\$} \{0,1\}^{|PSK|}$ and then query the extraction procedure for key PSK about $\delta_{\mathrm{id}} \oplus \Delta$. This gives

$$\mathsf{HKDF.Extract}(0, PSK \oplus \delta_{\mathrm{id}} \oplus \Delta) = \mathsf{HKDF.Extract}(0, PSK[\mathrm{id}] \oplus \Delta)$$

for $PSK[\mathrm{id}] = PSK \oplus \delta_{\mathrm{id}}$. For another query involving the same id we re-use the same value δ_{id}. Note that this is only a syntactical change.

Game_2. In the next game hop replace HKDF.Extract for key PSK by a random function R' (which takes values $\delta_{\mathrm{id}} \oplus \Delta$ as inputs). By the related key security this can decrease the advantage by at most the distinguishing advantage against HKDF.Extract.

Game_3. Replace R' by a random function R which takes the pair of values $(PSK[\mathrm{id}], PSK[\mathrm{id}] \oplus \Delta_i)$ as input as the two values which the variable $PSK[\mathrm{id}]$ can take during the evaluation. This is the actual attack with test bit $b = 1$. The only difference to the previous game is now that the random function R' always returns identical values for $\delta_{\mathrm{id}} \oplus \Delta = \delta_{\mathrm{id}'} \oplus \Delta'$ for some values Δ in a call to id and Δ' for id$'$. The actual random function R, however, would return different values (unless accidentally $\delta_{\text{id}} = \delta_{\text{id}'}$) because it takes $PSK[\text{id}] = PSK \oplus \delta_{\text{id}}$ resp. $PSK[\text{id}'] = PSK \oplus \delta_{\text{id}'}$ as additional input.

Assume that the first mismatch in the answers occurs in the ith call to R', i.e., $\delta_{\text{id}} \oplus \Delta = \delta_{\text{id}'} \oplus \Delta'$. Up to this point the adversary has only learned random (and independent) answers. Since it now picks the offset Δ independently of the uniformly distributed values PSK and $\delta_1, \ldots, \delta_{i-1}$, the probability of a collision with any of the other at most $i - 1$ values is $(i - 1) \cdot 2^{-|PSK|}$. Summing over all at most q queries gives the bound $\binom{q}{2} \cdot 2^{-|PSK|}$ for a collision. If no such collision occurs then the answers of R' and R are both uniform and independent.   □

6 Conclusion

We have shown how fault attacks can be used to mount successful attacks against TLS 1.3. This may not come as a surprise because TLS 1.3 for example has not been designed to withstand weak randomness or ephemeral state reveals, but instead focuses on basic security guarantees. Also, the recommended AEAD schemes are known to be insecure against nonce misuses. Still, we can provide positive results, showing that the PSK key derivation withstands differential fault attacks, and that one could harden attacks against faults by using rolling IVs.

One of the points which is not answered by our work is the one of composition. We have shown how to prevent nonce repetitions under (differential) fault attacks. Note that our adversary in the rIV$_{\text{TLS 1.3}}$ scheme can fault the nonce before it is output and potentially handed over to the AEAD scheme. This raises the question if, combined with a specific AEAD scheme, we obtain a fault-resistant channel protocol. Remarkably, the SIV approach does not seem to provide the desired security because the attack in [13] still applies. It is a worthwhile question if common schemes like a fault-resistant version of AES-GCM provide a resistant combination.

Acknowledgments. We thank the anonymous reviewers for valuable comments. Marc Fischlin has been [co-]funded by the Deutsche Forschungsgemeinschaft (DFG) – SFB 1119 – 236615297.

References

1. Aranha, D.F., Orlandi, C., Takahashi, A., Zaverucha, G.: Security of hedged fiat–shamir signatures under fault attacks. In: Canteaut, A., Ishai, Y. (eds.) EUROCRYPT 2020. LNCS, vol. 12105, pp. 644–674. Springer, Cham (2020). https://doi.org/10.1007/978-3-030-45721-1_23
2. Bellare, M., et al.: Hedged public-key encryption: how to protect against bad randomness. In: Matsui, M. (ed.) ASIACRYPT 2009. LNCS, vol. 5912, pp. 232–249. Springer, Heidelberg (2009). https://doi.org/10.1007/978-3-642-10366-7_14
3. Bellare, M., Kohno, T.: A theoretical treatment of related-key attacks: RKA-PRPs, RKA-PRFs, and applications. In: Biham, E. (ed.) EUROCRYPT 2003. LNCS, vol. 2656, pp. 491–506. Springer, Heidelberg (2003). https://doi.org/10.1007/3-540-39200-9_31

4. Biham, E., Shamir, A.: Differential fault analysis of secret key cryptosystems. In: Kaliski, B.S. (ed.) CRYPTO 1997. LNCS, vol. 1294, pp. 513–525. Springer, Heidelberg (1997). https://doi.org/10.1007/BFb0052259
5. Böck, H., Zauner, A., Devlin, S., Somorovsky, J., Jovanovic, P.: Nonce-disrespecting adversaries: practical forgery attacks on GCM in TLS. In: 10th USENIX Workshop on Offensive Technologies (WOOT 2016) (2016)
6. Boneh, D., DeMillo, R.A., Lipton, R.J.: On the importance of checking cryptographic protocols for faults. In: Fumy, W. (ed.) EUROCRYPT 1997. LNCS, vol. 1233, pp. 37–51. Springer, Heidelberg (1997). https://doi.org/10.1007/3-540-69053-0_4
7. Contini, S., Yin, Y.L.: Forgery and partial key-recovery attacks on HMAC and NMAC using hash collisions. In: Lai, X., Chen, K. (eds.) ASIACRYPT 2006. LNCS, vol. 4284, pp. 37–53. Springer, Heidelberg (2006). https://doi.org/10.1007/11935230_3
8. Dobraunig, C., Eichlseder, M., Mangard, S., Mendel, F., Unterluggauer, T.: ISAP - towards side-channel secure authenticated encryption. IACR Trans. Symmetric Cryptol. **2017**(1), 80–105 (2017)
9. Dowling, B., Fischlin, M., Günther, F., Stebila, D.: A cryptographic analysis of the TLS 1.3 handshake protocol candidates. In: Ray, I., Li, N., Kruegel, C. (eds.) Proceedings of the 22nd ACM SIGSAC Conference on Computer and Communications Security, Denver, CO, USA, 12–16 October 2015, pp. 1197–1210. ACM (2015)
10. Dowling, B., Fischlin, M., Günther, F., Stebila, D.: A cryptographic analysis of the TLS 1.3 handshake protocol. IACR Cryptol. ePrint Arch. **2020**, 1044 (2020). https://eprint.iacr.org/2020/1044
11. Dworkin, M.: Recommendation for block cipher modes of operation: The CCM mode for authentication and confidentiality. NIST Special Publication 800–38C (2004). https://doi.org/10.6028/NIST.SP.800-38C
12. Dworkin, M.: Recommendation for block cipher modes of operation: Galois/counter mode (GCM) and gmac. NIST Special Publication 800–38D (2007). https://doi.org/10.6028/NIST.SP.800-38D
13. Fischlin, M., Günther, F.: Modeling memory faults in signature and authenticated encryption schemes. In: Jarecki, S. (ed.) CT-RSA 2020. LNCS, vol. 12006, pp. 56–84. Springer, Cham (2020). https://doi.org/10.1007/978-3-030-40186-3_4
14. Fouque, P.-A., Leurent, G., Nguyen, P.Q.: Full key-recovery attacks on HMAC/NMAC-MD4 and NMAC-MD5. In: Menezes, A. (ed.) CRYPTO 2007. LNCS, vol. 4622, pp. 13–30. Springer, Heidelberg (2007). https://doi.org/10.1007/978-3-540-74143-5_2
15. Gennaro, R., Lysyanskaya, A., Malkin, T., Micali, S., Rabin, T.: Algorithmic Tamper-Proof (ATP) security: theoretical foundations for security against hardware tampering. In: Naor, M. (ed.) TCC 2004. LNCS, vol. 2951, pp. 258–277. Springer, Heidelberg (2004). https://doi.org/10.1007/978-3-540-24638-1_15
16. Gueron, S., Langley, A., Lindell, Y.: AES-GCM-SIV: Nonce Misuse-Resistant Authenticated Encryption. RFC 8452 (2019). https://doi.org/10.17487/RFC8452, https://rfc-editor.org/rfc/rfc8452.txt
17. Gueron, S., Lindell, Y.: GCM-SIV: full nonce misuse-resistant authenticated encryption at under one cycle per byte. In: Ray, I., Li, N., Kruegel, C. (eds.) Proceedings of the 22nd ACM SIGSAC Conference on Computer and Communications Security, Denver, CO, USA, 12–16 October 2015, pp. 109–119. ACM (2015)

18. Gueron, S., Lindell, Y.: Better bounds for block cipher modes of operation via nonce-based key derivation. In: Thuraisingham, B.M., Evans, D., Malkin, T., Xu, D. (eds.) Proceedings of the 2017 ACM SIGSAC Conference on Computer and Communications Security, CCS 2017, Dallas, TX, USA, 30 October–03 November 2017, pp. 1019–1036. ACM (2017)
19. Joux, A.: Authentication failures in NIST version of GCM. NIST Comment, p. 3 (2006)
20. Joye, M., Lenstra, A.K., Quisquater, J.: Chinese remaindering based cryptosystems in the presence of faults. J. Cryptol. **12**(4), 241–245 (1999)
21. Kim, Y., et al.: Flipping bits in memory without accessing them: an experimental study of DRAM disturbance errors. In: Proceeding of the 41st Annual International Symposium on Computer Architecuture, ISCA 2014, pp. 361–372. IEEE Press (2014)
22. McGrew, D.: An Interface and Algorithms for Authenticated Encryption. RFC 5116 (2008). https://doi.org/10.17487/RFC5116, https://rfc-editor.org/rfc/rfc5116.txt
23. Patton, C., Shrimpton, T.: Partially specified channels: the TLS 1.3 record layer without elision. In: Lie, D., Mannan, M., Backes, M., Wang, X. (eds.) Proceedings of the 2018 ACM SIGSAC Conference on Computer and Communications Security, CCS 2018, Toronto, ON, Canada, 15–19 October 2018, pp. 1415–1428. ACM (2018). https://doi.org/10.1145/3243734.3243789
24. Peyrin, T., Sasaki, Yu., Wang, L.: Generic related-key attacks for HMAC. In: Wang, X., Sako, K. (eds.) ASIACRYPT 2012. LNCS, vol. 7658, pp. 580–597. Springer, Heidelberg (2012). https://doi.org/10.1007/978-3-642-34961-4_35
25. Poddebniak, D., Somorovsky, J., Schinzel, S., Lochter, M., Rösler, P.: Attacking deterministic signature schemes using fault attacks. In: 2018 IEEE European Symposium on Security and Privacy, EuroS&P 2018, London, United Kingdom, 24–26 April 2018, pp. 338–352. IEEE (2018)
26. Razavi, K., Gras, B., Bosman, E., Preneel, B., Giuffrida, C., Bos, H.: Flip Feng Shui: Hammering a needle in the software stack. In: Holz, T., Savage, S. (eds.) 25th USENIX Security Symposium, USENIX Security 2016, Austin, TX, USA, 10–12 August 2016, pp. 1–18. USENIX Association (2016)
27. Rechberger, C., Rijmen, V.: New results on NMAC/HMAC when instantiated with popular hash functions. J. UCS **14**(3), 347–376 (2008)
28. Rescorla, E.: The Transport Layer Security (TLS) Protocol Version 1.3. RFC 8446 (2018). https://doi.org/10.17487/RFC8446, https://rfc-editor.org/rfc/rfc8446.txt
29. Rogaway, P.: Authenticated-encryption with associated-data. In: Atluri, V. (ed.) Proceedings of the 9th ACM Conference on Computer and Communications Security, CCS 2002, Washington, DC, USA, 18–22 November 2002, pp. 98–107. ACM (2002)
30. Rogaway, P., Shrimpton, T.: A provable-security treatment of the key-wrap problem. In: Vaudenay, S. (ed.) EUROCRYPT 2006. LNCS, vol. 4004, pp. 373–390. Springer, Heidelberg (2006). https://doi.org/10.1007/11761679_23
31. Romailler, Y., Pelissier, S.: Practical fault attack against the Ed25519 and EdDSA signature schemes. In: 2017 Workshop on Fault Diagnosis and Tolerance in Cryptography, FDTC 2017, Taipei, Taiwan, 25 September 2017, pp. 17–24. IEEE Computer Society (2017)

32. van der Veen, V., et al.: Drammer: deterministic rowhammer attacks on mobile platforms. In: Weippl, E.R., Katzenbeisser, S., Kruegel, C., Myers, A.C., Halevi, S. (eds.) Proceedings of the 2016 ACM SIGSAC Conference on Computer and Communications Security, Vienna, Austria, 24–28 October 2016, pp. 1675–1689. ACM (2016)
33. Yoav Nir, A.L.: ChaCha20 and Poly1305 for IETF Protocols. RFC 8439 (2018). https://doi.org/10.17487/RFC8439, https://rfc-editor.org/rfc/rfc8439.txt

On Internal Re-keying

Liliya Akhmetzyanova[✉], Evgeny Alekseev, Stanislav Smyshlyaev,
and Igor Oshkin

CryptoPro LLC, Moscow, Russia
ahmzliliya@gmail.com, {alekseev,svs,oshkin}@cryptopro.ru

Abstract. In this paper we introduce a classification of existing re-
keying-based approaches to increase the security of block cipher operation modes. We introduce the concepts of external and internal re-keying
putting the focus on the second one. Whereas the external re-keying approach is widely used and provides the mechanism of key usage control
on a message stream processing level, the internal re-keying approach is
the first known mechanism providing such a control on a single message
processing level. These approaches can be applied completely independently. The internal re-keying approach was already applied to the CTR
encryption mode and yielded the CTR-ACPKM mode. The mode is a
part of RFC 8645 "Re-keying Mechanisms for Symmetric Keys", which
represents the consensus of the Crypto Forum Research Group (CFRG)
of the Internet Research Task Force (IRTF).

In the current paper we apply the internal re-keying approach to the
well-known GCM authenticated encryption mode. The main results of
this paper are a new internally re-keyed GCM-ACPKM mode and its
security bounds. We estimate the security of the GCM-ACPKM mode
respecting standard security notions. We compare both security and performance of the GCM-ACPKM and GCM modes. The results show that
changing GCM mode by integrating the ACPKM internal re-keying procedure increases security, significantly extending the lifetime of a key
with a negligible loss in performance. Also we show how the re-keying
approaches could increase the security of TLS 1.3 and CMS cipher suites.

Keywords: Re-keying · Block cipher modes · AEAD · GCM ·
Provable security

1 Introduction

One of the main problems related to secure functioning of any cryptosystem is
the control of lifetimes of keys. Regarding symmetric keys the main concern is
constraining the key exposure by limiting the maximal amount of data processed
with one key. The restrictions can derive either from combinatorial properties
of the used cipher modes of operation (e.g. most modes of operation are secure
up to the birthday paradox bound [4]), or from resisting certain specific cryptographic attacks on the used block cipher, e.g. differential [11] or linear cryptanalysis [18]), including side-channel attacks [12] (in this case the restrictions

© Springer Nature Switzerland AG 2020
T. van der Merwe et al. (Eds.): SSR 2020, LNCS 12529, pp. 23–45, 2020.
https://doi.org/10.1007/978-3-030-64357-7_2

are the most severe ones). The adversary's opportunity to obtain an essential amount of data processed with the same key leads not only to theoretical but also to practical vulnerabilities (see, e.g., [9, 26]). Thus, when the total length of data processed with the same key reaches a threshold value, certain procedures on encryption keys are needed. This leads to several operating limitations, e.g. processing overhead caused by the new keys generation and the impossibility of long message processing.

In the context of high-level protocols, the most obvious way to overcome the above-mentioned limitations is a regular session key renegotiation. However, such an operation assumes interrupting payload transmissions, sending additional service-based data in the channel, using random number generators and even public key cryptography. Frequent key renegotiation is undesirable, since this would drastically reduce the total performance.

Another way is to deterministically transform a previously negotiated key. One mechanism, and the most common one in practice, is a key diversification (e.g. key hierarchy [21] and HKDF [24]). As soon as a given amount of whole messages is processed, the session key should be updated. Another mechanism, called key meshing [23], assumes the key transformation during separate message processing, which starts with the same key each time.

1.1 Related Work

Key Diversification. A key diversification scheme treats a shared key as a master key, which is never used directly for data processing. As soon as a given amount of whole messages is processed, a new session key should be derived (e.g. $2^{24.5}$ records in TLS 1.3 for a certain safety margin [24]).

Key diversification was addressed by Abdalla and Bellare in [1]—a motivation was given, criteria for such mechanisms and concrete security bounds were obtained, and two schemes were proposed (parallel and serial ones). One of the main points of this work is that the "satisfactory" key diversification technique allows you to essentially increase the key lifetime as compared to a direct usage of a key for data processing. The obtained security bound of the key diversified mode of operation allows to separately analyze the re-keying technique and the base mode of operation. Such a clear separation of security analysis is the definitive advantage of this mechanism. Another feature of this approach is a forward security property, as discussed in [8].

Key Meshing. Another mechanism to increase the key lifetime was presented for the first time in [23] and is called "CryptoPro Key Meshing" (CPKM). This solution assumes that each message is processed starting from the initially negotiated key, which is transformed as soon as a given relatively small amount of data is processed. Such a transformation does not require any additional secret values and uses the initial key directly for data processing. The security of this mechanism had not been analyzed for a long time until the security bound for the re-keyed CTR encryption mode was obtained in [2]. An operating disadvantages of CPKM is the usage of the decryption function. This can double the code size for some block cipher modes and, consequently, reduce the performance. Another disadvantage is that the probability of trivial-recovering the derived key is nonzero.

To negate the disadvantages mentioned above the new ACPKM (advanced CPKM) re-keying technique was proposed in CTCrypt 2018 for increasing the lifetime of keys used in CTR mode. This technique uses only the encryption function and the probability of trivial-recovering the derived keys is zero. The paper [3] contains the analysis of the internally re-keyed CTR-ACPKM mode for the standard IND-CPA notion. The obtained security bound shows that the usage of ACPKM increases the key lifetime compared to the base CTR mode.

The internally re-keyed CTR-ACPKM mode is a part of RFC 8645 "Re-keying Mechanisms for Symmetric Keys", which represents the consensus of the Crypto Forum Research Group (CFRG) of the Internet Research Task Force (IRTF) [32]. Possible usage in TLS cipher suites [33] is one of examples in the document. Also this mode is in the process of standardization in ISO ("Amendment 1: CTR-ACPKM Mode of operation" to ISO/IEC 10116:2017, in development in ISO/IEC JTC1 SC27 WG2 working group, currently on the DAM stage).

1.2 Our Contribution

In the current paper we introduce concepts of internal and external re-keying approaches—generalizations of key diversification and key meshing mechanisms. We discuss the advantages and disadvantages of both the internal and external re-keying approaches, the relationship between them and their application fields. We show that the internal re-keying approach can be treated not as an alternative of the external approach analyzed in [1] but rather as its powerful extension. It allows us to avoid such an operating problem as the message length limitation in the case when the key lifetime is rather strict [26]. Using the examples of TLS 1.3 and CMS we show that these approaches essentially increase the key lifetime.

In the current paper we integrate the ACPKM key update procedure into the well-known GCM authenticated encryption mode. The main results of this paper are a new internally re-keyed GCM-ACPKM mode and its security bounds respecting both Privacy and Authenticity notions. We show that the ACPKM re-keying improves not only privacy, that was already shown in [3] for the quite similar CTR encryption mode, but also authenticity. The considered mode is also a part of RFC 8645.

The ACPKM technique is chosen with performance aspects in mind—the key transformation needs relatively small amount of encryption operations, which code is already initialized and presented in the cache. We compare the performance of the base GCM mode and the internally re-keyed GCM-ACPKM mode with different section sizes. We consider base block cipher AES-256 with hardware support. Slowdown due to using the ACPKM technique does not exceed 3% for any section size.

2   Preliminaries

For a bit string $M \in \{0,1\}^*$ and a positive integer $\ell \leqslant |M|$ let $\text{msb}_\ell(M)$ ($\text{lsb}_\ell(M)$) be the string, consisting of the leftmost (rightmost) ℓ bits of M. For nonnegative integers ℓ and i let $\text{str}_\ell(i)$ be ℓ-bit representation of i with the least significant bit on the right. For a nonnegative integer ℓ and a bit string $M \in \{0,1\}^\ell$ let $\text{int}(M)$ be an integer i such that $\text{str}_\ell(i) = M$. For any set S, define $Perm(S)$ as the set of all bijective mappings on S (permutations on S), and $Func(S)$ as the set of all mappings from S to S. A block cipher E (or just a cipher) with a block size n and a key size k is the permutation family $\left(E_K \in Perm(\{0,1\}^n) \mid K \in \{0,1\}^k\right)$, where K is a key. Throughout this paper, we fix a blockcipher E with the block size $n = 128$. For a bit string U we denote by $U_i \in \{0,1\}^n$, $1 \leqslant i \leqslant \lceil |U|/n \rceil - 1$, and $U_{\lceil |U|/n \rceil} \in \{0,1\}^h$, $h \leqslant n$, such strings that $U = U_1 \| U_2 \| \dots \| U_{\lceil |U|/n \rceil}$ and call them blocks of the string U. We denote by $|U|_n = \lceil |U|/n \rceil$ the length of the string U in n-bit blocks. If the value s is chosen from a set S uniformly at random, then we denote $s \in_{\mathcal{U}} S$.

We model an adversary using a probabilistic algorithm that has access to one or more oracles. Denote by $\mathcal{A}^{\mathcal{O}_1, \mathcal{O}_2, \dots}$ an adversary $\mathcal{A}$ that interacts with oracles $\mathcal{O}_1, \mathcal{O}_2, \dots$ by making queries. Notation $\mathcal{A}^{\mathcal{O}_1, \mathcal{O}_2, \dots} \Rightarrow 1$ means that the algorithm $\mathcal{A}$, after interacting with oracles $\mathcal{O}_1, \mathcal{O}_2, \dots$, outputs 1. The resources of $\mathcal{A}$ are measured in terms of time and query complexities. For a fixed model of computation and a method of encoding the time complexity includes the description size of $\mathcal{A}$. The query complexity usually includes the number of queries and the maximal length of queries.

3   Block Cipher Modes and Re-keying

A block cipher is the permutation family, which on its own do not provide such application-level security properties as integrity, confidentiality or authenticity (see, e.g., [6]). The cipher is usually used as a base function for constructing other schemes or protocols that solve the above-mentioned cryptographic challenges. The security of such constructions is usually proven under assumption that the block cipher is secure. In the paradigm of practice-oriented provable security (see [7]) we should quantify the security as a function of the used primitive security for given notions.

The above-mentioned cryptographic challenges can be solved with the use of "block cipher modes of operation". The modes define how to use the underlying block cipher to process messages which can consist of more than one block. Thus, a single key can be used for processing a large number of blocks. To achieve the sufficient security level this number should be limited. The main reasons for this are pointed out in Introduction.

Re-keying is an approach, which is widely used to overcome the above-mentioned limitation for block cipher modes of operation. The main idea behind this approach is as follows: the data is processed with a sequence of keys derived from an initial "truly" random key.

In this section we introduce the classifications of existing re-keying approaches (*internal* and *external*) and of accompanying key update techniques (with a *master key* and without a master key). These classifications are also described in [32]. Two out of four possible combinations were mentioned in Introduction: external re-keying with master key (key diversification) and internal re-keying without master key (key meshing). In this section we consider the common approaches and discuss their properties, advantages and disadvantages. We put the focus on the internal re-keying approach, since its properties were not considered carefully.

3.1 External Re-keying

The main concept of this approach is as follows: a key, derived according to a certain key update technique (we will also call it "subkey"), is intended to process the fixed number of separate messages, after which the key should be updated. Using external re-keying jointly with the block cipher mode of operation does not change the mode internal structure, therefore we call this approach "external re-keying". The number of separate messages processed with the certain key before it is updated is usually parameterised and is called "subkey lifetime". The main idea behind it is presented in Fig. 1.

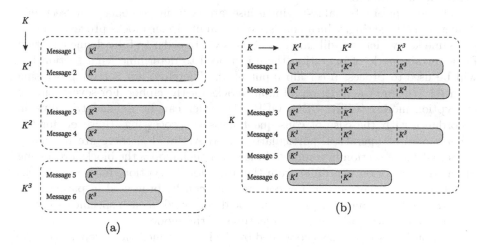

Fig. 1. Idea behind external (a) and internal (b) re-keying. For simplicity, a case with only six messages and the subkey lifetime equal to 2 is shown. In the case (a) every two messages are processed under the corresponding subkey K^i. In the case (b) each message is processed starting from the first derived section key K_1 and this key is changed each time a data section of fixed length has been processed.

Doubtless advantage of external re-keying is the possibility to explicitly use the obtained security bounds for the base mode to quantify security of the corresponding externally re-keyed mode (see [1]).

External re-keying is proposed to be performed each time a given amount of messages is processed. However, the key lifetime is defined by the total length of the processed messages and not by their number. In order to satisfy a certain requirement on the key lifetime limitation, one should fix the maximal message length. If this requirement is restrictive enough (e.g., to resist side-channel attacks), it leads to some problems. Thus, long message processing requires additional fragmentation. Such a fragmentation can lead to frequent re-using a random number generator for generating new IVs (e.g., in the case of data processing in the CBC or CFB modes), that significantly affects the performance.

External re-keying is recommended for the usage in protocols, which process quite small messages, since the maximum gain in increasing the key lifetime is achieved by increasing the number of messages.

3.2   Internal Re-keying

The internal re-keying approach modifies the base mode of operation in such a way that each message is processed starting from the same key, which is changed using the certain key update technique during processing of the current message. It is integrated into the base mode of operation and changes its internal structure, therefore we call it "internal re-keying". The main idea behind internal re-keying is presented in Fig. 1b.

The concept of internal re-keying is inseparable from the concept of "section". A section is the string, which consists of all input cipher blocks processed using the same key, which we will call a "section key". In order to fully define a section for a certain mode of operation there is a need to determine what section key will be used to process a certain input block. Therefore, for correct processing we need to define the order on all input blocks for the cipher. For several simple encryption modes (CTR, CBC, OFB) the order can be defined trivially—in accordance with the case of consequent message processing. However, for the other modes of operation, particularly for AEAD modes, there are too many ways to define a section in common. Indeed, for such modes the blocks processing order for encryption can differ from the order for decryption, moreover, blocks for plaintext encryption and tag computation can be processed in parallel. So, we stress that internal re-keying should be determined in each specific case with respect to security and operational features of the mode.

Obviously a section size is bounded by the key lifetime, which depends on the combinatorial properties of the used operation mode or existing attacks on the base block cipher including side-channel attacks. A certain section size can be chosen optionally for different cases, because it affects the operating properties and limits the number of messages: the larger the section size, the faster message processing, but the smaller the section size, the greater the number of separate processed messages.

Security analysis of internally re-keyed modes leads to the analysis of the abstract modes where section keys are chosen independently at random. For standard encryption modes of operation the security of corresponding modes with random keys can be easily analyzed, using the technique of hybrid argument. To obtain security bounds for more complicated modes (AEAD, MAC types), where sections are not consistent, their base proof should be rethought.

Summing up the above-mentioned issues, we can conclude that internal re-keying should be treated as a technique, which produces a new set of the re-keyed modes of operation.

Internal re-keying mechanisms are recommended to be used in protocols, which process large single messages (e.g., CMS messages), since the maximum gain in increasing the key lifetime is achieved by increasing the length of a message, while it provides almost no increase in the number of messages, which can be processed with a single key.

3.3   Composition of Internal and External Re-keying

Both external re-keying and internal re-keying have their own advantages and disadvantages discussed above. For instance using external re-keying can essentially limit the message length, while in the case of internal re-keying the section size, which can be chosen the maximal possible for operational properties, limits the number of separate messages. There is no technique, which is more preferable, because the choice of technique can depend on certain protocol features. For example, for protocols, which allow out-of-order delivery and lost records (e.g., [28,29]), external re-keying is preferable to be used, but if a protocol assumes processing a significant amount of ordered records, which can be considered as a single data stream (e.g., [30,31]), internal re-keying is better suited.

In order to negate the mentioned disadvantages, the composition of external and internal re-keying approaches can be applied. It can be easily done due to the concepts of external and internal re-keying. Indeed, external re-keying controls key lifetime on the protocol level (a message stream) and internal re-keying controls key lifetime on the block cipher mode level (a single message). This allows to compose these techniques independently.

3.4   Key Update Techniques

In the previous subsections we discussed the approaches to data processing with a sequence of derived keys. The current subsection is dedicated to the several techniques of producing such keys.

We distinguish two key update techniques: with a master key and without a master key. The first one has the following property: a shared initial key is never used directly for data processing but is used only for subkey derivation. Using this technique in the internal and external ways allows to combine the arbitrary key update function with the arbitrary mode of operation and to bound security of the construction, separately analyzing the used components:

– for external re-keying—the key update technique and the base mode of operation [1];

– for internal re-keying—the key update technique and the abstract mode with random section keys.

Another advantage is the possibility to protect keys for some pieces of data even in the case when keys for the other pieces are compromised.

The second technique directly uses the initial key as the first key for data processing, and each next key is computed from the previous one. It seems to be mostly useful in the case when the total amount of data for an initial key is not known beforehand: we will not lose performance on useless operations if the data is rather short, and we will not lack security when it occurs to be large. We will derive new keys only when they are needed. As distinct from the first technique we cannot consider the concrete key update function separately from the mode of operation. In order to illustrate the importance of considering the key update function and the mode of operation as a whole, we will show the following example.

Consider the CBC-MAC mode providing message authenticity. We give a rough specification of CBC-MAC: for the input message $M = M_1\| \ldots \|M_\ell$, $\ell = |M|_n$ the authentication tag T is computed as follows:

$$T = E_K(E_K(\ldots E_K(E_K(M_1) \oplus M_2)\ldots) \oplus M_\ell).$$

Here we assume that the input message length is a multiple of the block size. CBC-MAC is known to be provably secure up to the birthday paradox bound when applied to prefix free message space [5].

Suppose $k = n$ for the used block cipher and message length be at least 2 blocks. Let us internally extend the base mode with the following key update function:

$$K^1 = K, \qquad K^{i+1} = E_{K^i}(C_0) \oplus E_{K^i}(C_1), \quad i = 2, \ldots,$$

where $K \in \{0,1\}^k$ is the initially shared key, $C_0, C_1 \in \{0,1\}^n$ are arbitrary different constants. Let the section size be at least 2 blocks.

Due to the message length limitations (at least 2 blocks) the adversary is not able to obtain the values of encrypted C_0, C_1 just by querying the authentication tags for one-block messages C_0 and C_1. However, this key update technique does not increase the security of the base mode, because there is the attack, which allows to find out the key of the second section with probability 1 and $2 \cdot 2^{n/2}$ pairs (M, T) for chosen M, $|M|_n = 2$. The adversary requests authentication tags for $2^{n/2}$ messages $C_0\|R_1\|0^{n/2}$ and $2^{n/2}$ messages $C_1\|0^{n/2}\|R_2$, where R_1 and R_2 take all strings from $\{0,1\}^{n/2}$. Note that all messages are prefix-free. Obviously, there is the collision $T_1 = T_2$ with probability 1, where $T_1 = E_K(E_K(C_0) \oplus R_1\|0^{n/2})$ and $T_2 = E_K(E_K(C_1) \oplus 0^{n/2}\|R_2)$. Thus, the next section key $K^2 = E_K(C_0) \oplus E_K(C_1)$ is $R_1\|R_2$. The revealed next section key allows to trivially forge the tag for long (more than section) messages. The similar attack can be applied to the OMAC mode (see [14,15,20]).

We may conclude that the proposed key update function is "bad", but for such encryption modes as CBC, OFB, CFB the considered attack is not applicable because of using random initialization vector. Therefore, to be convinced that the proposed key update function is good, we should provide the security proof in both cases of external and internal re-keying.

4 GCM and GCM-ACPKM Modes

In the current section we introduce an internally re-keyed authenticated encryption with associated data (AEAD) mode called GCM-ACPKM.

4.1 Description

Firstly recall the description of the GCM mode according to [19]. We consider the GCM mode with the nonce length restricted to 96 bits.

GCM. Denote by GCM_E the GCM mode that uses a blockcipher E with the block size $n = 128$.

Before considering the GCM mode in details define the auxiliary functions. For bit strings A, B of arbitrary (may be zero) lengths and $H \in \{0,1\}^n$ we have the function

$$\mathrm{GHASH}_H(A, B) = \sum_{i=1}^{m} X_i \cdot H^{m+1-i},$$

where "$\sum$" and "$\cdot$" are addition and multiplication in $GF(2^n)$, and the string $X = X_1 \| \ldots \| X_m$, $X_i \in \{0,1\}^n$ is computed as follows. Let $a = n \cdot |A|_n - |A|$, $b = n \cdot |B|_n - |B|$, $m = |A|_n + |B|_n + 1$, then $X = A \| 0^a \| B \| 0^b \| \mathrm{str}_{n/2}(|A|) \| \mathrm{str}_{n/2}(|B|)$.

For $0 \leqslant a < n$ let $\mathrm{incr}_a : \{0,1\}^n \to \{0,1\}^n$ be the encoding function, which takes the input $I \in \{0,1\}^n$, and outputs the string

$$\mathrm{msb}_{n-a}(I) \| \mathrm{str}_a(\mathrm{int}(\mathrm{lsb}_a(I)) + 1 \bmod 2^a).$$

Authenticated Encryption in the GCM Mode. A processed message for authenticated encryption in the GCM_E mode is (N, A, M), where N is a nonce, $|N| = 96$, A is an associated data, $0 \leqslant |A| \leqslant 2^{n/2} - 1$, and M is a plaintext, $0 \leqslant |M| \leqslant n(2^{32} - 2)$. The result of GCM encryption under a key K is a pair (C, T), where $C \in \{0,1\}^{|M|}$ is a ciphertext of M and $T \in \{0,1\}^n$ is an authentication tag, which are computed as follows:

$$C = M \oplus \mathrm{msb}_{|M|}(E_K(I_1) \| \ldots \| E_K(I_{|M|_n})),$$
$$T = E_K(I_0) \oplus \mathrm{GHASH}_H(A, C).$$

Here $H = E_K(0^n)$, $I_i = \mathrm{incr}_{32}(I_{i-1})$, $1 \leqslant i \leqslant |M|_n$, where $I_0 = N \| 0^{31} 1$. The nonces N are different for different messages processed with the same key K.

Now we introduce the internally re-keyed GCM-ACPKM mode.

GCM-ACPKM. Firstly, define the auxiliary function $\varphi_i : \{0,1\}^n \to \{0,1\}$, $\varphi_i(X) = X_{(i)}$, $0 \leqslant i < n$. This function returns the i-th bit of string (counting from left to right starting at zero).

Unlike GCM, for GCM-ACPKM we allow to choose the nonce length, introducing a parameter $n/2 \leqslant c < n$ denoted a nonce bit length. For the fixed value of c key updating for the GCM-ACPKM encryption mode is defined as follows:

$$K^1 = K, \quad K^{i+1} = \text{ACPKM}(K^i) = \text{msb}_k(E_{K^i}(D_1)\| \dots \|E_{K^i}(D_s)),$$

where $s = \lceil k/n \rceil$, $D_1, \dots, D_s \in \{0,1\}^n$ are pairwise different arbitrary constants such that $\varphi_c(D_1) = \dots = \varphi_c(D_s) = 1$ and K is an initially shared key.

We denote by $\text{GCM-ACPKM}_{E,c,\ell}$ the GCM_E mode of operation with c-bits nonces N, $|N| = c$, that takes the key updating according to the ACPKM technique after each ℓ processed blocks of the plaintext M (without consideration of the associated data A). The internal state (counter) of the mode is not reset for each new section. There is a certain reason for that: in order to protect against a key-collision attack (see [10]), we should provide different input blocks for encryption under different keys. The key for computing values $E_K(I_0)$ and $H = E_K(0^n)$ is not updated and is equal to the initial key. So, the encryption in the GCM-ACPKM mode is proceeded as follows:

$$C = M \oplus \text{msb}_{|M|}(E_{K^1}(I_1)\| \dots \|E_{K^1}(I_\ell)\| \dots \|E_{K^h}(I_{h(\ell-1)+1})\| \dots \|E_{K^h}(I_{|M|_n})),$$

$$T = E_{K^1}(I_0) \oplus \text{GHASH}_H(A, C),$$

where $h = \lceil |M|_n / \ell \rceil$, $I_i = \text{incr}_{n-c}(I_{i-1})$, $1 \leqslant i \leqslant |M|_n$, where $I_0 = N\|0^{n-c-1}1$. The nonces N are different for different messages processed with the same key K.

The plaintext length should be at most $m_{\max} = \min(2^{n-c-1} - 2, \frac{2^{n/2-1}}{n})$ blocks. This restriction and the restriction on the constants $D_1, \dots, D_s$ guarantee that blocks of the next key K^j never appear in a set of blocks $E_{K^{j-1}}(I_i)$, where $1 \leqslant i \leqslant |M|_n$.

4.2   Security Bounds

Firstly, recall several security notions.

Block Cipher. Standard security notion for block ciphers is PRP-CPA ("PseudoRandom Permutation under Chosen Plaintext Attack"). We will denote by $\mathbf{Adv}_E^{\text{PRP-CPA}}(\mathcal{A})$ the advantage of an adversary $\mathcal{A}$ succeeding in distinguishing E_K from a random permutation (for formal definitions see Appendix A).

AEAD Mode. For the AEAD modes we consider security notions Privacy and Authenticity. We will denote by $\mathbf{Adv}_{\text{AEAD}_E}^{\text{Priv}}(\mathcal{A})$ and $\mathbf{Adv}_{\text{AEAD}_E}^{\text{Auth}}(\mathcal{A})$ the advantage of an adversary $\mathcal{A}$ succeeding in breaking the privacy properties and authenticity properties of the AEAD_E mode respectively, where E is the underlined cipher with parameters n and k. The privacy advantage is the increase in the probability that an adversary is able to successfully distinguish an AEAD ciphertext from the output of an ideal cipher. The authenticity advantage is the probability that an adversary is able to forge a ciphertext that will be accepted as valid (for formal definitions see Appendix A).

GCM. Below we consider known results on the security of the GCM mode that are obtained in [19] for the first time and then repaired and improved in [16,22].

Corollary 1 ([16]). *Let E be the parameters of GCM. Then for any adversary $\mathcal{A}$ with time complexity at most t that makes at most q queries, where the total plaintext length is at most σ blocks and the nonce length is restricted to 96 bits, there exists an adversary $\mathcal{A}'$ such that*

$$Adv_{GCM_E}^{Priv}(\mathcal{A}) \leqslant Adv_E^{PRP\text{-}CPA}(\mathcal{A}') + \frac{(\sigma + q + 1)^2}{2^{n+1}}, \tag{1}$$

where $\mathcal{A}'$ makes at most $\sigma + q + 1$ queries. Furthermore, the time complexity of $\mathcal{A}'$ is at most $t + cn\sigma_A$, where σ_A is the total input queries length, c is a constant that depends only on the model of computation and the method of encoding.

Corollary 2 ([22]). *Let E be the parameters of GCM. Then for any adversary $\mathcal{A}$ with time complexity at most t that makes at most q encryption queries and q' decryption queries, where the total plaintext length is at most σ blocks, the nonce length is restricted to 96 bits and the maximal summary length of plaintext or ciphertext and associated data in query is at most m_A blocks, there exists an adversary $\mathcal{A}'$ such that*

$$Adv_{GCM_E}^{Auth}(\mathcal{A}) \leqslant Adv_E^{PRP\text{-}CPA}(\mathcal{A}') + \left[\frac{q'(m_A + 1)}{2^n}\right] \cdot \exp\left(\frac{4\sigma q}{2^n}\right). \tag{2}$$

where $\mathcal{A}'$ makes at most $\sigma + q + q' + 1$ queries. Furthermore, the time complexity of $\mathcal{A}'$ is at most $t + cn\sigma_A$, where σ_A is the total queries length, c is a constant that depends only on the model of computation and the method of encoding.

GCM-ACPKM. Below we present the main results on the security of the internally re-keyed GCM-ACPKM mode. The obtained results allow to claim that this mode is secure if the base block cipher is secure and that the usage of the ACPKM internal re-keying technique increases security, essentially extending the lifetime of a key as compared to the base GCM mode.

Since the plaintext encryption for GCM-ACPKM is quite similar to the encryption for CTR-ACPKM the security bound for Privacy is obtained by the same way as described in [3]. Below we present the theorem for GCM-ACPKM that shows the security bound for Privacy.

Theorem 1. *Let E, c and ℓ be the parameters of GCM-ACPKM mode. Then for any adversary $\mathcal{A}$ with time complexity at most t that makes at most q queries, where the maximal plaintext length is at most m blocks and the total plaintext length is at most σ blocks, there exists an adversary $\mathcal{A}'$ such that*

$$Adv_{GCM\text{-}ACPKM_{E,c,\ell}}^{Priv}(\mathcal{A}) \leqslant h \cdot Adv_E^{PRP\text{-}CPA}(\mathcal{A}') + \frac{(\sigma_1 + q + s + 1)^2}{2^{n+1}} +$$
$$+ \frac{(\sigma_2 + s)^2 + \ldots + (\sigma_{h-1} + s)^2 + (\sigma_h)^2}{2^{n+1}}, \tag{3}$$

where $s = \lceil k/n \rceil$, $h = \lceil m/\ell \rceil$, σ_j is the total data block length processed during q plaintexts encryption under the section key K^j and $\sigma_1 + \ldots + \sigma_h = \sigma$. The adversary $\mathcal{A}'$ makes at most $\sigma_1 + q + s + 1$ queries. Furthermore, the time complexity of $\mathcal{A}'$ is at most $t + cn\sigma_A$, where σ_A is the total input queries length, c is a constant that depends only on the model of computation and the method of encoding.

The proof can be found in Appendix B.

Remark 1. Note that the re-keyed mode is secure if the value $s = \lceil k/n \rceil$ is rather small. For the common block ciphers (AES-256 and AES-128) this condition is satisfied: $s \in \{1, 2\}$. Note that if $m \leqslant \ell$ (that is the case when the ACPKM mechanism is not applied, $\sigma_1 = \sigma$, $h = 1$) then the bound (3) totally coincides with the bound (1) since GCM-ACPKM with $\ell \geqslant m$ is exactly the GCM mode with c-bits nonces. The bound for the internally re-keyed mode shows that the insecurity of the mode reaches minimum if $\sigma_1 = \ldots = \sigma_h$, i.e. if all messages are of the same length.

Now consider the security bound for Authenticity.

Theorem 2. *Let E, c and ℓ be the parameters of GCM-ACPKM mode. Then for any $\mathcal{A}$ with time complexity at most t, which makes at most q encryption queries and q' decryption queries, where the maximal summary length of plaintext or ciphertext and associated data in query is at most m_A blocks and the total plaintext length is at most σ blocks, there exists an adversary $\mathcal{A}'$ such that*

$$\mathbf{Adv}^{Auth}_{GCM\text{-}ACPKM_{E,c,\ell}}(\mathcal{A}) \leqslant \mathbf{Adv}^{PRP\text{-}CPA}_{E}(\mathcal{A}') + \left[\frac{q'(m_A + 1)}{2^n}\right] \exp\left(\frac{4(\sigma_1 + s)q}{2^n}\right), \quad (4)$$

where $s = \lceil k/n \rceil$, σ_1 is the total data block length processed during q plaintexts encryption under then section key $K = K^1$, $\sigma_1 + s \leqslant 2^{n-1}$. The adversary $\mathcal{A}'$ makes at most $\sigma_1 + q + q' + s + 1$ queries. Furthermore, the time complexity of $\mathcal{A}'$ is at most $t + cn\sigma_A$, where σ_A is the total input queries length, c is a constant, which depends only on the model of computation and the method of encoding.

The proof can be found in Appendix C.

Remark 2. Note that if $m \leqslant \ell$ (that is the case when the ACPKM mechanism is not applied, $\sigma_1 = \sigma$, $h = 1$) then the bound (4) totally coincides with the bound (2) since GCM-ACPKM with $\ell \geqslant m$ is entirely the GCM mode with nonce length restricted to variable number of bits.

4.3   Comparison of Bounds

Compare the security bounds of the GCM and GCM-ACPKM modes for a cipher E such that $s = \lceil k/n \rceil = 2$.

Note that the obtained bounds for the GCM mode are tight. For the Privacy notion it conventionally holds and for the Authenticity notions it follows from the recently obtained results [17, 22].

Privacy. If $t \ll 2^k$ then for any adversary $\mathcal{A}$ with time complexity at most t that makes at most q queries, where the total plaintext length is at most σ blocks and the maximal plaintext length is at most m blocks

$$\mathbf{Adv}_{\mathrm{GCM}_E}^{\mathrm{Priv}}(\mathcal{A}) \approx \frac{(\sigma + q)^2}{2^{n+1}},$$

$$\mathbf{Adv}_{\mathrm{GCM\text{-}ACPKM}_{E,c,\ell}}^{\mathrm{Priv}}(\mathcal{A}) \approx \frac{(\sigma_1 + q)^2 + \sigma_2^2 + \ldots + \sigma_{h-1}^2 + \sigma_h^2}{2^{n+1}},$$

where $h = \lceil m/\ell \rceil$. Here we neglect the constants and suppose $\mathbf{Adv}_E^{\mathrm{PRP\text{-}CPA}}(\mathcal{A}')$ to be zero.

These relations indicate that the security of the GCM-ACPKM mode is improved compared to the security of the base GCM mode for the Privacy notion in the most typical cases due to $\sigma^2 \geqslant \sigma_1^2 + \ldots + \sigma_h^2$ for all $\sigma = \sigma_1 + \ldots + \sigma_h$.

Authenticity. For the same reasons for any adversary $\mathcal{A}$ with time complexity at most t that makes at most q encryption queries and q' decryption queries, where the total plaintext length is at most σ blocks and the maximal summary length of plaintext or ciphertext and associated data in query is at most m_A blocks,

$$\mathbf{Adv}_{\mathrm{GCM}_E}^{\mathrm{Auth}}(\mathcal{A}) \approx \frac{q' m_A}{2^n} \cdot \exp\left(\frac{4\sigma q}{2^n}\right),$$

$$\mathbf{Adv}_{\mathrm{GCM\text{-}ACPKM}_{E,c,\ell}}^{\mathrm{Auth}}(\mathcal{A}) \approx \frac{q' m_A}{2^n} \cdot \exp\left(\frac{4\sigma_1 q}{2^n}\right).$$

The authenticity security of the GCM-ACPKM mode is also improved compared to the security of the base GCM mode for all typical cases since $\sigma_1 < \sigma$.

Remark 3. The paper [22] proposes the attack that recovers the hash-key H of GCM with probability at least $\frac{1}{2}$ based on $\sqrt{n/m} \cdot 2^{n/2}$ encryption queries, where m is the number of blocks present in plaintext of encryption queries. In the case of GCM-ACPKM we need for now $\sqrt{n/\ell} \cdot 2^{n/2}$ encryption queries to recover the hash-key H using the same attack where ℓ is the section size.

The considered bounds can be rewritten in the term of the q and m parameters using $\sigma \leqslant qm$ and $\sigma_i \leqslant q\ell$ for all i:

$$\mathbf{Adv}_{\mathrm{GCM}_E}^{\mathrm{Priv}}(\mathcal{A}) \approx \frac{(qm + q)^2}{2^{n+1}}, \quad \mathbf{Adv}_{\mathrm{GCM\text{-}ACPKM}_{E,c,\ell}}^{\mathrm{Priv}}(\mathcal{A}) \approx \frac{m}{\ell} \cdot \frac{(q\ell + q)^2}{2^{n+1}},$$

$$\mathbf{Adv}_{\mathrm{GCM\text{-}ACPKM}_{E,c,\ell}}^{\mathrm{Auth}}(\mathcal{A}) \approx \frac{q' m_A}{2^n} \cdot \exp\left(\frac{4\ell q^2}{2^n}\right).$$

Let fix a safety margin of privacy, which allows to process q messages with plaintext length exactly m blocks in the base GCM_E mode. Note that the case of equal length messages is practical: messages can be padded in purpose of achieving a length-hiding property. According to the approximate security bounds presented above the plaintext length can be (without loss in security) increased by internal re-keying up to $\min\left(\frac{m+1}{\ell+1}\cdot m,\ m_{\max}\right)$. Herewith, if the length of an associated data (e.g. a header) is negligible compared to the maximal plaintext length, then the forgery probability for $q'=1$ is still at $\frac{1}{2^c}$ as long as

$$q \leqslant \frac{2^{n/2}-1}{\sqrt{\ell}}.$$

4.4 Performance

We analyze the correlation between efficiency of the internally re-keyed encryption mode and the section size ℓ. The results are presented in Table 1, where the first row is the section size in kilobytes and the second one is the appropriate processing speed in megabytes per second. The last row shows loss of performance compared to the base GCM mode (in percent). We measure the processing speed during the encryption of one long message in the GCM and GCM-ACPKM modes with the hardware-supported AES-256 block cipher (using OpenSSL source [27]). The computer with the following characteristics was used: Intel Core i5-6500 CPU 3.20GHz, L1 D-Cache 32 KB x 4, L1 I-Cache 32 KB x 4, L2 Cache 256 KB x 4. Speed of the encryption process in the base GCM mode with the hardware-supported AES-256 cipher is 2690 MB/s.

Table 1. The performance of the GCM-ACPKM mode with the AES-256 cipher.

KB	64	128	256	512	1024	2048	4096
MB/s	2614.2	2628.2	2647.5	2661.6	2670.2	2680.1	2687.0
%	2.8	2.2	1.6	1.1	0.7	0.4	0.1

The section size can be varied depending on the different purposes. Obviously processing speed is proportional to the section size. However, when choosing this parameter, the following condition should be satisfied: the value $q\ell$ (where q is the number of separate processed messages, ℓ is the section size) should be no greater than the lifetime of a key.

5 Practical Significance

Consider the security bounds for GCM, for GCM-ACPKM, for key diversified (externally re-keyed with master key) GCM (denoted by $\overline{\text{GCM}}$) and for key diversified GCM-ACPKM (denoted by $\overline{\text{GCM-ACPKM}}$). The next theorem was originally formulated for the LOR-CPA notion in [1]. For convenience we convert it to the bound for the Privacy notion by the obvious reduction.

Theorem 3. ([1]). *Let $\mathcal{SE}$ be a base encryption scheme with key size k, $\mathcal{G}$ be a stateful generator with block size k and p be a subkey lifetime. Let $\overline{\mathcal{SE}}^p$ be the associated re-keyed encryption scheme. Then for any adversary $\mathcal{A}$ with time complexity at most t, which makes at most q encryption queries, where the maximal plaintext length is at most m blocks, there exist adversaries $\mathcal{A}'$ and $\mathcal{A}''$ such that*

$$Adv_{\overline{\mathcal{SE}}^p}^{Priv}(\mathcal{A}) \leqslant 2 \cdot Adv_{\mathcal{G},N}^{PRG}(\mathcal{A}') + \left\lceil \frac{q}{p} \right\rceil \cdot Adv_{\mathcal{SE}}^{Priv}(\mathcal{A}''),$$

where $\mathcal{A}'$ makes at most q queries with the maximal plaintext length at most m blocks, and the time complexities of $\mathcal{A}'$ and $\mathcal{A}''$ are at most t.

Corollary 3. *The same bound can be applied for the Authenticity notion:*

$$Adv_{\overline{\mathcal{SE}}^p}^{Auth}(\mathcal{A}) \leqslant 2 \cdot Adv_{\mathcal{G},N}^{PRG}(\mathcal{A}') + \left\lceil \frac{q}{p} \right\rceil \cdot Adv_{\mathcal{SE}}^{Auth}(\mathcal{A}'').$$

If one assumes the approximations considered in Sect. 4.3 for the adversary $\mathcal{A}$, which makes q encryption queries, each of which consists of plaintext of the m-blocks length without associated data (thus, $\sigma < qm$), and one decryption query, then the approximations presented in Table 2 will be obtained.

Table 2. Approximate security bounds for the re-keyed GCM modes. Here q is the number of queries to the encryption oracle, m is the number of plaintext blocks in query, p (subkey lifetime) and ℓ (section size) are the parameters of the external and internal re-keying techniques.

$\mathcal{SE}$	$Adv_{\mathcal{SE}}^{Priv}(\mathcal{A})$	$Adv_{\mathcal{SE}}^{Auth}(\mathcal{A})$
GCM_E	$\dfrac{(qm+q)^2}{2^n}$	$\dfrac{m}{2^n} \cdot \exp\left(\dfrac{4mq^2}{2^n}\right)$
$\overline{GCM_E}^p$	$\dfrac{q}{p} \cdot \dfrac{(pm+p)^2}{2^n}$	$\dfrac{q}{p} \cdot \dfrac{m}{2^n} \cdot \exp\left(\dfrac{4mp^2}{2^n}\right)$
$GCM\text{-}ACPKM_{E,c,\ell}$	$\dfrac{m}{\ell} \cdot \dfrac{(q\ell+q)^2}{2^n}$	$\dfrac{m}{2^n} \cdot \exp\left(\dfrac{4\ell q^2}{2^n}\right)$
$\overline{GCM\text{-}ACPKM_{E,c,\ell}}^p$	$\dfrac{qm}{p\ell} \cdot \dfrac{(p\ell+p)^2}{2^n}$	$\dfrac{q}{p} \cdot \dfrac{m}{2^n} \cdot \exp\left(\dfrac{4\ell p^2}{2^n}\right)$

Now consider re-keyed GCM modes with $n = 128$, the subkey lifetime $p = 2^6$ for external re-keying and the section size $\ell = 2^6$ for internal re-keying. Technically, these parameters mean that the initial key should be diversified after every 64 messages and each diversified subkey should be internally updated after every kilobyte. Here we compare security bounds for these modes, taking into account the following metrics:

– number of records equal to q in TLS 1.3 protocol [24], where the record size (plaintext length) m is at most 2^{10} blocks or 2^{14} bytes.

– plaintext length equal to m in CMS protocol [25], where only one message can be processed under a single key (i.e. $q = 1$).

The comparison results are presented in Table 3 and in Table 4, where the first column contains the number of processed records q or the plaintext length m and the following columns contain the corresponding upper bounds for success probabilities of attack on privacy (δ_{priv}) and of a forgery (δ_{auth}). The success probabilities were calculated using the approximate security bounds presented in Table 2 and $\exp(4x/2^{128}) \leqslant 2$ for $x \leqslant 2^{126}$.

Table 3. Key lifetime limitations in TLS 1.3 with record size (message length) $m = 2^{10}$ blocks (16 kilobytes) for GCM, $\overline{\text{GCM}}$, $\overline{\text{GCM}}$-ACPKM with parameters $n = 128$ bits, $p = 2^6$ records (1 megabyte), $\ell = 2^6$ blocks (1 kilobyte).

q	GCM		$\overline{\text{GCM}}$		GCM-ACPKM	
	δ_{priv}	δ_{auth}	δ_{priv}	δ_{auth}	δ_{priv}	δ_{auth}
2^{34}	2^{-40}	2^{-115}	2^{-68}	2^{-89}	2^{-72}	2^{-89}
2^{44}	2^{-20}	2^{-115}	2^{-58}	2^{-79}	2^{-62}	2^{-79}
2^{54}	1	2^{-115}	2^{-48}	2^{-69}	2^{-52}	2^{-69}
2^{64}	1	1	2^{-38}	2^{-59}	2^{-42}	2^{-59}

The results presented in Table 3 show that after processing maximum possible in TLS 1.3 number of records (2^{64}) with GCM, both privacy and integrity will be totally corrupted. Herewith, the $\overline{\text{GCM}}$ mode still remains secure up to 2^{-38} for privacy and 2^{-59} for integrity. Thus, using the TLS 1.3 KeyUpdate technique for key diversification allows to drastically increase the key lifetime in TLS 1.3. Note that the ACPKM technique for key meshing improves the security bound (2^{-42} for privacy) only a little, since in TLS 1.3 the message length is rather small. Therefore, the ACPKM technique is better to be used for increasing the parameter p without loss in security. For example, for the section size $\ell = 2^6$, the subkey lifetime p can be set to 2^{10} and both privacy and integrity will still be on the same level as for the $\overline{\text{GCM}}$ mode. Increasing p may lead to performance increase despite adding the ACPKM transformation. Indeed, in TLS 1.3 the relatively slow Expand function is called and an additional Key Update message is formed and sent to the channel each time key is updated, while the ACPKM function is integrated in the mode and is based on the fast block cipher. Moreover, $\frac{m}{\ell} = 2^4 = 16$ section keys for every new subkey can be precomputed.

The significant growth in security because of using ACPKM is provided in the protocols like CMS where the long messages can be processed. Note that using key diversification technique (external re-keying) is meaningless there, since only one message is processed under a single key. The base GCM mode allows to process no more than $2^{32} - 2$ blocks providing high enough security.

Table 4. Key lifetime limitations in CMS with number of messages $Q = 1$ for GCM and GCM-ACPKM with parameters $n = 128$ bits, $\ell = 2^6$ blocks (1 kilobyte). Dash in the column means that corresponding plaintext length m is not allowed to be processed by the corresponding mode. The probability after the slash sign corresponds to the modification of the GCM mode which allows longer message processing (the message length is increased in the same way as in GCM-ACPKM, see Sect. 4.1 for detail).

m	GCM		GCM-ACPKM	
	δ_{priv}	δ_{auth}	δ_{priv}	δ_{auth}
$2^{32} - 2$	2^{-64}	2^{-96}	2^{-91}	2^{-96}
2^{44}	$-/2^{-40}$	$-/2^{-83}$	2^{-78}	2^{-83}
2^{54}	$-/2^{-20}$	$-/2^{-73}$	2^{-68}	2^{-73}

The GCM-ACPKM mode does not have such a limit: by choosing an appropriate nonce length we can increase the maximal plaintext length. The results in Table 4 show that GCM-ACPKM allows to process messages of 2^{54}-blocks length remaining secure up to 2^{-68} for privacy and 2^{-63} for integrity, while for the GCM mode (with increased message length in the same way as in GCM-ACPKM) the privacy bound is not small enough (2^{-20}).

6   Conclusion

In this paper, we have introduced the clear classification of existing re-keying approaches and have discussed their advantages and disadvantages. We have proposed a new internally re-keyed GCM-ACPKM mode and have studied its security, respecting the standard notions. We have shown that the security for the Privacy and Authenticity notion is increased compared to the base mode. Therefore we are convinced that the overall security of GCM is drastically increased by the ACPKM re-keying technique with only a minor loss in performance. Also we have considered the internal and external re-keying approaches in more detail and have provided certain parameters leading to improvements in applications, particularly in TLS 1.3 and CMS.

One of the most interesting open problems is the analysis of the re-keying influence on a multi-key, or multi-user, security of the proposed modes. This notion challenges cryptographic algorithms to maintain high levels of security when used with many different keys by many different users.

Acknowledgement. The authors are very grateful to Nikolay P. Varnovsky, Ekaterina S. Griboedova, and Lolita A. Sonina for their valuable comments and suggestions concerning the text of the article.

A   Security Notions

Define the PRP-CPA notion. For a cipher E with parameters n and k define

$$\mathbf{Adv}_E^{\text{PRP-CPA}}(\mathcal{A}) = \Pr\left[K \in_{\mathcal{U}} \{0,1\}^k : \mathcal{A}^{E_K} \Rightarrow 1\right] -$$
$$-\Pr\left[\pi \in_{\mathcal{U}} Perm(\{0,1\}^n) : \mathcal{A}^\pi \Rightarrow 1\right],$$

where the probabilities are defined over the randomness of $\mathcal{A}$, and the choices of K and π. Also further we will use the PRF notion. The PRF notion is defined in the same way as PRP-CPA except for the random permutation π, which is replaced by the random function $\rho \in_{\mathcal{U}} Func(\{0,1\}^n)$.

Privacy. We consider an adversary $\mathcal{A}$ that has access to an encryption oracle $\mathcal{E}$ or a random-bits oracle \$. Before starting the work the encryption oracle chooses a key $K \in_{\mathcal{U}} \{0,1\}^k$. The adversary makes queries (N, A, M), where N is a nonce, A is an associated data and M is a plaintext. The random-bits oracle in response returns (C, T), where $C\|T \in_{\mathcal{U}} \{0,1\}^{|M|+n}$, n is a tag size. The encryption oracle returns (C, T), $C \in \{0,1\}^{|M|}$, $T \in \{0,1\}^n$,—the result of AEAD encryption of (N, A, M) under the key K. For the AEAD mode define

$$\mathbf{Adv}_{\text{AEAD}}^{\text{Priv}}(\mathcal{A}) = \Pr\left[K \in_{\mathcal{U}} \{0,1\}^k : \mathcal{A}^{\mathcal{E}} \Rightarrow 1\right] - \Pr\left[\mathcal{A}^{\$} \Rightarrow 1\right],$$

where the probabilities are defined over the randomness of $\mathcal{A}$, the choices of K and randomness of the random-bits oracle, respectively. We consider a set of nonce-respecting adversaries, which choose N unique for each query.

Authenticity. We consider an adversary $\mathcal{A}$ that has access to an encryption oracle $\mathcal{E}$ and a decryption oracle $\mathcal{D}$. Before starting the work both oracles choose a common key $K \in_{\mathcal{U}} \{0,1\}^k$. The adversary interacts with the encryption oracle in the same way as described in the Privacy notion. Additionally the adversary can make queries (N, A, C, T) to the decryption oracle, where N is a nonce, A is an associated data, C is a ciphertext and T is an authentication tag. It returns the result of AEAD_E decryption of (N, A, C, T) under the key K: $M \in \{0,1\}^{|C|}$ or $\perp$.

The adversary forges if the decryption oracle returns a bit string (other than $\perp$) for a query (N, A, C, T), but (C, T) was not previously returned to $\mathcal{A}$ from the encryption oracle for a query (N, A, M) with some M. As in the Privacy notion, we assume that $\mathcal{A}$ is nonce-respecting to encryption oracle. We remark that nonces used for the encryption queries can be used for decryption queries and vice-versa, and that the same nonce can be repeated for decryption queries. For the AEAD mode define

$$\mathbf{Adv}_{\text{AEAD}}^{\text{Auth}}(\mathcal{A}) = \Pr\left[K \in_{\mathcal{U}} \{0,1\}^k : \mathcal{A}^{\mathcal{E},\mathcal{D}} \text{ forges}\right],$$

where the probability is defined over the randomness of $\mathcal{A}$ and the choice of K.

B   Proof of Theorem 1

Proof. Define the hybrid experiments $Hybrid_j(\mathcal{A})$, $j = 0, 1, \ldots, h$. In the experiment $Hybrid_j(\mathcal{A})$ the oracle in the Privacy notion is replaced by the oracle, which operates in the following way:

- The oracle chooses key $K^{j+1} \in_{\mathcal{U}} \{0,1\}^k$;
- In response to a query (N, A, M) the oracle returns a pair (C, T) which is calculated as follows.
  A ciphertext $C = M \oplus \mathrm{msb}_{|M|}(G' \| G^{j+1} \| \ldots \| G^h)$, where $G' \in_{\mathcal{U}} \{0,1\}^{n\ell j}$ and $G^i = E_{K^i}(I_{(i-1)l+1}) \| \ldots \| E_{K^i}(I_{i\ell})$, $i = (j+1), \ldots, h$, is the concatenation of the appropriate ℓ encrypted counter blocks under the K^i section key. Note that the $(j+1)$-th section is processed under the truly random K^{j+1} key and each next key is produced from previous one according to ACPKM.
  An authentication tag $T = Z \oplus \mathrm{GHASH}_H(A, C)$, where $Z = E_{K^1}(I_0)$, $H = E_{K^1}(0^n)$ if $j = 0$, and $Z, H \in_{\mathcal{U}} \{0,1\}^n$, otherwise.

The result of any experiment described above is what the adversary $\mathcal{A}$ returns as a result. Further we denote by $Hybrid_j(\mathcal{A}) \Rightarrow 1$ an event, which occurs if the result of the experiment $Hybrid_j(\mathcal{A})$ is 1.

Note that for the adversary $\mathcal{A}$ the oracle in the experiment $Hybrid_h(\mathcal{A})$ totally coincides with the oracle \$, and the oracle in the experiment $Hybrid_0(\mathcal{A})$ coincides with the oracle $\mathcal{E}$, i.e. the following equalities hold:

$$\Pr\left[Hybrid_h(\mathcal{A}) \Rightarrow 1\right] = \Pr\left[\mathcal{A}^\$ \Rightarrow 1\right],$$

$$\Pr\left[Hybrid_0(\mathcal{A}) \Rightarrow 1\right] = \Pr\left[K \in_{\mathcal{U}} \{0,1\}^k : \mathcal{A}^\mathcal{E} \Rightarrow 1\right].$$

Construct a set of adversaries $\mathcal{A}'_j$, $j = 1, \ldots, h$, for the block cipher E in the PRF model, which uses $\mathcal{A}$ as a black box.

After receiving a query (N, A, M) from $\mathcal{A}$ the adversary $\mathcal{A}'_j$ processes this query as in the $Hybrid_j(\mathcal{A})$ experiment but the encrypted blocks for masking the j-th section and blocks of the $(j+1)$-th section key are obtained by making queries to the oracles ρ or E_K provided by the PRF experiment. The adversary $\mathcal{A}'_j$ returns 1, if the adversary $\mathcal{A}$ returns 1, and returns 0, otherwise. Note that

- $\mathcal{A}'_1$ makes at most $\sigma_1 + q + s + 1$ queries (to obtain hash key H, s blocks of the second section key, q masking values Z_i and σ_1 blocks needed to process the fist sections of q messages);
- $\mathcal{A}'_j$, $j = 2, \ldots, h-1$, makes at most $\sigma_j + s$ (to obtain s blocks of the next section key and σ_j blocks needed to process the fist sections of q messages) queries;
- $\mathcal{A}'_h$ makes at most σ_h queries (σ_h blocks needed to process the fist sections of q messages).

Note that $\Pr\left[K \in_{\mathcal{U}} \{0,1\}^k : (\mathcal{A}'_j)^{E_K} \Rightarrow 1\right] = \Pr\left[Hybrid_{j-1}(\mathcal{A}) \Rightarrow 1\right]$ and $\Pr\left[\rho \in_{\mathcal{U}} Func(\{0,1\}^n) : (\mathcal{A}'_j)^\rho \Rightarrow 1\right] = \Pr\left[Hybrid_j(\mathcal{A}) \Rightarrow 1\right]$. The last equality is proceeded from that the input blocks for producing the K^{j+1} section key and the input blocks for masking the j-th section and producing the Z and H values are different for the random function. Therefore, the K^{j+1} variable distribution is statistically indistinguishable from the uniform one. Then for the advantages of the adversaries $\mathcal{A}'_j$

$$
\sum_{j=1}^{h} \mathbf{Adv}_E^{\mathrm{PRF}}\left(\mathcal{A}'_j\right) = \sum_{j=1}^{h} \Big(\Pr\left[K \in_{\mathcal{U}} \{0,1\}^k : (\mathcal{A}'_j)^{E_K} \Rightarrow 1\right]
$$

$$
-\Pr\left[\rho \in_{\mathcal{U}} Func(\{0,1\}^n) : (\mathcal{A}'_j)^{\rho} \Rightarrow 1\right]\Big)
$$

$$
= \sum_{j=1}^{h} \Pr\left[Hybrid_{j-1}(\mathcal{A}) \Rightarrow 1\right] - \sum_{j=1}^{h} \Pr\left[Hybrid_j(\mathcal{A}) \Rightarrow 1\right]
$$

$$
= \Pr\left[Hybrid_0(\mathcal{A}) \Rightarrow 1\right] - \Pr\left[Hybrid_h(\mathcal{A}) \Rightarrow 1\right] = \mathbf{Adv}_{\mathrm{GCM\text{-}ACPKM}_{E,c,\ell}}^{\mathrm{Priv}}(\mathcal{A}).
$$

From the PRP/PRF switching lemma [13] for any block cipher E and any adversary $\mathcal{A}'$ making at most q queries we have

$$
\mathbf{Adv}_E^{\mathrm{PRF}}\left(\mathcal{A}'\right) \leqslant \mathbf{Adv}_E^{\mathrm{PRP\text{-}CPA}}\left(\mathcal{A}'\right) + \frac{q(q-1)}{2^{n+1}} \leqslant \mathbf{Adv}_E^{\mathrm{PRP\text{-}CPA}}\left(\mathcal{A}'\right) + \frac{q^2}{2^{n+1}}.
$$

Thus,

$$
\mathbf{Adv}_{\mathrm{GCM\text{-}ACPKM}_{E,c,\ell}}^{\mathrm{Priv}}(\mathcal{A}) = \sum_{j=1}^{h} \mathbf{Adv}_E^{\mathrm{PRF}}\left(\mathcal{A}'_j\right)
$$

$$
\leqslant \left(\mathbf{Adv}_E^{\mathrm{PRP\text{-}CPA}}\left(\mathcal{A}'_1\right) + \frac{(\sigma_1 + q + s + 1)^2}{2^{n+1}}\right)
$$

$$
+ \sum_{j=2}^{h-1} \left(\mathbf{Adv}_E^{\mathrm{PRP\text{-}CPA}}\left(\mathcal{A}'_j\right) + \frac{(\sigma_j + s)^2}{2^{n+1}}\right) + \left(\mathbf{Adv}_E^{\mathrm{PRP\text{-}CPA}}\left(\mathcal{A}'_h\right) + \frac{\sigma_h^2}{2^{n+1}}\right)
$$

$$
\leqslant h \cdot \mathbf{Adv}_E^{\mathrm{PRP\text{-}CPA}}\left(\mathcal{A}'\right) + \frac{(\sigma_1 + q + s + 1)^2}{2^{n+1}}
$$

$$
+ \frac{(\sigma_2 + s)^2 + \ldots + (\sigma_{h-1} + s)^2 + \sigma_h^2}{2^{n+1}},
$$

where $\mathcal{A}'$ is an adversary which makes at most $\sigma_1 + q + s + 1$ queries. The last relation is due to $\sigma_1 \geqslant \ldots \geqslant \sigma_h$ and $\mathbf{Adv}_E^{\mathrm{PRP\text{-}CPA}}\left(\mathcal{A}''\right) \leqslant \mathbf{Adv}_E^{\mathrm{PRP\text{-}CPA}}\left(\mathcal{A}'\right)$ for such adversaries $\mathcal{A}'$ and $\mathcal{A}''$ with the same computational resources that the queries number made by $\mathcal{A}''$ is less than the queries number made by $\mathcal{A}'$. □

C   Proof of Theorem 2

Proof. Without loss of generality, we assume a key size k be multiple of a block size n, and $s = k/n$.

We firstly consider the modification of the target mode – the abstract GCM-ACPKM* mode – that works as follows. The only modification is that instead of generating the initial key $K = K^1$ the permutation π is chosen uniformly at random from $Perm(\{0,1\}^n)$. This permutation replaces the E_{K^1} function, i.e. it is used to produce the following values:

- the hash key $H = \pi(0^n)$,
- blocks of the second section key $\pi(D_1)$, ..., $\pi(D_s)$, $K^2 = \pi(D_1)\|\ldots\|\pi(D_s)$,
- q masking values $Z_i = \pi(N_i\|0^{n-c-1}1)$, $1 \leqslant i \leqslant q$,
- blocks needed to process the fist sections of q messages, i.e. $\Gamma_i^j = \pi(N_i\|\mathrm{str}_{n-c}(j+1))$, $1 \leqslant j \leqslant \ell_i \leqslant \ell$, $1 \leqslant i \leqslant q$ (note that $\ell_1 + \ell_2 + \cdots + \ell_q = \sigma_1$).

The other section is processed using E_{K^i}, where $K^2 = \pi(D_1)\|\ldots\|\pi(D_s)$ and $K^i = \mathrm{ACPKM}(K^{i-1})$, $i \geqslant 3$.

By the obvious reduction we obtain the following inequality

$$\mathbf{Adv}_{\mathrm{GCM\text{-}ACPKM}_{E,c,\ell}}^{\mathrm{Auth}}(\mathcal{A}) \leqslant \mathbf{Adv}_E^{\mathrm{PRP\text{-}CPA}}(\mathcal{A}') + \mathbf{Adv}_{\mathrm{GCM\text{-}ACPKM}_{c,\ell}^*}^{\mathrm{Auth}}(\mathcal{A}),$$

where $\mathcal{A}'$ makes at most $\sigma_1 + q + s + 1$ queries.

Now consider the following modification of the Authenticity mode (Auth*): the adversary at the beginning of the game additionally takes as input blocks $\pi(D_1)$, ..., $\pi(D_s)$. Note that the advantage of the adversary in this game is not less then the same advantage in the initial game since in the Auth* game the adversary is just given more information. Thus,

$$\mathbf{Adv}_{\mathrm{GCM\text{-}ACPKM}_{c,\ell}^*}^{\mathrm{Auth}}(\mathcal{A}) \leqslant \mathbf{Adv}_{\mathrm{GCM\text{-}ACPKM}_{c,\ell}^*}^{\mathrm{Auth}^*}(\mathcal{A}),$$

The goal of this modification is to show that giving to the adversary all information about all section keys except for the first section key cannot break the authenticity. Indeed, the ciphertext calculation process influences the authenticity only by giving the additional inputs-outputs of π to the adversary. Key updating technique allows to limit this information only to the inputs-outputs which are used for the first section processing and producing blocks of the second section key.

For the proposed GCM-ACPKM* mode the proof of security in the Auth* model is the same as for Theorem 5 [22]. Below we present the light overview of this proof (for details see the original paper).

Without loss of generality we assume that $\mathcal{A}$ is deterministic and the nonce N' in the forging attempt (N', A', C', T') is one of the nonce N_i in the encryption queries (N_i, A_i, M_i) responsed with (C_i, T_i) (since otherwise the bound can be shown to be smaller). Thus, the forgery probability is equal to the probability of the event that $\mathrm{GHASH}_H(A, C) \oplus \mathrm{GHASH}_H(A', C') = T \oplus T'$.

Note that fixing the transcript of interaction between the challenger and the adversary we fix all variables in this equation except for H. Thus, for fixed transcript we can estimate this probability by $\frac{m_A+1}{2^n}$, since the equation has only m_A solutions in the Galois field (equal to polynomial degree). The next step is to estimate the conditional probability of the event that such a fixed transcript is realized (where the appropriate $H = \pi(0^n)$ is conditioned). It easy to see that the fixed transcript is fully determined by the values T_i, Γ_i^j, K^2, which in it turns are determined by additionally fixing $q + \sigma_1 + s$ input-output of π. Therefore this conditioned probability should be $\frac{1}{(2^n - 1)_{q + \sigma_1 + s}}$, where $(a)_b = a \cdot (a - 1) \cdots (a - b + 1)$. The total probability over all possible transcripts defined by T_i, Γ_i^j, K^2 is estimated exactly as in [22] using Bernstein's upper bound of the interpolation probability of a random permutation. $\qquad\square$

References

1. Abdalla, M., Bellare, M.: Increasing the lifetime of a key: a comparative analysis of the security of re-keying techniques. In: Okamoto, T. (ed.) ASIACRYPT 2000. LNCS, vol. 1976, pp. 546–559. Springer, Heidelberg (2000). https://doi.org/10.1007/3-540-44448-3_42
2. Ahmetzyanova, L., Alekseev, E., Oshkin, I., Smyshlyaev, S., Sonina, L.: On the properties of the CTR encryption mode of the Magma and Kuznyechik block ciphers with re-keying method based on CryptoPro Key Meshing. IACR Cryptology ePrint Archive, 2016:628 (2016)
3. Ahmetzyanova, L., Alekseev, E., Smyshlyaev, S.: Security bound for CTR-ACPKM internally re-keyed encryption mode. IACR Cryptology ePrint Archive, 2018:950 (2018)
4. Bellare, M., Desai, A., Jokipii, E., Rogaway, P.: A concrete security treatment of symmetric encryption. In: Proceedings of 38th Annual Symposium on Foundations of Computer Science (FOCS 1997), USA, pp. 394–403. IEEE Press (1997)
5. Bellare, M., Pietrzak, K., Rogaway, P.: Improved security analyses for CBC MACs. In: Shoup, V. (ed.) CRYPTO 2005. LNCS, vol. 3621, pp. 527–545. Springer, Heidelberg (2005). https://doi.org/10.1007/11535218_32
6. Bellare, M., Rogaway, P.: Introduction to modern cryptography (2005). http://cseweb.ucsd.edu/~mihir/cse207/classnotes.html
7. Bellare, M.: Practice-oriented provable-security. In: Damgård, I.B. (ed.) EEF School 1998. LNCS, vol. 1561, pp. 1–15. Springer, Heidelberg (1999). https://doi.org/10.1007/3-540-48969-X_1
8. Bellare, M., Yee, B.: Forward-security in private-key cryptography. In: Joye, M. (ed.) CT-RSA 2003. LNCS, vol. 2612, pp. 1–18. Springer, Heidelberg (2003). https://doi.org/10.1007/3-540-36563-X_1
9. Bhargavan, K., Leurent, G.: On the Practical (In-)Security of 64-bit Block Ciphers: Collision Attacks on HTTP over TLS and OpenVPN. IACR Cryptology ePrint Archive, 2016:798 (2016)
10. Biham, E.: How to forge DES-encrypted messages in 2^{28} steps. Technion Computer Science Department Technical Report CS0884 (1996)
11. Biham, E., Shamir, A.: Differential cryptanalysis of DES-like cryptosystems. J. Cryptol. 537, 2–21 (1990)
12. Standaert, F.X.: Introduction to side-channel attacks. In: Verbauwhede, I. (ed.) Secure Integrated Circuits and Systems. Integrated Circuits and Systems. Springer, Boston (2010). https://doi.org/10.1007/978-0-387-71829-3_2
13. Chang, D., Nandi, M.: A Short Proof of the PRP/PRF Switching Lemma. IACR Cryptology ePrint Archive, 2008:078 (2008)

14. Iwata, T., Kurosawa, K.: OMAC: one-key CBC MAC. In: Johansson, T. (ed.) FSE 2003. LNCS, vol. 2887, pp. 129–153. Springer, Heidelberg (2003). https://doi.org/10.1007/978-3-540-39887-5_11

15. Iwata, T., Kurosawa, K.: Stronger security bounds for OMAC, TMAC, and XCBC. In: Johansson, T., Maitra, S. (eds.) INDOCRYPT 2003. LNCS, vol. 2904, pp. 402–415. Springer, Heidelberg (2003). https://doi.org/10.1007/978-3-540-24582-7_30

16. Iwata, T., Ohashi, K., Minematsu, K.: Breaking and repairing GCM security proofs. In: Safavi-Naini, R., Canetti, R. (eds.) CRYPTO 2012. LNCS, vol. 7417, pp. 31–49. Springer, Heidelberg (2012). https://doi.org/10.1007/978-3-642-32009-5_3

17. Luykx, A., Preneel, B.: Optimal forgeries against polynomial-based MACs and GCM. In: Nielsen, J.B., Rijmen, V. (eds.) EUROCRYPT 2018. LNCS, vol. 10820, pp. 445–467. Springer, Cham (2018). https://doi.org/10.1007/978-3-319-78381-9_17

18. Matsui, M.: Linear cryptanalysis method for DES cipher. In: Helleseth, T. (ed.) EUROCRYPT 1993. LNCS, vol. 765, pp. 386–397. Springer, Heidelberg (1994). https://doi.org/10.1007/3-540-48285-7_33

19. McGrew, D.A., Viega, J.: The security and performance of the Galois/Counter Mode (GCM) of operation. In: Canteaut, A., Viswanathan, K. (eds.) INDOCRYPT 2004. LNCS, vol. 3348, pp. 343–355. Springer, Heidelberg (2004). https://doi.org/10.1007/978-3-540-30556-9_27

20. Mitchell, C.J.: On the security of XCBC, TMAC and OMAC. Technical report RHUL-MA-2003-4, 19 August 2003. http://www.rhul.ac.uk/mathematics/techreports

21. Chen, L.: NIST Special Publication 800–108. Recommendation for Key Derivation Using Pseudorandom Functions (Revised) (2009)

22. Nandi, M.: Bernstein bound on WCS is tight. In: Shacham, H., Boldyreva, A. (eds.) CRYPTO 2018. LNCS, vol. 10992, pp. 213–238. Springer, Cham (2018). https://doi.org/10.1007/978-3-319-96881-0_8

23. Popov, V., Kurepkin, I., Leontiev, S.: Additional cryptographic algorithms for use with GOST 28147–89, GOST R 34.10-94, GOST R 34.10-2001, and GOST R 34.11-94 algorithms. RFC 4357 (2007)

24. Rescorla, E., RTFM, Inc.: The Transport Layer Security (TLS) Protocol Version 1.3, RFC 8446, August 2018

25. Housley, R.: Using AES-CCM and AES-GCM Authenticated Encryption in the Cryptographic Message Syntax (CMS), RFC 5084, November 2007

26. Ramsay, C., Lohuis, J.: TEMPEST attacks against AES. Covertly stealing keys for €200 (2017). https://www.fox-it.com

27. https://www.openssl.org/

28. Rescorla, E., Modadugu, N.: Datagram Transport Layer Security Version 1.2, RFC 6347, January 2012.https://doi.org/10.17487/RFC6347

29. Kent, S.: IP Encapsulating Security Payload (ESP), RFC 4303, December 2005. https://doi.org/10.17487/RFC4303

30. Dierks, T., Rescorla, E.: The Transport Layer Security (TLS) Protocol Version 1.2, RFC 5246, August 2008. https://doi.org/10.17487/RFC5246

31. Ylonen, T., Lonvick, C. (ed.): The Secure Shell (SSH) Transport Layer Protocol, RFC 4253, January 2006. https://doi.org/10.17487/RFC4253

32. Smyshlyaev, S.: Re-keying Mechanisms for Symmetric Keys, RFC8645, August 2019

33. Smyshlyaev, S.: GOST Cipher Suites for Transport Layer Security (TLS) Protocol Version 1.2, draft-smyshlyaev-tls12-gost-suites-04, 29 December 2018

A Systematic Appraisal of Side Channel Evaluation Strategies

Melissa Azouaoui[1,2], Davide Bellizia[2], Ileana Buhan[3], Nicolas Debande[4],
Sèbastien Duval[2], Christophe Giraud[4], Èliane Jaulmes[5], François Koeune[2],
Elisabeth Oswald[6,7(✉)], François-Xavier Standaert[2], and Carolyn Whitnall[7]

[1] NXP Semiconductors, Hamburg, Germany
[2] ICTEAM, UCLouvain, Louvain-la-Neuve, Belgium
[3] Radboud University, Nijmegen, The Netherlands
[4] IDEMIA, Paris, France
[5] SGDSN, Paris, France
[6] AAU, Klagenfurt, Austria
Elisabeth.Oswald@aau.at
[7] UoB, Bristol, UK

Abstract. In this paper we examine the central question that is how well do side channel evaluation regimes capture the true security level of a product. Concretely, answering this question requires considering the optimality of the attack/evaluation strategy selected by the evaluator, and the various steps to instantiate it. We draw on a number of published works and discuss whether state-of-the-art solutions for the different steps of a side-channel security evaluation offer bounds or guarantees of optimality, or if they are inherently heuristic. We use this discussion to provide an informal rating of the steps' optimality and to put forward where risks of overstated security levels remain.

Keywords: Side channels · Evaluation · Certification

1 Introduction

Testing for side channel vulnerabilities is a central aspect of security evaluations of implementations featuring cryptography. The effort that goes into testing is considerable, and the stakes for companies are high. There exist two testing/evaluation regimes at present. The first regime operates within the Common

This work has been funded in parts by the European Union (EU) via the H2020 project 731591 (acronym REASSURE), the ERC project 724725 (acronym SWORD) and the ERC project 725042 (acronym SEAL). François-Xavier Standaert is a senior research associate of the Belgian Fund for Scientific Research (FNRS-F.R.S.). Ileana Buhan was with Riscure at the time of conducting this research.

T. van der Merwe et al. (Eds.): SSR 2020, LNCS 12529, pp. 46–66, 2020.
https://doi.org/10.1007/978-3-030-64357-7_3

Criteria (CC) framework [23][1] whereby side channel (and other implementation related) attacks have been picked up early as a threat that warrants specialist consideration, in particular in the context of smart cards. The second regime operates within the framework of FIPS 140 [36]; there is a transition effort currently ongoing to move from 140-2 towards 140-3, the latter explicitly considers side channel attacks.

Within the context of CC, stakeholder groups such as JHAS[2], are concerned with achieving a *balance between sound evaluation practices and the cost of evaluations*. Their approach is to discuss and in some sense categorise attacks (they maintain a confidential list of attack vectors that need to be attempted during an evaluation), and come to a shared understanding of the difficulty of mounting attacks via a specific rating system [48].

In contrast, the FIPS 140 approach is to keep the *cost of evaluation to an absolute minimum* by mandating no more than conformance style testing as specified in ISO 17825:2016 [24]. FIPS 140-3 (which has been agreed on in 2019 and will become effective later in 2020) adopts a variation of the so-called Test Vector Leakage Assessment (TVLA) framework [16] to assess the threat of side channel attacks.

Contributions. In this paper we are concerned with the central question of how well do such evaluation regimes capture the true security level of a product. Concretely, answering this question requires considering the optimality of the attack/evaluation strategy selected by the evaluator, and the various steps to instantiate it. We also point towards a third evaluation strategy, based on working backwards from the worst-case adversary, which has emerged in the academic literature. We draw on a number of published works and discuss whether state-of-the-art solutions for the different steps of a side-channel security evaluation offer bounds or guarantees of optimality, or if they are inherently heuristic. We use this discussion to provide an informal rating of the steps' optimality and to put forward where risks of overstated security levels remain.

1.1 Organisation and Outline of This Paper

We provide a brief explanation of the two evaluation regimes (Common Criteria and FIPS 140) in Sect. 2. We suggest a third technique (we call this the worst case adversary) in Sect. 3, and discuss some examples where such an approach was in fact used in the academic community. Then we consider the optimality of the steps or components that are the constituent parts of the three evaluation approaches and comment on the overall assurance that contemporary evaluations offer in Sect. 4.

---

[1] The most recent version of all documents relating to CC evaluations can be found on www.commoncriteriaportal.com.

[2] (JIL Hardware Attacks Subgroup), they operate within the International Security Certification Initiative (ISCI).

2   State-of-the-Art Industrial Evaluation Approaches

Whilst there are a number of security evaluation approaches possible in principle, two schemes (and derivatives thereof) dominate in industrial practice. Common Criteria evaluations are "attack driven" and aim to systematically capture and categorise attack vectors. The Common Criteria methodology is adopted as an international standard via ISO 15408. Common criteria features a range of assurance levels (so called EALs), and to reach the higher level requires more rigorous testing. The goal of a Common Criteria evaluation is to check the security claims made by a manufacturer and testing against side channels is typically included.

FIPS 140 evaluations are "conformance style" evaluations that rely on checking some minimum criteria relating to the security of a product. FIPS 140-2 is mandated in the US (FIPS 140-3 will replace FIPS 140-2 late in 2020), it is also used in Canada and some other countries (e.g. Japan), have begun adopting it as well. FIPS 140 is represented by a set of ISO standards (ISO/IEC 19790:2012(E) and ISO/IEC 24759:2017(E)), and the difference between FIPS 140-2 and FIPS 140-3 is the inclusion of testing against side-channel attacks (the methodology for this is given in ISO/IEC 17825:2016, with setups and calibration defined in ISO/IEC 20085-1 and 20085-2).

Both approaches require that the product is tested by an accredited testing laboratory and a government agency oversees this process.

2.1   CC

CC evaluations are complex and governed by several documents. The product which is being certified is called the Target of Evaluation (TOE). For a TOE two documents are of relevance: the Protection Profile (PP) and the Security Target (ST). The Protection Profile is a generic document for a category of product (e.g. Travel documents, Java Cards, IC, *etc.*), often created by a user community. It provides an implementation independent specification of security requirements for a "class of devices": it lists threats, security objectives, assumptions, security functional requirements (SFRs), security assurance requirements (SARs) and rationales. Such document insures that a product is conform to a security goal and provides the expected security features. It is not mandatory to rely on a PP, but if one exists for a kind of products, it is recommended to use it. The Security Target details the secure implementation of the TOE and may use (or not) a PP as reference. It uniquely identifies the product and describes the assets, the threats, the security objectives (both on the TOE and on the environment), the perimeter of the evaluation, the SFRs and the life cycle. Vendors often make the Security Target details available to their customers.

During the Common Criteria evaluation process, vendors must state an envisioned security level. This is called the Evaluation Assurance Level (EAL). The EAL indicates a minimal level for each subclass (development process, guidance, conformity of security target, vulnerability assessment, *etc.*) that will be taken into account during the evaluation. It reflects the rigour of the evaluation. There are seven levels of EALs, with EAL 1 being the most basic and level 7 being the most rigorous. One can pick a level and "augment" it with specific requirements from a higher level. It is imperative to understand that higher EALs do not necessarily imply a higher level of security, they imply that the claimed security assurance of the TOE has been more rigorously verified. Among all subclasses, the more relevant for practical security is AVA_VAN (vulnerability assessment), with levels going from 1 (resistance to basic attackers) to 5 (resistance to attackers with high attack potential). It describes the search for vulnerabilities and define a rating scale for attacks, depending on the means of the adversary.

Smart Card/Integrated Circuit Evaluations. In the specific case of smart cards, the International Security Certification Initiative (ISCI) brings together stakeholders from every aspect of smart card security evaluations: certification bodies, evaluation laboratories, hardware vendors, software vendors, card vendors and service providers. ISCI has two working groups: ISCI-WG1, which aims to define methodology and best practice for smart security device evaluation, and ISCI-WG2 (also known as JHAS), which defines and maintains the state of the art in potential attacks against smart security devices.

Two documents are essential for the evaluation of smart cards. The "Application of Attack Potential to Smart Cards" [48] provides a "rating system" for attacks. The "Attack Methods for Smart Cards and Similar Devices" [49] is a confidential document and describes attack vectors that are considered "relevant". The purpose of the rating system is grounded in the need to be able to compare the "security strength" of different products. The rating system is designed to reduce subjectivity and it results in a total score. This score is the sum of several factors during both the "Identification" and the "Exploitation" phase of an attack (for reference: identification is broadly speaking about finding, and characterising, leaks and corresponding attack vectors for the first time; exploitation refers to attacks utilising the results from identification). The factors that are considered are: Elapsed time, Expertise, Knowledge of TOE, Access to TOE, Used equipment, Open samples[3]. The same rating scheme is also used by EMVCo (a "derivative" of the CC approach that we discuss).

2.2 FIPS 140-3

This Federal Information Processing Standard (140-2, and, from late 2020 on, FIPS 140-3) specifies the security requirements for cryptographic modules. It has four increasing, qualitative levels intended to cover a wide range of potential applications and environments. FIPS 140-3 covers side-channel attacks via a link to several ISO standards: a side-channel test regime is given in ISO/IEC 17825:2016, with setups and calibration defined in ISO/IEC 20085-1 and 20085-2 (NIST special publications SP800-140 A-F may modify these in the future).

For testing against basic power analysis attacks in the context of symmetric encryption, ISO/IEC 17825:2016 relies on using leakage detection procedures

---

[3] For the sake of succinctness we refer the reader to the JHAS documentation for a precise definition of these factors [48].

instead of attempting attacks. In all other scenarios it requires to test against standard DPA style attacks (the type of attacks/methodology are listed in the standard). Leakage detection involves producing evidence for the presence of leaks using statistical hypothesis testing. It has been advertised as a "cheaper process" than running full blown attacks, and ISO/IEC 17825:2016 suggests it may be done *instead* of attacks. ISO/IEC 17825:2016 adopts a modified version of the Test Vector Leakage Assessment (TVLA), which is a methodology to test side-channel resistance. As such, it is a black-box tool that gathers evidence against the absence/presence of leaks.

3   An Alternative: Backwards Evaluations

The goal of an evaluation is to ascertain the true security level of a product (either in absolute terms by checking explicit claims by the manufacturer or in relative terms via ensuring that it is at least as secure as given by some minimum criteria) and our research question for this work is how well existing evaluation regimes capture the true security level of a product. The NIST/FIPS approach for side channels (via ISO/IEC 17825:2016) sets the bar rather low by mandating a testing regime that captures a well resourced and capable adversary (we a provide a more in-depth critique in the next section). But it is far from mandating even a "best practical adversary" (as it happens in the CC approach). Defining the "best practical adversary" is hard because "practical" is somewhat subjective and tends to change over time. In contrast, the definition of a worst-case adversary (and working backwards, i.e. relaxing assumptions) is often less ambiguous and therefore academic works have increasingly utilised this approach. Such a worst-case adversary will utilize multiple leaking intermediate variables, a multivariate characterization of each leaking intermediate variable, divide-and-conquer or analytical information extraction and enumeration capabilities. For this, various types of capabilities, for example in terms of knowledge of the target implementation and profiling abilities, can be granted to the adversary. Academic research has featured this type of adversary in published works, and we will link to two concrete such examples in the next section.

3.1   Worst-Case Adversary

The worst-case adversary is assumed to be able to measure one or multiple side channels from the target, and have full control over all inputs (plaintexts or ciphertexts) as well as over the secret parameters (keys, randomness). They can turn off any countermeasures (should the target allow turning them off), and has detailed implementation knowledge (e.g., source code in the case of software implementations, or a hardware level description in the case of hardware implementations). The worst-case adversary is pushing the separation between the identification of the attack and its exploitation to the extreme: *it essentially enables practically unbounded profiling efforts in order to reach the strongest online attack.*

For instance in case of an AES hardware implementation that employs a special logic style that does not require extra randomness, the worst-case adversary would have full information about the properties of that logic style, and he would be able to choose keys and inputs. They would also have full information about the AES architecture. With this information, a profiling attack should be attempted (using either statistical modelling, machine learning or deep learning).

In case of an AES software implementation that employs software masking and shuffling, the worst-case adversary would have the source code, control over inputs (plaintexts/ciphertexts), key, and knowledge of randomness (for both masking and shuffling). This is because in software it is realistic to output randomness without significantly changing the leakage characteristics of the rest of the implementation (therefore the countermeasure can be made accessible during evaluation, but this access can be completely removed when the software is deployed). With these assumptions, the evaluator can again conduct a profiling attack and we describe in a subsequent section one such concrete example.

During an evaluation, a natural goal is therefore to come as close as possible to the worst-case adversary, by first granting them with the maximum (even if not always realistic) capabilities. Thanks to such advanced capabilities, it is in general possible to (i) identify (from the documentation) the predictable target values that may occur separated in the time domain, and the predictable target values that occur within each clock cycle, (ii) attempt characterization (potentially by using a biased trace set if documentation suggests when masks may leak)[4]. As a result, a backwards evaluation suggests to start from such a powerful (yet easier to specify) adversary and, once concretely analyzed, to discuss the consequences of relaxing different adversarial capabilities for the feasibility of the attack, and the additional (profiling or online) attack complexity this relaxation implies. Arguing from this angle provides at least a stable starting point, and a fairly well defined set of steps which fit to processes which are (to the best of our knowledge) already standard.

Thus this approach advocates that, if at all possible, an attack for the worst-case adversary should be demonstrated. After the feasibility of a worst-case attack has been considered, and if there are sound reasons that explain why this may not be possible, then the adversarial assumptions or capabilities can be gradually relaxed, and attacks be considered and demonstrated for the considered relaxed assumptions. The impact of relaxing these strong adversarial capabilities on the attack complexity should be discussed, in order to assess the possible complexity gaps between worst-case attacks and ones with fewer assumptions.

Because every evaluation requires a number of (potentially iterative) steps, it is important to consider and spell out assumptions for each of the steps, which will ultimately determine the assurance of the evaluation.

---

[4] A target value is an intermediate value that the adversary/evaluator can predict based on knowing (parts of) the input and guessing parts of the key.

3.2 Evaluation Steps

We propose to consider any evaluation as a composition (possibly iterative) of the following key steps:

1. **Measurement and preprocessing.** This step provides the adversary (evaluators) with leakages (e.g., the power consumption or electromagnetic radiation of a chip, or their simulation in case simulated analyses are considered) based on their input control, and possibly performs data-independent preprocessing in order to improve the quality of these measurements.
2. **Leakage detection and mapping.** In leakage detection, the adversary (evaluator) aims to detect the presence of any data-dependent leakage (independent of whether this data-dependency is exploitable in a realistic attack). Leakage mapping further aims to connect the detected samples to specific operations performed by the target implementation.
3. **Leakage exploitation.** In this last step, the adversary (evaluator) aims to exploit the leakages in order to perform an attack (e.g., a key recovery). It is usually divided in three phases:
   (a) **(Optional) modelling phase.** In this phase, the adversary (evaluator) takes advantage of their profiling abilities to estimate a model for the leakages.
   (b) **Information extraction phase.** In this phase, the adversary (evaluator) extracts information about intermediate values manipulated by their target implementation thanks to a model (that can be obtained from a modelling phase or assumed a priori).
   (c) **Information processing.** In this final phase, the adversary (evaluator) combines the partial information they extracted from their target implementation and aggregates this information in order to recover some secret parameter (e.g., a master key).

We now illustrate the backwards approach based on the Worst-Case Adversary with reference to two concrete papers that were published recently: a masked AES implementation proposed by the French ANSSI (Agence Nationale de la Sécurité des Systèmes d'Information) [2], recently analyzed in [5], and an (unprotected) ECC scalar multiplication analyzed in [1,40].

3.3 Case Study: Masked AES Implementation

Instantiation of a Worst-Case Adversary. The ANSSI implementation that was analysed by [5] is a protected implementation combining additive and multiplicative secret sharing into an affine masking scheme [14], which is additionally mixed with a shuffled execution [20]. It is running on an ARM Cortex-M4 architecture. Preliminary leakage assessments did not reveal data dependencies with up to 100,000 measurements (i.e. following a TVLA style leakage assessment). Bronchain and Standaert considered a worst-case adversary with no specific device preparation, a single device sample, full control of the AES inputs and outputs, full profiling capabilities (i.e., knowledge of the key and randomness during profiling), knowledge of the (open source) software implementation, limited knowledge of the hardware details (i.e., the general architecture of the ARM Cortex family), with a simple measurement setup worth a few thousands of euros. The attack steps listed in Sect. 3.2 of their worst-case attack can be detailed as follows.

Measurement Setup: The target board has been modified by removing decoupling capacitors and measurements were taken at $1\,[Gsamples/s]$ with a PicoScope (while the chip was running at $48\,MHz$). The probe position was optimized in function of the Signal-to-Noise Ratio (SNR) [32] of the multiplicative mask. No additional preprocessing (e.g., filtering) was performed on the traces. The SNR of the computation samples was typically in the 0.1 range, while it was significantly higher (more than 10) for the memory accesses needed during the precomputations of the multiplicative mask tables.

Leakage Detection and Mapping: Most target intermediate variables are identified based on the SNR metric. In the case of the multiplicative mask precomputations, a dimensionality reduction based on principal component analysis (PCA) was additionally performed (which allowed recovering this mask in full).

Modelling: All the randomized target intermediate variables can be modeled with Gaussian mixtures as per [52,55]. Thanks to the knowledge of the randomness during profiling, this was done straightforwardly by estimating first-order (sometimes multivariate) Gaussian templates [9].

Information Extraction: Bronchain and Standaert considered the dissection of countermeasures. That is, they targeted the different countermeasures (i.e., the additive mask, the multiplicative mask and the shuffling) independently in order to reduce the physical noise amplification they respectively imply. Thanks to this approach, the multiplicative mask was recovered in full, the shuffling permutation was recovered with high probability, leaving the adversary with the need to attack a two-share Boolean masking scheme with multivariate templates.

Finally, the information extracted on the different target intermediate variables was accumulated on the long-term key using a standard maximum likelihood approach. Key information was then post-processed with a key enumeration algorithm [39]. As a result, the best attack was able to reduce the 128-bit key rank below 2^{32} with less than 2,000 measurements.

Relaxing Capabilities. Compared to the leakage assessment in [2], the main improvement in the dissection attack described above is that it exploits multiple target intermediate variables and multiple leakage samples per target. For this purpose, the two most critical adversarial capabilities are (i) the implementation knowledge made available thanks to the open source library and (ii) the possibility to profile models efficiently thanks to the randomness knowledge. As discussed in [5], removing these capabilities makes the attack substantially harder.

On the one hand, purely black box approaches (e.g., based on machine learning) seem unable to efficiently identify the different countermeasures as exploited in a dissection attack [5]. So in absence of implementation knowledge, it is unlikely that an attack can directly target the additive and multiplicative masks and the shuffling separately, implying a significant (multiplicative) increase of the overall attack cost. Such a difficulty could be overcome with advanced techniques such as [12] which are, however, less studied and understood than standard side-channel attacks.

On the other hand, profiling Gaussian mixtures without mask knowledge is known to be a hard task. A work by Lerman et al. discusses options for this purpose [29], but the profiling cost is significantly higher than in the known randomness case (another solution is [28]). Alternatively, one can attack using a non-profiled higher-order side-channel attack [43]. However such a strategy (based on the estimation of a higher-order statistical moment rather than a mixture) becomes increasingly suboptimal as the level of noise in the implementation decreases [50]. When combined together, the lack of implementation knowledge and the unknown randomness during profiling additionally imply that tuples of Points-of-Interest (POIs) must be detected exhaustively, which is also known to be a hard task [6,11]. For illustration, the complexities of the worst-case attack put forward by Bronchain and Standaert and the single-target attack discussed in the preliminary security assessment of the ANSSI implementation differ by a factor $> \frac{100,000}{2,000} = 50$.

3.4   Case Study: ECC Scalar Multiplication

Instantiating a Worst-Case Adversary. The ECSM implementation analyzed in [1,40] is a constant-time Montgomery ladder using Jacobian coordinates on the NIST P-256 curve and the target device is an ARM cortex-M4 with no specific preparation. The worst-case adversary is assumed to have full control of the inputs and full profiling capabilities. The generic evaluation framework designed by Poussier et al. [40] is horizontal (i.e. it utilises multiple leakage points per leakage trace) and allows extracting most of the information in the leakage traces. The main vector of the attack is that for each scalar bit a regular ECSM performs a fixed and predictable sequence of operations. These operations lead to several leakages on intermediate values that depend on the scalar bit and the input point. Following an Extend and Prune (E&P) strategy, once one bit is recovered, the internal state of the ECSM is known and the following bit can be recovered in the same way. The general steps of the evaluation, as outlined in Sect. 3.2, are summarised below.

Measurement Setup: The voltage variation was monitored using a $4.7\,\Omega$ resistor. The traces were acquired using a Lecroy WaveRunner HRO 66 ZI oscilloscope running at 200 MHz. The target micro-controller runs at 100 MHz. No preprocessing was applied to the traces. The average SNR achieved by the targeted ALU operations was around 0.018.

Leakage Detection and Mapping: POIs corresponding to target intermediate values are identified using classical selection techniques such as correlation [11] (based on a simple estimated model) or SNR based ones.

Modelling: Once the time locations of all the target intermediates are found, they can be modelled using classical Gaussian templates [9], but a full profiling (i.e. assuming that all 32 bits in a variable can interact) on 32-bit variables is too measurement intensive. As a result, Poussier et al. rather use a regression based approach with only a linear 32-bit basis [45], which significantly speeds up the modelling phase of the 32-bit target registers.

Information Extraction: Using the previous regression based modeling and a single side-channel trace, the conditional probabilities of all the target intermediates are evaluated.

Finally, all the information is processed by simply multiplying all the intermediate's probabilities to evaluate the most likely value for the scalar bit. Based on the E&P strategy, to recover the following bit at index $i+1$, the intermediate values are not only predicted based on the value of the bit at index $i + 1$ but also on the previously guessed value of the bit at index i. This is due to the recursive nature of ECSM algorithms. On the target implementation, a scalar bit is recovered with high confidence when 1000 or more intermediate values are exploited.

While all previous steps were described for a single scalar bit, they can be easily extended to consider words of the scalar. For example instead of considering only two possible sequences of intermediate values, the analysis can be extended to n-bit limbs (n is typically small) and thus now the attack requires to predict 2^n intermediate value sequences instead of 2. After the previous attack, in the case of ECDH, computational power can be exploited in order to mitigate a possible lack of information using enumeration [27], and to recover the full value of the scalar. For ECDSA, a potential strategy is to partially attack the random nonces, recover their first few bits, and apply lattice cryptanalysis in order to recover the secret scalar [37]. Lattice attacks are hindered by errors on the nonces' bits. However based on the nonces' probabilities after a side-channel attack, it is possible to select only a few nonces' with a probability above a certain threshold, and discard the others to maximize the success of the lattice attack. Based on this combination of tools, the ECDSA key can be recovered using 4 bits of 140 nonces.

Relaxing Capabilities. The previously described evaluation strategy is designed to exploit the leakage of all the intermediate values computed during the execution of the ECSM. This is made easy by the detailed knowledge of the code that an open evaluation enables. However, even when the attacker is not assumed to have access to this information, a similar evaluation strategy is still possible for a lower (yet still high) number of intermediate values that the attacker can guess. That is, while reverse engineering the ECSM code is a possible but tedious option, the structure of the elliptic curve and the fact that ECSM algorithms always perform point addition and point doubling routines make it possible for the adversary to test a few "natural" options for how point and field operations are implemented in practice. This step could be emulated by the evaluator/adversary based on openly available ECC implementations, for example.

Typically, the original attack of Poussier et al. [40] exploits 1,600 intermediate values based on the knowledge of the multiplication algorithm. By mapping some intermediate values to the side-channel traces, it is possible for an attacker to try identifying the multiplication, addition and modular reduction algorithms used. For instance (i.e., based on the above experiment), an attacker who has knowledge of the multiplication algorithm could exploit roughly 46% of the key dependent leakage, an attacker able to identify the addition algorithm (which is in most cases the easiest to recover) can exploit 3% of the key dependent leakage and an attacker having access to the modular reduction code can additionally exploit over 50% of the leakage.

Tools such as the shortcut formula given by Azouaoui et al. [1] can then help evaluators to predict the success rate of the previous attack for a varying number of intermediate values, without having to implement the attack in full and with minimal modeling.

Overall, we conclude that while the knowledge of the implementation details is helpful to rapidly reach a close to worst-case attack, strong horizontal attacks are still possible without this knowledge. This is in contrast with the case of a masked AES implementation in the previous section. The main reason of this observation is that an unprotected ECSM implementation has many targets that can be very efficiently identified with simple (correlation or SNR) tools.

4   Optimality of Evaluation Steps

We now discuss the optimality of the state-of-the-art tools that can be used for various attack steps in the context of the three evaluation approaches that we have introduced.

4.1   Measurement and Preprocessing

In general, a measurement setup is composed of several elements, such as a probe, preamplifiers, physical filters and a digital storage oscilloscope, that has to deploy some specific characteristics, such as low-noise capability, suitable bandwidth and sampling rate, as also reported in ISO/IEC 20085-1.

The choice of those components and how they interact with each other impact greatly on the final outcome of the practical evaluation of a device. Based on the knowledge of the device's operating parameters (e.g., clock frequency, range of admitted operating power supply voltage, etc.), the measurement setup has to be designed in order to fulfil the expected leakage characteristics in order to deploy a sound evaluation.

Due to its physical nature, the optimality of the measurement and preprocessing step is hard to quantify. The quality of a measurement setup is indeed mostly dependent on hard to evaluate engineering expertise. A badly designed setup may lead to higher noise in the time and amplitude domains that directly affect the attack complexity [32], and the impact of which exponentially increases whenever combined with countermeasures such as masking [10].

Preprocessing is similarly heuristic. Many published solutions exist to filter the noise [38,41] and to resynchronise the traces [47,53], but their effectiveness is typically application dependent. Based on this state-of-the-art, the best mitigation plan currently is to make measurement setups and preprocessing steps as open and reproducible as possible so that the quality of the measurements they provide can be compared thanks to simple and established metrics (e.g., the SNR for univariate evaluations [19,32] and information theoretic metrics for multivariate evaluations [51]).

In the context of CC/JHAS and the worst case approach the emphasis is on working towards the best setup. In the FIPS 140 case, the corresponding public ISO standards advocate checking against some set target devices in order to argue the quality of a setup. Neither approach is able to substantially change the heuristic nature of setups and configurations, thus there cannot be any claims towards optimality.

4.2 Detection and Mapping

The term leakage in the context of leakage detection refers to the presence of sensitive data dependency in the trace measurements. Mapping of leaks is about associating identified leaks with intermediate values. Leakage can be detected using statistical hypothesis tests for independence. These can be based on (non-parametric) comparisons between generic distributional features or on (parametric) comparisons between moments and related quantities, and vary in complexity and scope depending on whether one is interested in univariate or multivariate settings. There are two potential end results aimed at by a detection test:

Certifying vulnerability: Find a leak in **at least one** trace point. In such a case it is important to control the number of false positives (that is, concluding there is a leak where there is none).

Certifying security: Find **no leaks** having tested thoroughly. Here false negatives (failure to find leaks that are really there) become a concern.

The statistical methods used for leakage detection cannot "prove" that there is no effect, they can at best conclude that there is no evidence of a leak. Hence it is especially important to design tests with **'statistical power'** in mind – that is, to make sure the sample size is large enough to detect a present effect of a certain size with reasonable probability. Then, in the event that no leak is discovered, these constructed features of the test form the basis of a reasoned interpretation. A further, considerable challenge implicit to this goal is the necessity to be convincingly exhaustive in the range of tests performed – that is, to target "all possible" intermediates and all relevant higher-order combinations of points. (This suggests analogues with the idea of *coverage* in software testing).

Typically leakage detection is a precursor to leakage exploitation. However in conformance style testing as detailed in ISO 17825:2016, leakage detection is seen as a replacement for leakage attacks in specific circumstances (in particular in the case of testing block ciphers against standard DPA attacks). We therefore consider the case of an evaluation with detection as precursor to attack, and the case of an evaluation that uses detection only.

Detect and Then Attack: CC and Worst Case Approach. It is *impossible to eliminate* errors in statistical hypothesis testing; the aim is rather to understand and minimise them. The decision to reject a null hypothesis when it is in fact true is called a Type I error, a.k.a. 'false positive' (e.g. finding leakage when in fact there is none). The acceptable rate of false positives is explicitly set by the analyst at a significance level α. A Type II error, a.k.a. 'false negative' is a failure to reject the null hypothesis when it is in fact false (e.g. failing to find leakage when in reality there is some). The Type II error rate of an hypothesis test is denoted β and the **power** of the test is $1 - \beta$, that is, the probability of correctly rejecting a false null in favour of a true alternative.

It is well known that the two errors can be traded-off against one another, and mitigated (but not eliminated) by:

- Increasing the **sample size**, intuitively resulting in more evidence from which to draw a conclusion.
- Increasing the minimum **effect size** of interest, which in our case implies increasing the magnitude of leakage that one would be willing to dismiss as 'negligible'. This is possible via an improved setup.
- Choosing a different statistical test that is more efficient with respect to the sample size. In the case of first order leakage analysis, the t-test is already the most trace efficient technique [35].

If detection is followed by attacks, then the purpose of detection is in line with "certifying vulnerability": i.e. we want to find any leaks and are particularly interested to avoid false positives. Recall that false positives are trace points that indicate a leak but there is none. If attacks are based on false positives, they are likely to be inconclusive, and they waste evaluators' time. Controlling false positives in the context of leakage traces (which have many potentially correlated leakage points) is all but straightforward. The principal difficulty is that for any methods that are not detrimental to the detection power, something has to be already known about the distribution of leaks in the leakage traces. This obviously represents a catch-22 if detection precedes further analysis. However, in the case where attacks follow detection, the consequences of missing out on some leaks (because of a lack of statistical power) is not as severe (as a test with a lower power is still o.k.), because any detected leak that is confirmed via an attack leads to the rejection of the security claim about the device.

Note that in the open context of a worst-case adversary, the detection is expected to be successful and it is only these positive results that are easy to interpret. By contrast, and as we argued before, negative detection results in the context of a closed source protected (e.g., masked) implementation are not necessarily indicative of a secure implementation [50].

A similar observation holds for the mapping step, which can be instantiated using a variety of simple statistical tools [11]. By contrast, if one is not in the worst case adversary setting, the dimensionality reduction problem may become hard with no optimal solutions (in the context of higher-order and multivariate attacks [6]).

Detect and Then Stop: ISO 17825. The goal of evaluations typically is to "certify security", and if this is based on leakage detection only as in the case of ISO 17825 (for symmetric encryption), this is particularly difficult to achieve. In this case we cannot tolerate low powered tests as any missed leak may enable a device to pass certification. As explained before, the confidence level of a test, the power of a test, the number of traces, the effect size and the trace variance all play off each other. Setup manipulations may enable to increase the effect size and/or decrease the trace variance, and an increase of the number of traces enables to achieve better confidence and power simultaneously. Consequently the trace "budgets" are very important factors in an evaluation that relies exclusively on leakage detection.

In ISO 17825:2016, the security levels 3 and 4 are separated by the resources (sample size = number of traces) available to perform the leakage detection, and the degree of data pre-processing. For level 3 10.000 traces are mandated; for level 4 100.000 traces are mandated. These criteria seem to be directly inherited from FIPS 140-2, which originally was based on attacks (like CC and EMVCo evaluations). The standard leaves ambiguous whether the sample size specifications apply per acquisition or for both fixed and random trace sets combined; similarly whether they are intended per repetition or for both the first and the confirmatory analysis combined.

Whitnall and Oswald [56] studied methods to account for multiple testing and concluded that utilising the Bonferroni adjustment represents the best method to retain both detection power and deal with long traces. They show that ISO 17825 needs to mandate more traces in the case of relying on detection only (which it does in the context of testing implementations of symmetric cryptography).

We have so far ignored implementations that perhaps do not show any leakage in the first moment. Generic leakage detection approaches that rely on mutual information [35], or tests that rely on preprocessing to make higher order leaks visible via first order statistics [46] can be utilised. However, these approaches typically require more traces per se, are lower power powered than first order statistics, or miss leakages that do not sit in central moments. A recent discussion on this topic can also be found in [4].

4.3   Attacks and Exploitation

In the context of FIPS 140, leakage exploitation is foreseen only in the case of implementations of public key cryptosystems (see ISO 17825:2016). The attacks are somewhat categorised and an upper time limit is provided as well as an upper trace limit. The consideration of worst-case adversaries is not foreseen (limited profiling). Consequently, it is unlikely that in this context an evaluation would come close to an optimal, worst-case adversary.

In CC evaluations, considerably more rigour and effort goes into ascertaining the possibility of worst-case attacks. Interaction between evaluators and implementers/vendors is foreseen, and, thanks to JHAS, a list of up to date attack vectors is maintained. However, as there are no scientific grounds for inclusion (or exclusion) for this list provided, it is unclear if such a list can ever truly represent the state-of-the-art, or the worst-case adversary. Whilst evaluators select methods from this list (and their own expertise) it is also unclear if in any concrete evaluation the optimal practical adversary is indeed considered (what if that adversary is a combination of attack methods not yet on the list?).

In the remainder of this section we hence concentrate on arguing how confident we can be (in the context of the worst-case approach) to actually reach the worst-case adversary with state-of-the-art methods.

Leakage Modeling (Profiling). In the current state of the art, optimally modelling a (multivariate and higher-order) leakage function remains a complex problem even when the source code and randomness are given to the evaluator. The main reason for this is that the best model should be chosen in function of the implementation's security order (i.e., the lowest statistical moment of the leakage distribution that depends on the key) and finding this security order becomes expensive as the number of shares in a masking scheme increases. For low security orders, the best known approach is to try higher-order detection on selected tuples of samples (provided by the detection and mapping step) [46]. This is for example possible for the two additive shares of the ANSSI software implementation analysed by Bronchain and Standaert in [5]. For high security orders, this exhaustive approach remains expensive and may require considering security margins [26].

From another perspective, the problem of accurate and efficient leakage modeling is well illustrated by the numerous attempts to evaluate security with machine learning and deep learning algorithms [7,21,30,31]. Such approaches generally work with minimum assumptions on the underlying leakage distribution (e.g., they do not assume the independence of consecutive leakage samples). But the cost of this generality is (in the current literature) a more expensive profiling step. Since the independence of leakage samples is also the origin of the security order reductions that make the optimal modelling of leakage distributions challenging, it is an important open problem to better understand the best tools to deal with this problem in a systematic manner. Summarising, modelling is challenging and well understood techniques can often only be utilised by worst case adversaries.

Information Extraction. Given well detected Points-of-Interest (POIs) and well estimated templates that accurately model the leakage distribution, the extraction of information for the relevant target intermediate values in an implementation can simply be performed by evaluating the templates with fresh samples. This part of the attack is not expected to lead to sub-optimalities (and can be easily automated).

Information Processing. For this last step, one should first distinguish between (what we next denote as) simple approaches and (what we next denote as) advanced ones.

Simple approaches include Divide-and-Conquer (D&C) attacks in the context of symmetric cryptography and Extend-and-Prune (E&P) attacks in the context of asymmetric cryptography. In this context, the information about different parts of the target secret are first combined in a maximum likelihood manner (which is optimal [9]). For symmetric algorithms, the remaining (full key) candidates can then be enumerated or their rank can be bounded (thanks to key knowledge). There is a large body of work on rank estimation that provides tight bounds, see for example [15,33,34,39], and these state-of-the-art solutions should be close enough to optimal. The case of asymmetric cryptography is less covered but dedicated approaches have also been proposed there [27].

Advanced approaches include the algebraic (resp., analytical) attacks that target the secret key at once, as for example considered in [44] (resp., [54]) in the context of block ciphers, or in [42] for asymmetric cryptography. These attacks are in general more difficult to mount and to evaluate, due to their higher computational cost and sensitivity to various inherently heuristic parameters (e.g., to deal with cycles in the circuit graphs) [17,18]. It implies risks of security overstatements whenever such attacks provide a significant gain over the simpler D&C and E&P ones.

The different depths of understanding between simple and advanced approaches motivate the suggestion to study both approaches in a backwards evaluation, so that the distance between them can provide an indication of the risk related to the more heuristic nature of advanced approaches.

5   Summary

An informal summary of the state-of-the-art solutions that can be used is given in Table 1. As illustrated by the colour code (red signals most uncertainty, followed by orange, yellow and green which indicates least uncertainty), some attack steps are quite well understood (in this context, where adversaries are given full access to randomness and keys) and there are various working solutions for them. This is typically the case of detection and mapping, information extraction, and simple (D&C and E&P) approaches to information processing, as discussed before.

The measurement and preprocessing step is introducing a first source of (moderate) risk, as there are no (and probably cannot be) theoretical ways to design optimal measurement setups. This step is determining the noise level of the measurements, which is a key parameter for most algorithmic side-channel countermeasures (e.g., masking [8,22], shuffling [20,55], ...). Yet, this risk can

Table 1. Remaining uncertainty in evaluation steps.

Attack steps		CC	WCA	FIPS-SK	FIPS-PK
Measurement and preprocessing		●	●	●	●
Detection and mapping		●	○	●	●
Leakage Modeling (Profiling)		●	○	-	-
Information extraction		○	○	-	-
Information Processing	Simple (D&C, E&P)	○	○	-	○
	Advanced (analytical)	●	●	-	-
Overall		●	○	●	●

and should be mitigated by the sound comparison of standard measurement boards and the sharing of good practices, possibly combined with some security margins for the expected measurement noise level.

Advanced information processing (with algebraic or analytical attacks) is bringing another source of (moderate) risk due to their more heuristic nature. Current practical evaluations however suggest that the security loss due to sub-optimalities in these attacks is generally limited and can be captured by small security margins as well.

6   Conclusions

Based on the previous summary we conclude that the main source of risk in side-channel security evaluations remains in the modelling step. On the one hand, this is where the impact of strong adversarial capabilities is the most critical. On the other to accurately estimate higher-order and multivariate distributions is likely to remain a hard problem with a need of risk management to be further investigated.

Because leakage modelling is not within the scope of FIPS/ISO 17825, the lack thereof implies that any resulting evaluation only provides very loose guarantees.

A key difference between the CC approach and backwards evaluations (the approach that considers the worst case adversary first) is that in a backwards evaluation it is much more likely that simpler tools can be deployed during modelling and this lowers the risk of incorrectly estimating the true security level of a product (it also implies less guesswork and therefore faster/cheaper evaluations).

Our research suggest that any optimality can only ever be achieved when considering worst case adversaries. These are adversaries that get full access to implementation details, can select secret parameters, and thereby control countermeasures during an initial profiling/modelling phase. The reason for this is that only in this setting, can we utilise tools which are well understood and for which we can assess/argue their optimality. Any attack vector which requires dealing with higher order or multivariate data leads to a loss of theoretical guarantees in relation to "best methods".

References

1. Azouaoui, M., Poussier, R., Standaert, F.-X.: Fast side-channel security evaluation of ECC implementations: shortcut formulas for horizontal side-channel attacks against ECSM with the montgomery ladder. In: Polian, I., Stöttinger, M. (eds.) COSADE 2019. LNCS, vol. 11421, pp. 25–42. Springer, Cham (2019). https://doi.org/10.1007/978-3-030-16350-1_3
2. Benadjila, R., Khati, L., Prouff, E., Thillard, A. https://github.com/ANSSI-FR/SecAESSTM32
3. Bilgin, B., Fischer, J.-B. (eds.): CARDIS 2018. LNCS, vol. 11389. Springer, Cham (2019). https://doi.org/10.1007/978-3-030-15462-2
4. Bronchain, O., Schneider, T., Standaert, F.: Multi-tuple leakage detection and the dependent signal issue. IACR Trans. Cryptogr. Hardw. Embed. Syst. **2019**(2), 318–345 (2019)
5. Bronchain, O., Standaert, F.: Side-channel countermeasures' dissection and the limits of closed source security evaluations. IACR Trans. Cryptogr. Hardw. Embed. Syst. **2020**(2), 1 25 (2020)
6. Cagli, E., Dumas, C., Prouff, E.: Kernel discriminant analysis for information extraction in the presence of masking. In: Lemke-Rust, K., Tunstall, M. (eds.) CARDIS 2016. LNCS, vol. 10146, pp. 1–22. Springer, Cham (2017). https://doi.org/10.1007/978-3-319-54669-8_1
7. Cagli, E., Dumas, C., Prouff, E.: Convolutional neural networks with data augmentation against jitter-based countermeasures - profiling attacks without preprocessing. In: Fischer and Homma [13], pp. 45–68
8. Chari, S., Jutla, C.S., Rao, J.R., Rohatgi, P.: Towards sound approaches to counteract power-analysis attacks. In: Wiener, M. (ed.) CRYPTO 1999. LNCS, vol. 1666, pp. 398–412. Springer, Heidelberg (1999). https://doi.org/10.1007/3-540-48405-1_26
9. Chari, S., Rao, J.R., Rohatgi, P.: Template attacks. In: Kaliski, B.S., Koç, K., Paar, C. (eds.) CHES 2002. LNCS, vol. 2523, pp. 13–28. Springer, Heidelberg (2003). https://doi.org/10.1007/3-540-36400-5_3
10. Duc, A., Faust, S., Standaert, F.-X.: Making masking security proofs concrete (or how to evaluate the security of any leaking device), extended version. J. Cryptol. **32**(4), 1263–1297 (2018). https://doi.org/10.1007/s00145-018-9277-0
11. Durvaux, F., Standaert, F.-X.: From improved leakage detection to the detection of points of interests in leakage traces. In: Fischlin, M., Coron, J.-S. (eds.) EUROCRYPT 2016, Part I. LNCS, vol. 9665, pp. 240–262. Springer, Heidelberg (2016). https://doi.org/10.1007/978-3-662-49890-3_10
12. Eisenbarth, T., Paar, C., Weghenkel, B.: Building a side channel based disassembler. In: Gavrilova, M.L., Tan, C.J.K., Moreno, E.D. (eds.) Transactions on Computational Science X. LNCS, vol. 6340, pp. 78–99. Springer, Heidelberg (2010). https://doi.org/10.1007/978-3-642-17499-5_4
13. Fischer, W., Homma, N. (eds.): CHES 2017. LNCS, vol. 10529. Springer, Cham (2017). https://doi.org/10.1007/978-3-319-66787-4

14. Fumaroli, G., Martinelli, A., Prouff, E., Rivain, M.: Affine masking against higher-order side channel analysis. In: Biryukov, A., Gong, G., Stinson, D.R. (eds.) SAC 2010. LNCS, vol. 6544, pp. 262–280. Springer, Heidelberg (2011). https://doi.org/10.1007/978-3-642-19574-7_18

15. Glowacz, C., Grosso, V., Poussier, R., Schüth, J., Standaert, F.-X.: Simpler and more efficient rank estimation for side-channel security assessment. In: Leander, G. (ed.) FSE 2015. LNCS, vol. 9054, pp. 117–129. Springer, Heidelberg (2015). https://doi.org/10.1007/978-3-662-48116-5_6

16. Goodwill, G., Jun, B., Jaffe, J., Rohatgi, P.: A testing methodology for side-channel resistance validation. In: NIST Non-Invasive Attack Testing Workshop (2011)

17. Green, J., Roy, A., Oswald, E.: A systematic study of the impact of graphical models on inference-based attacks on AES. In: Bilgin and Fischer [3], pp. 18–34

18. Grosso, V., Standaert, F.: ASCA, SASCA and DPA with enumeration: which one beats the other and when? In: Iwata and Cheon [25], pp. 291–312

19. Guilley, S., Maghrebi, H., Souissi, Y., Sauvage, L., Danger, J.: Quantifying the quality of side channel acquisitions. COSADE, February 2011

20. Herbst, C., Oswald, E., Mangard, S.: An AES smart card implementation resistant to power analysis attacks. In: Zhou, J., Yung, M., Bao, F. (eds.) ACNS 2006. LNCS, vol. 3989, pp. 239–252. Springer, Heidelberg (2006). https://doi.org/10.1007/11767480_16

21. Heuser, A., Zohner, M.: Intelligent machine homicide: breaking cryptographic devices using support vector machines. In: Schindler, W., Huss, S.A. (eds.) COSADE 2012. LNCS, vol. 7275, pp. 249–264. Springer, Heidelberg (2012). https://doi.org/10.1007/978-3-642-29912-4_18

22. Ishai, Y., Sahai, A., Wagner, D.: Private circuits: securing hardware against probing attacks. In: Boneh, D. (ed.) CRYPTO 2003. LNCS, vol. 2729, pp. 463–481. Springer, Heidelberg (2003). https://doi.org/10.1007/978-3-540-45146-4_27

23. ISO/IEC JTC 1/SC 27: ISO/IEC 15408-1: Information technology - Security techniques - Evaluation criteria for IT security - Part 1: Introduction and general model. International Organization for Standardization, Geneva, CH (2009)

24. ISO/IEC JTC 1/SC 27: ISO/IEC 17825: Information technology - Security techniques - Testing methods for the mitigation of non-invasive attack classes against cryptographic modules. International Organization for Standardization, Geneva, CH (2016)

25. Iwata, T., Cheon, J.H. (eds.): ASIACRYPT 2015, Part II. LNCS, vol. 9453. Springer, Heidelberg (2015). https://doi.org/10.1007/978-3-662-48800-3

26. Journault, A., Standaert, F.: Very high order masking: efficient implementation and security evaluation. In: Fischer and Homma [13], pp. 623–643

27. Lange, T., van Vredendaal, C., Wakker, M.: Kangaroos in side-channel attacks. In: Joye, M., Moradi, A. (eds.) CARDIS 2014. LNCS, vol. 8968, pp. 104–121. Springer, Cham (2015). https://doi.org/10.1007/978-3-319-16763-3_7

28. Lemke-Rust, K., Paar, C.: Gaussian mixture models for higher-order side channel analysis. In: Paillier, P., Verbauwhede, I. (eds.) CHES 2007. LNCS, vol. 4727, pp. 14–27. Springer, Heidelberg (2007). https://doi.org/10.1007/978-3-540-74735-2_2

29. Lerman, L., Markowitch, O.: Efficient profiled attacks on masking schemes. IEEE Trans. Inf. Forensics Secur. 14(6), 1445–1454 (2019)

30. Lerman, L., Medeiros, S.F., Bontempi, G., Markowitch, O.: A machine learning approach against a masked AES. In: Francillon, A., Rohatgi, P. (eds.) CARDIS 2013. LNCS, vol. 8419, pp. 61–75. Springer, Cham (2014). https://doi.org/10.1007/978-3-319-08302-5_5

31. Lerman, L., Poussier, R., Bontempi, G., Markowitch, O., Standaert, F.-X.: Template attacks vs. machine learning revisited (and the curse of dimensionality in side-channel analysis). In: Mangard, S., Poschmann, A.Y. (eds.) COSADE 2014. LNCS, vol. 9064, pp. 20–33. Springer, Cham (2015). https://doi.org/10.1007/978-3-319-21476-4_2

32. Mangard, S.: Hardware countermeasures against DPA – a statistical analysis of their effectiveness. In: Okamoto, T. (ed.) CT-RSA 2004. LNCS, vol. 2964, pp. 222–235. Springer, Heidelberg (2004). https://doi.org/10.1007/978-3-540-24660-2_18

33. Martin, D.P., Mather, L., Oswald, E.: Two sides of the same coin: counting and enumerating keys post side-channel attacks revisited. In: Smart, N.P. (ed.) CT-RSA 2018. LNCS, vol. 10808, pp. 394–412. Springer, Cham (2018). https://doi.org/10.1007/978-3-319-76953-0_21

34. Martin, D.P., O'Connell, J.F., Oswald, E., Stam, M.: Counting keys in parallel after a side channel attack. In: Iwata and Cheon [25], pp. 313–337

35. Mather, L., Oswald, E., Bandenburg, J., Wójcik, M.: Does my device leak information? An a priori statistical power analysis of leakage detection tests. In: Sako, K., Sarkar, P. (eds.) ASIACRYPT 2013, Part I. LNCS, vol. 8269, pp. 486–505. Springer, Heidelberg (2013). https://doi.org/10.1007/978-3-642-42033-7_25

36. National Institute of Standards and Technology: NIST FIPS 140-3. Information Technology Laboratory, NIST, Gaithersburg, MD 20899-8900

37. Nguyen, P.Q., Shparlinski, I.E.: The insecurity of the elliptic curve digital signature algorithm with partially known nonces. Des. Codes Cryptogr. 30(2), 201–217 (2003). https://doi.org/10.1023/A:1025436905711

38. Oswald, D., Paar, C.: Improving side-channel analysis with optimal linear transforms. In: Mangard, S. (ed.) CARDIS 2012. LNCS, vol. 7771, pp. 219–233. Springer, Heidelberg (2013). https://doi.org/10.1007/978-3-642-37288-9_15

39. Poussier, R., Standaert, F.-X., Grosso, V.: Simple key enumeration (and rank estimation) using histograms: an integrated approach. In: Gierlichs, B., Poschmann, A.Y. (eds.) CHES 2016. LNCS, vol. 9813, pp. 61–81. Springer, Heidelberg (2016). https://doi.org/10.1007/978-3-662-53140-2_4

40. Poussier, R., Zhou, Y., Standaert, F.: A systematic approach to the side-channel analysis of ECC implementations with worst-case horizontal attacks. In: Fischer and Homma [13], pp. 534–554

41. Merino Del Pozo, S., Standaert, F.-X.: Blind source separation from single measurements using singular spectrum analysis. In: Güneysu, T., Handschuh, H. (eds.) CHES 2015. LNCS, vol. 9293, pp. 42–59. Springer, Heidelberg (2015). https://doi.org/10.1007/978-3-662-48324-4_3

42. Primas, R., Pessl, P., Mangard, S.: Single-trace side-channel attacks on masked lattice-based encryption. In: Fischer and Homma [13], pp. 513–533

43. Prouff, E., Rivain, M., Bevan, R.: Statistical analysis of second order differential power analysis. IACR Cryptology ePrint Archive, 2010, 646 (2010)

44. Renauld, M., Standaert, F.-X., Veyrat-Charvillon, N.: Algebraic side-channel attacks on the AES: why time also matters in DPA. In: Clavier, C., Gaj, K. (eds.) CHES 2009. LNCS, vol. 5747, pp. 97–111. Springer, Heidelberg (2009). https://doi.org/10.1007/978-3-642-04138-9_8

45. Schindler, W., Lemke, K., Paar, C.: A stochastic model for differential side channel cryptanalysis. In: Rao, J.R., Sunar, B. (eds.) CHES 2005. LNCS, vol. 3659, pp. 30–46. Springer, Heidelberg (2005). https://doi.org/10.1007/11545262_3

46. Schneider, T., Moradi, A.: Leakage assessment methodology - extended version. J. Cryptogr. Eng. 6(2), 85–99 (2016). https://doi.org/10.1007/s13389-016-0120-y

47. Skorobogatov, S.: Synchronization method for SCA and fault attacks. J. Cryptogr. Eng. **1**(1), 71–77 (2011). https://doi.org/10.1007/s13389-011-0004-0
48. SOG-IS: Application of attack potential to smartcards and similar devices (2019)
49. SOG-IS: Attack methods for smartcards and similar devices (2020)
50. Standaert, F.: How (not) to use Welch's t-test in side-channel security evaluations. In: Bilgin and Fischer [3], pp. 65–79
51. Standaert, F.-X., Malkin, T.G., Yung, M.: A unified framework for the analysis of side-channel key recovery attacks. In: Joux, A. (ed.) EUROCRYPT 2009. LNCS, vol. 5479, pp. 443–461. Springer, Heidelberg (2009). https://doi.org/10.1007/978-3-642-01001-9_26
52. Standaert, F.-X., et al.: The world is not enough: another look on second-order DPA. In: Abe, M. (ed.) ASIACRYPT 2010. LNCS, vol. 6477, pp. 112–129. Springer, Heidelberg (2010). https://doi.org/10.1007/978-3-642-17373-8_7
53. van Woudenberg, J.G.J., Witteman, M.F., Bakker, B.: Improving differential power analysis by elastic alignment. In: Kiayias, A. (ed.) CT-RSA 2011. LNCS, vol. 6558, pp. 104–119. Springer, Heidelberg (2011). https://doi.org/10.1007/978-3-642-19074-2_8
54. Veyrat-Charvillon, N., Gérard, B., Standaert, F.-X.: Soft analytical side-channel attacks. In: Sarkar, P., Iwata, T. (eds.) ASIACRYPT 2014, Part I. LNCS, vol. 8873, pp. 282–296. Springer, Heidelberg (2014). https://doi.org/10.1007/978-3-662-45611-8_15
55. Veyrat-Charvillon, N., Medwed, M., Kerckhof, S., Standaert, F.-X.: Shuffling against side-channel attacks: a comprehensive study with cautionary note. In: Wang, X., Sako, K. (eds.) ASIACRYPT 2012. LNCS, vol. 7658, pp. 740–757. Springer, Heidelberg (2012). https://doi.org/10.1007/978-3-642-34961-4_44
56. Whitnall, C., Oswald, E.: A critical analysis of ISO 17825 ('Testing Methods for the mitigation of non-invasive attack classes against cryptographic modules'). In: Galbraith, S.D., Moriai, S. (eds.) ASIACRYPT 2019, Part III. LNCS, vol. 11923, pp. 256–284. Springer, Cham (2019). https://doi.org/10.1007/978-3-030-34618-8_9

Taming the Many EdDSAs

Konstantinos Chalkias, François Garillot, and Valeria Nikolaenko$^{(\boxtimes)}$

Novi/Facebook, Cambridge, USA
{kostascrypto,fga,valerini}@fb.com

Abstract. This paper analyses security of concrete instantiations of EdDSA by identifying exploitable inconsistencies between standardization recommendations and Ed25519 implementations. We mainly focus on current ambiguity regarding signature verification equations, binding and malleability guarantees, and incompatibilities between randomized batch and single verification. We give a formulation of Ed25519 signature scheme that achieves the highest level of security, explaining how each step of the algorithm links with the formal security properties. We develop optimizations to allow for more efficient secure implementations. Finally, we designed a set of edge-case test-vectors and run them by some of the most popular Ed25519 libraries. The results allowed to understand the security level of those implementations and showed that most libraries do not comply with the latest standardization recommendations. The methodology allows to test compatibility of different Ed25519 implementations which is of practical importance for consensus-driven applications.

Keywords: EdDSA · Ed25519 · Malleability · Blockchain · Cofactor

1 Introduction

The Edwards-Curve Digital Signature Algorithm (EdDSA) [5] is a deterministic Schnorr signature [38] variant using twisted Edwards curves rather than Weierstrass curves, at a significant performance gain. As of today, Ed25519 is the most popular instance of EdDSA and is based on the Edwards Curve25519 providing ∼128-bits of security.

Due to its superior efficiency among Elliptic Curve schemes and better security guarantees against side-channel attacks under weak randomness sources, Ed25519 is widely adopted by such protocols as TLS 1.3, SSH, Tor, GnuPGP, Signal and more [18]. It is also the preferred signature scheme of several blockchain systems, such as Corda [16], Tezos [14], Stellar [3], and Libra [22].

Seeking to reap more performance and security benefits, some applications even rely on properties of Ed25519 beyond the usual staple of digital signature algorithms. Those "extras" include for instance fast batch verification, non-repudiation, strong unforgeability and correctness consistency. Serving these demands with—at first—little specification guidance, libraries implementing Ed25519 have introduced tweaks to the original scheme that we will

© Springer Nature Switzerland AG 2020
T. van der Merwe et al. (Eds.): SSR 2020, LNCS 12529, pp. 67–90, 2020.
https://doi.org/10.1007/978-3-030-64357-7_4

explore in depth. Today, the wide adoption of Ed25519 heightens concerns about backwards-compatibility, while clarity on the exact security guarantees of close variants of EdDSA has progressed but recently [8]. It is therefore no wonder that we have observed no agreement on the exact set of correct signatures between different implementations.

Nonetheless, two standardization efforts for Ed25519 have made attempts at such an agreement, one from IETF, RFC 8032 [20] (active since 2015 and still sees modifications) and a recent one from NIST as part of FIPS 186–5 [34] (published as a draft in October 2019). Although these efforts are similar, one of the most divisive topics relating to EdDSA standardization is the discrepancy in correctness definitions, i.e. in the verification equations, between standards and software libraries. Specifically, RFC 8032 [20] allows optionality between using a permissive verification equation (*cofactored*) and a more strict verification equation (*cofactorless*)[1].

For base point B, public key A and signature (R, S), RFC 8032 states:

Check the group equation $[8][S]B = [8]R + [8][k]A$. It's sufficient, but not required, to instead check $[S]B = R + [k]A$.

By contrast, NIST's draft [34] allows no such optionality and only suggests a more permissive (*cofactored*) verification equation. This comes in contradiction to the choice of almost all software libraries, which use the more strict verification equation (*cofactorless*), most likely for performance reasons.

Beyond the discrepancies that do occur in EdDSA standards, we also note considerations they neglect. For instance, none of the standards formulate the scheme in a way that offers non-repudiation, or resilience to key substitution attacks (see Appendix A for an example). This choice makes it difficult to use the scheme for such applications as

Contract Signing: if company A signed an agreement with company B using a key that allows for repudiation, it can later claim that it signed a completely different deal.

Electronic Voting: malicious voters may pick special keys that allow for repudiation on purpose in order to create friction in the process and deny results, as their signed vote might be verified against multiple candidates.

Transactions: a blockchain transaction of amount X might also be valid for another amount Y, creating potential problems for consensus and dispute resolution.

Finally, we highlight that the application domain of Ed25519 has changed over the years. For instance, Blockchain technology is a booming field, which gained hundreds of billions of US dollars in market capitalization in the time since the publication of the original EdDSA paper [4]. It features cryptographic

---

[1] Cofactored means interpreting the verification equation modulo 8, which is a cofactor of the Curve25519. Any signature accepted by a "cofactorless" equation will be accepted by a "cofactored" equation, though the converse is false.

signatures pervasively, and places a premium on performance. Yet, being strongly reliant on Byzantine consensus algorithms, blockchains are vulnerable to any disagreement on the validity of signatures between different implementations: a sequence of carefully crafted signatures exploiting such a disagreement could slow most consensus algorithms to a crawl.

Moreover, the adversarial ecosystem exploiting cryptographic flaws in blockchains is now well-developed, and the stakes of even minor flaws of cryptographic schemes have become consequential [11,17].

In order to stem the rapidly rising costs of the conflicting approaches to Ed25519, we hope standardization bodies will lead the way for Ed25519 developers and equip them with the guidance necessary to produce high assurance libraries that conform with each other. Specifically, the cryptographic community at large would benefit if standards offered a set of more precise recommendations and test vectors that check for all the difficult edge cases left open by the mathematics of EdDSA. We offer a first incarnation of those elements here.

Note that although this research paper focuses on Ed25519, the same methods apply to Ed448 and potentially to other non-prime order curves as well.

Our Contributions. In this paper, we give a precise formulation of Ed25519 signature scheme that achieves the highest level of security—strong unforgeability and resilience to repudiation—with a minimal number of additional inexpensive checks, and we explain why each of these checks is required. In doing so, we precisely link those checks with the formal security properties usually considered in the establishment of a signature standard, but incorporate more modern considerations as well, such as compatibility with EdDSA's batch verification. To make it easy for both the standards and the libraries to add the checks we recommend, we equip the reader with specific procedures that perform them optimally. This single scheme relieves developers from the burden of making distinct choices based on their intended applications, and so it is our hope that it can help the Ed25519 ecosystem to converge to a single interoperable scheme, one compatible with the degree of determinism required by blockchain applications. But even if a standard body was to disagree on some of our approach, we expect that our systematic analysis will offer practical tools for crafting better Ed25519 implementations: for instance we highlight that beyond their differences on the style of verification equation, neither standards nor software libraries offer non-repudiation. We explain how to add non-repudiation via an inexpensive check on the public key.

We also provide test vectors that help surface the differences between implementation choices as well as find common blunders in the wild. We run the test vectors against most of the popular cryptographic libraries, and from the results we deduce which libraries offer strong unforgeability, which guarantee non-repudiation and which of them do cofactored verification. We carefully explain the methodology, making it easy to analyze other libraries in the same way. The test vectors can be used for blockchain applications to make sure the participants agree on acceptance/rejection of those vectors, which should give high assurance in that the participants would agree on the validity of all possible signatures.

Outline. In Sect. 2.1 we explain various security and malleability notions for a signature scheme, in Sect. 2.2 we show the stakes of precise correctness definitions (as surfaced recently in consensus-driven applications). We start Sect. 3 recalling the structure of the Curve25519 group, including the structure of the small-order subgroup, and we point out caveats regarding the checks for non-canonical encodings, before detailing the Ed25519 key and signature generation algorithms. In Sect. 3.1 we formulate a single signature verification algorithm that achieves the strongest notion of security. We explain each line of the algorithm in detail and eliminate ambigious implementation choices. In Sect. 3.2 we formulate batch verification algorithm. We explain why only cofactored form of single signature verification is compatible with batch verification. In Sect. 4 we explain how to optimize the verification algorithm, especially the additional checks. In Sect. 5 we provide the test vectors and analyse the existing libraries using those vectors. Related work is given in Sect. 6.

2 Background

2.1 Signatures Security

There are four security properties relevant to EdDSA which we sketc.h at a high level here (the exact game-based definitions can be found in, e.g., Brendel et al. [8]).

EUF-CMA (existential unforgeability under chosen message attacks) is usually the minimal security property required of a signature scheme. It guarantees that any efficient adversary who has the public key pk of the signer and received an arbitrary number of signatures on messages of its choice (in an adaptive manner): $\{m_i, \sigma_i\}_{i=1}^N$, cannot output a valid signature σ^* for a new message $m^* \notin \{m_i\}_{i=1}^N$ (except with negligible probability). In case the attacker outputs a valid signature on a new message: (m^*, σ^*), it is called an *existential forgery*.

SUF-CMA (strong unforgeability under chosen message attacks) is a stronger notion than EUF-CMA. It guarantees that for any efficient adversary who has the public key pk of the signer and received an arbitrary number of signatures on messages of its choice: $\{m_i, \sigma_i\}_{i=1}^N$, it cannot output a new valid signature pair (m^*, σ^*), s.t. $(m^*, \sigma^*) \notin \{m_i, \sigma_i\}_{i=1}^N$ (except with negligible probability).

Strong unforgeability implies that an adversary cannot only sign new messages, but also cannot find a new signature on an old message. Strongly unforgeable signatures are used to build chosen ciphertext secure encryption schemes and group signatures [7]. This property is highly desirable for blockchain applications, e.g., ECDSA signatures in Bitcoin are not strongly unforgeable, and multiple attempts to fix the problem [25,41] only ended with a soft fork fixing the signature serialization format [42]. As was shown in [8], additional checks in the verification procedure makes Ed25519 signature scheme satisfy SUF-CMA.

Binding Signature (BS). We say that a signature scheme is binding if *no efficient signer* can output a tuple $[pk, m, m', \sigma]$, where both (m, σ) and (m', σ)

are valid message signature pairs under the public key pk and $m \neq m'$ (except with negligible probability).

A binding signature makes it impossible for the signer to claim later [to a judge] that it has signed a different message, the signature binds the signer to the message. If the signer is able to produce another message for which the same signature is valid, we say that the signer *repudiates* or breaks the *non-repudiation* property of the signature scheme (see [43]).

Strongly Binding Signature (SBS). Certain applications may require a signature to not only be binding to the message but also be binding to the public key. We say that a signature scheme is *strongly-binding* if any efficient signer can not output a tuple $[\mathsf{pk}, m, \mathsf{pk}', m', \sigma]$, where (m, σ) is a valid signature for the public key pk and (m', σ) is a valid signature for the public key pk' and either $m' \neq m$ or $\mathsf{pk} \neq \mathsf{pk}'$, or both (except with negligible probability).

As was shown in [8] certain variants of EdDSA (in particular, the one described in the RFC8032 [20]) are not binding—there are special types of public keys that allow the signer to repudiate. Rejecting those keys makes the ed25519 scheme strongly binding which we prove in Sect. 3.1. We extend the result of Brendel et al. [8] giving a simpler check that helps achieve strong binding. We define the SBS security as follows (this notion is stronger than M-S-UEO [8]).

Definition 1. *A signature scheme with verification algorithm* Verify *is strongly binding (SBS-secure) if for any probablistic polynomial time algorithm $\mathcal{A}$ the following probability is negligible:*

$$\Pr \left[\begin{array}{l} (m \neq m' \vee pk \neq pk') \wedge \\ \mathsf{Verify}(pk, \sigma, m) \wedge \\ \mathsf{Verify}(pk', \sigma, m') \end{array} \middle| (pk, pk', \sigma, m, m') \xleftarrow{\$} \mathcal{A}() \right] < negl.$$

Malleable Signature: Signature malleability gets different meanings in different contexts, in this writing we say that the signature is malleable if it is either not strongly unforgeable or it is not strongly binding, or both. In other words, we will call the signature scheme malleable if it does not satisfy the strongest notion of security. Note that only the signature security property (EUF-CMA) is necessary for any deployment of a signature scheme, the absence of the rest of the properties might not necessarily weaken the security of the application, but we advocate for any modern standard to design schemes with the highest security guarantees.[2]

To see why these definitions cover all the possibilities for attacks, we recall in Fig. 1 different capabilities for the signer and for the external (public) attacker to alter parts of the public key, message, signature triplet.

Often, a signature scheme is proven to be secure at a certain level, but the specific implementations may degrade the security level because of inappropriate padding, ambiguous serialization or non-unique encoding.

---

[2] Note that a malicious signer can always bypass the correct signing execution by picking a random R and thus output two different signatures for the same message. Thus, EdDSA cannot guarantee the signature-uniqueness property.

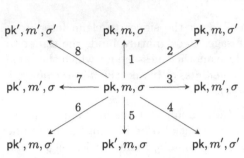

	Security property preventing the alteration by a (possibly malicious)	
Alteration to (pk, m, σ) triplet		
Fig 1a	signer	public attacker
5	SBS	SBS
3	BS	EUF-CMA
2	uniqueness *	SUF-CMA
4	N/A	EUF-CMA
7	SBS	SBS
6,8	N/A	N/A

(a) Signature transformations
We assume $pk \neq pk'$, $m \neq m'$ and $\sigma \neq \sigma'$.

(b) Here N/A means that an alteration of this type is expected from the signature scheme and does not concern us in this writing. Note (*) that the EdDSA signatures are deterministic but not unique, i.e. a dishonest signer can always produce multiple signatures for the same message.

Fig. 1. Different ways of altering signatures

In Sect. 3 we state the variant of Ed25519 that is strongly-unforgeable and strongly-binding. We also highlight multiple caveats for implementing the Ed25519 signature scheme securely.

2.2 Correctness of Cryptographic Signatures

Increasing number of applications are in need of unambigious description for the set of valid signatures. It is most important for consensus-driven protocols, where participants need to agree beforehand on the exact format of a valid signature. An adversary may create a malformed signature such that half of the participants will accept it as valid and half will not thus create issues for consensus decisions on whether the signature is valid or not, potentially slowing down applications. In particular, nearly all consensus mechanisms rely on a 2/3 majority of (honest) nodes reaching the same accept or reject decision on a particular value for liveness. Imagine two signatures σ_1 and σ_2, where half of the parties accept the first, but reject the second and the other half on the contrary accept the second, but reject the first, the consensus might come to a halt.

We observe the discrepancy between the verification equations in the standards (IETF and NIST) and almost all the cryptographic libraries. We present test vectors that surface the exact nature of these discrepancies in Sect. 5.

3   Ed25519 Signatures

The signature scheme is defined over the elliptic curve group

$$E = \{(x, y) \in F_q \times F_q : -x^2 + y^2 = 1 + dx^2y^2\}$$

where $d = -121665/121666 \in F_q$ and $q = 2^{255} - 19$. The neutral element of the group is $0 = (0, 1)$, the complete twisted Edwards addition law is:

Algorithm 1. Ed25519 Algorithm: Key Generation and Signature Generation

---

Key Generation

1: Sample uniformly random sk $\in \{0, 1\}^{256}$.
2: Expand the secret with a hash function: $(h_0, h_1, \ldots, h_{511}) \leftarrow$ SHA512(sk).
3: Compute a secret scalar $s = 2^{254} + h_{253} \cdot 2^{253} + \cdots + h_3 \cdot 2^3$ [3].
4: Compute the public key pk $= A$, where $A = s \cdot B$.

Signature Generation on message M and secret key $(h_{256}, \ldots, h_{511})$ and s

5: Generate a 512-bits pseudorandom nonce $r := $ SHA512$(h_{256}|| \ldots ||h_{511}||M)$.
6: Interpret the nonce as a scalar and obtain a curve point: $R := r \cdot B$.
7: Compute the scalar $S := (r + $ SHA512$(R||A||M) * s)$ mod L.
8: Encode the scalar S canonically (i.e. reduce S mod L prior to serializing).
9: Encode the curve point R canonically (i.e. reduce the $R.y$ mod $2^{255} - 19$ prior to serializing).

$$(x_1, y_1) + (x_2, y_2) = \left(\frac{x_1 y_2 + x_2 y_1}{1 + dx_1 x_2 y_1 y_2}, \frac{y_1 y_2 + x_1 x_2}{1 - dx_1 x_2 y_1 y_2} \right).$$

The number of points on the elliptic curve is $|E| = 8 \times L$, where $L = 2^{252} + 27742317777372353535851937790883648493$ is prime. The base point B, specified in the RFC (Sect. 5.1 [20]), has order L. It has been chosen to be the point with the smallest u coordinate in Montgomery representation ($u = 9$, see Appendix A, in [21]).

Note that the presence of the co-factor of 8 in the curve-order makes it harder to use this curve in applications where a prime-order group is required for the cryptographic proof. For example in [24], an adversary may send a key exchange group element that lies in a small subgroup of order 8 instead of the correct subgroup and use the honest user's response to deduce some bits of this user's secret exponent.

Group Structure, Small-Order Subgroup: Elliptic curve group E is isomorphic to $\mathbb{Z}_L \times \mathbb{Z}_8$. A base point $B \in E$ generates a subgroup of order L and there is a small torsion point $T_8 \in E$ that generates a subgroup of order 8. Any point P of the group E can be uniquely represented as a linear combination of B and T_8: $P = b \cdot B + t \cdot T_8$, where $b \in 0, \ldots, L - 1$ and $t \in 0, \ldots, 7$. We say that the discrete log of P base B is b. We say that a point P is of *"small order"* iff $b = 0$, *"mixed order"* iff $t \neq 0$ and $b \neq 0$, and *"order L"* iff $b \neq 0$ and $t = 0$.

Table 1 shows the small order points with their orders. Any of the points of order 8 can serve as a small subgroup generator, T_8. For four intermediate rows

---

[3] The least significant three bits of the scalar are unset to allow using the same secret key in the DH-key agreement, where the EC point of another party is raised to the secret key. Raising to the exponent divisible by 8 there erases the small-subgroup component and defends against attacks that exploit the non-trivial co-factor of 8. The most significant bit is unset to make sure that the number is indeed the multiple of 8 and was not wrapped around the modulus. The second most significant bit is being set to prevent variable-time implementation of multiplication that first looks for the first most significant bit that is set. Note however that the secret key has 251 pseudo-random bits and is not uniformly random mod a 253-bits prime L, though this loss of a few bits of random bits is deemed acceptable.

exact formulas exist, but they are cumbersome and irrelevant for our writing. We will just mention that for one of these points $y = \left(\sqrt{\frac{-1+\sqrt{1+d}}{d}} \right)$, $x = \sqrt{-1} \cdot y$, and the remaining 3 points are combinations of x and y with various signs: $(-x, y)$, $(x, -y)$ and $(-x, -y)$. Full hexidecimal encodings of the small-order points can be found in Appendix B.

Encodings, Non-canonical Encodings: An element of the scalar field mod L is encoded with a 256-bits string in little-endian format. If the scalar is reduced mod L its encoding is called *canonical*, otherwise it is called *non-canonical*.

A group element (x, y) is encoded as a 256-bits string, that consists of 255-bits encoding of y (in little-endian format: bytes placed from left to right and from least significant to most significant) followed by a sign bit which is 1 iff x is negative. Given the serialization, the x coordinate is restored as $x = \pm\sqrt{(y^2 - 1)/(dy^2 + 1)}$. If the y coordinate in the encoding of point (x, y) is reduced mod q the encoding is called *canonical*, otherwise it is called *non-canonical*. Two special points with $x = 0$ ($y = 1$ or $y = 2^{255} - 20$) are canonically encoded only with a sign bit 0, otherwise the encodings are non-canonical.

There are 19 elliptic curve points that can be encoded in a non-canonical form. Those points have y coordinates in the range $[2^{255} - 19, \ldots, 2^{255} - 1]$.

Table 1. Small order points of Curve25519 in its twisted Edwards form.

#	Order	Point	Serialized point
Canonical serializations			
1	1	$(0, 1)$	010000..0000
2	2	$(0, -1)$	ECFFFF..FF7F
3	4	$(-\sqrt{-1}, 0)$	000000..0080
4	4	$(\sqrt{-1}, 0)$	000000..0000
5	8	...	C7176A..037A
6	8	...	C7176A..03FA
7	8	...	26E895..FC05
8	8	...	26E895..FC85
Non-canonical serializations			
9	1	$(-0, 1)$	010000..0080
10	2	$(-0, -1)$	ECFFFF..FFFF
11	1	$(0, 2^{255} - 18)$	EEFFFF..FF7F
12	1	$(-0, 2^{255} - 18)$	EEFFFF..FFFF
13	4	$(-\sqrt{-1}, 2^{255} - 19)$	EDFFFF..FFFF
14	4	$(\sqrt{-1}, 2^{255} - 19)$	EDFFFF..FF7F

Table 2. Non-canonically encoded points.

y	$y + 2^{255} - 19$	Valid	Order
0	$2^{255} - 19$	✓	4
1	$2^{255} - 18$	✓	0
2	$2^{255} - 17$	✗	-
3	$2^{255} - 16$	✓	$8 \cdot L$
4	$2^{255} - 15$	✓	$4 \cdot L$
5	$2^{255} - 14$	✓	$8 \cdot L$
6	$2^{255} - 13$	✓	$8 \cdot L$
7	$2^{255} - 12$	✗	-
8	$2^{255} - 11$	✗	-
9	$2^{255} - 10$	✓	$2 \cdot L$
10	$2^{255} - 9$	✓	$8 \cdot L$
11	$2^{255} - 8$	✗	-
12	$2^{255} - 7$	✗	-
13	$2^{255} - 6$	✗	-
14	$2^{255} - 5$	✓	$8 \cdot L$
15	$2^{255} - 4$	✓	$4 \cdot L$
16	$2^{255} - 3$	✓	$8 \cdot L$
17	$2^{255} - 2$	✗	-
18	$2^{255} - 1$	✓	$4 \cdot L$

Among these points there are 2 points of small order and from the remaining 17 y-coordinates only 10 decode to valid curve points all of mixed order. The details are given in Table 2. No evidence suggests that the discrete log base B of any of those points is known except for the first two (the discrete log is zero base B for those). Note that the base point was chosen "somewhat" verifiably arbitrarily: it has y coordinate $y = 4/5 \pmod{2^{255} - 19}$.

3.1 Single Signature Verification

The Ed25519 signature scheme, as shown in Algorithm 2, achieves the strongest notion of security (SUF-CMA + SBS); we explain all the extra-checks and important caveats for correct deployment. Algorithm 2 generally conforms with the standards [20,34], except for an addition of line #2. The implementations which we analyse in Sect. 5 do disagree with the Algorithm in various ways.

Algorithm 2. Ed25519 Algorithm: single signature verification

---

 Signature Verification on message M, public key A and signature $\sigma = (R, S)$
1: Reject the signature if $S \notin \{0, \ldots, L - 1\}$.
2: Reject the signature if the public key A is one of 8 small order points.
3: Reject the signature if A or R are non-canonical.
4: Compute the hash $\mathsf{SHA512}(R\|A\|M)$ and reduce it mod L to get a scalar h.
5: Accept if $8(S \cdot B) - 8R - 8(h \cdot A) = 0$.

Reject $S \geq L$ (line #1, Algorithm 2): This check makes the scheme strongly existentially unforgeable [8] (SUF-CMA). Many approaches have been used in research or production-ready Ed25519 libraries to perform this validation and unfortunately sometimes the check is incomplete or not optimized.

Reject Small Order A (line #2, Algorithm 2): This check makes the scheme strongly binding (SBS-secure, see Definition 1 in Sect. 2), i.e. resilient to key/message substitution attacks, as we prove in Theorem 1 (the proof resembles the proof of Theorem 7 in [8]). Although this additional check is not part of any standard yet and rarely appears in the libraries. The check can be done very efficiently by simply verifying that 32-byte array of A received for verification is not in the set of 14 small order points (including the non-canonical encodings) shown on Table 1 with extended version in Appendix B. Note that for binding the rejection of small order R is not required.

Theorem 1. *Let* Verify *be Algorithm 2 with the hash function assumed to act as a random oracle H with output length at least 2λ. Then* Verify *is SBS secure.*

Proof. To successfully break SBS security the adversary $\mathcal{A}$ needs to output two public keys $A = aB + tT_8$ and $A' = a'B + t'T_8$, a signature $\sigma = (R, S)$ and two messages m and m', s.t. $(m \neq m')$ or $(A \neq A')$ and $\mathsf{Verify}(A, \sigma, m)$ and

Verify(A', σ, m') both accept. The success of the verifications imply that $a \neq 0$ and $a' \neq 0$ (since small order public keys are rejected) and

$$8SB = 8R + 8H(R|A|m)A \text{ and } 8SB = 8R + 8H(R|A'|m')A'.$$

It follows that $8H(R|A|m)A = 8H(R|A'|m')A'$. Which implies $H(R|A|m)a = H(R|A'|m')a' \bmod L$. Since $a' \neq 0$, it follows that

$$H(R|A'|m')a'(a)^{-1} = H(R|A|m) \bmod L. \tag{1}$$

For some fixed a, m', a' the probability for a random m to satisfy the equation is $\frac{\lceil 2^{2\lambda}/L \rceil}{2^{2\lambda}}$. Assuming the adversary can make up to Q_h random oracle queries, the probability of finding a collision that satisfies Eq. 1 and thus the probability of a successful attack is $\frac{\lceil 2^{2\lambda}/L \rceil}{2^{2\lambda}} \cdot Q_h^2$. Given that the adversary runs in time polynomial in λ, Q_h is bounded by some polynomial in λ. Having that the bit-length of L is close to λ, the overall probability of success is negligible. □

On Rejecting Non-canonical Encodings of A and R (line #3, Algorithm 2): The RFC 8032 and the NIST FIPS186-5 draft both require to reject non-canonically encoded points, and as we show in Sect. 5 not all of the implementations follow those guidelines. For consistency with the standard, the non-canonical points should be rejected. The non-canonical points of which the discrete log is known are all of small order as explained in the beginning of this section, therefore the security level of the scheme is judged by the acceptance/rejection of small order points, not by acceptance/rejection of non-canonical subset of those.

On Computing SHA512 (line #4, Algorithm 2): If non-canonical points are accepted, there are two possible ways to put them into the SHA512 hash: [1] re-encode them in a canonical form or [2] put them in the hash as they were received. This can cause discrepancy between implementations, thus it is recommended to reject non-canonical points.

Note that if an implementation uses *cofactorless* verifcation (discussed next), then it is absolutely required to fully reduce the scalar SHA512($R||A||M$) to $[0, L)$ range before multiplying it by A. Otherwise, the implementations might disagree on the validity of a signature with a public key of mixed order. Indeed, consider a public key of mixed order: $A = bB + tT_8$, where B is the base point, T_8 is a point of order 8 and $0 < t \leq 7$. Consider an unreduced integer $h' \geq L$ which is an output of SHA512 and a reduced scalar $h = h' \bmod L$. With high probability for a random h: $((h \cdot t \neq h' \cdot t) \bmod 8)$ (e.g., with probability 7/8 for $t = 1$), then $h \cdot A \neq h' \cdot A$ causing the verifications to disagree depending on whether they reduce the scalar or not. Despite this discrepancy, an implemtation will incure significant performance loss if the scalar is not fully reduced prior to scalar-to-point multiplication, therefore we never see this problem in practice. However, if the RFC8032 [20] is read precicely it says to interpret the 64-octet digest as an "integer" k and compute $[k]A$, where $[n]X$ is defined as "X added to itself n times", whereas instead it should say to take the digest, reduce is as an integer to get $0 \leq k < L$. In general other applications where Curve25519 is used should be very careful and not rely on the fact that $(n \bmod L)((m \bmod L)P) = ((nm) \bmod L)P$ as this is not generally true for a composite order point P.

On Cofactored vs. Cofactorless Verification (line #5, Algorithm 2): The verification equation of Algorithm 2 is called *cofactored*. If implementation computes the verification equation as stated on line #5, then the multiplication by 8 should be done as a separate scalar-to-point multiplication, i.e. it is incorrect to first compute $(8h) \bmod L$ as the resulting scalar might not be divisible by 8 as an integer and thus will not clear the low order component from A, if it exists. This is a recommended way to verify EdDSA signatures in the standards [20, 34]. The original paper of Bernstein et al. [5] on line 5 of Algorithm 2 was not multiplying by 8, which is called *cofactorless* verification. Almost all the cryptographic libraries use the cofactorless version to make verification slighly faster. In the next section we explain why multiplying by a cofactor is required for applications that want to take advantage of batch verification. We therefore would recommend to use cofactored verfication as it conforms with the standard, it enables batch verification that could bring substantial speed-up (around 2x) and in addition enables novel methods for faster single signature verification [32].

3.2 Batch Signature Verification

A batch verification technique allows verifying several signatures in a single operation, much faster than verifying signatures one-by-one (e.g., using the dalek ed25519 library [19] on a 2.9 GHz 6-Core Intel Core i9 CPU single signature verification takes 50 μs, while batch verification with more than 20 signature costs 20 μs per signature). Bernstein et al. [5] proposed to use random linear combinations to verify the batch of signatures, in Algorithm 3 we restate the technique with a small alteration (i.e. in a cofactored form) that makes it compatible with single signature verifcation.

Algorithm 3. Ed25519 Algorithm: batch signature verification

Batch Signature Verification on n tuples $\{M_i, pk_i = A_i, \sigma_i = (R_i, S_i)\}_{i=1}^{n}$
1: Reject the batch if any of the signatures fail any of the checks 1,2 or 3 of single signature verification, Algorithm 2.
2: Sample n uniformly random integers $z_i \in \{0, 1\}^{128}$.
3: Compute $\mathsf{SHA512}(R_i\|A_i\|M_i)$ and reduce it $\bmod L$ to get a scalar h_i.
4: Accept if $\left(8\left(-\sum_i z_i S_i \bmod L\right)\right) B + 8(\sum_i z_i R_i) + 8(\sum_i (z_i h_i \bmod L)A_i) = 0$.

The batch verification equation stated on line 4, Algorithm 3 is called *cofactored*. The original paper of Bernstein et al. [5] on line 4, Algorithm 3 was not multiplying by 8 which is called *cofactorless* verification. We claim that only *cofactored* verifications, single and batch, are compatible with each other[4]. Other combinations (cofactorless-single with cofactorless-batch; cofactorless-signle with cofactored-batch; cofactored-single with cofactorless-batch) are all incompatible.

Consider the following sequence of signatures of length $n \geq 1$, we construct a first signature maliciously (deviating from the standard signature generation algorithm) and we construct the rest of the signatures in an ordinary way:

1. Given small integers t_A and t_R (where $0 \leq t_A, t_R \leq 7$), generate the first signature in a special way:
   (a) Set $A_1 := s \cdot B + t_A \cdot T_8$ for some secret scalar s.
   (b) Set $R_1 := r \cdot B + t_R \cdot T_8$ for some secret scalar r.
   (c) Set $S_1 := r + \mathsf{SHA512}(R_1 \| A_1 \| M)s$.
   (d) Set $\sigma_1 = (R_1, S_1)$.
2. For $i = 2..n$, construct the rest of the signatures $\sigma_2, \ldots, \sigma_n$ in an ordinary way, following the standard procedure for signature generation (Algorithm 1).

Table 3 demonstrates that *only* cofactorless single with cofactorless batch verifications agree with each other accepting the signatures with overwhelming probability, other combinations do disagree with each other. Batch verification is run on the batch constructed above, single verification is run on σ_1 from the batch. For cofactorless single signature verification, the $\checkmark_p$ (or $\boldsymbol{\times}_p$) indicates that we search for M that succeeds (or fails) the verification which happens with probability p for a random M. Next for cofactorless batch verification given M from the previous column, the $\checkmark_q$ (or $\boldsymbol{\times}_q$) indicates that with probability q over the choice of the first random scalar z_1, the batch verification will succeed (or fail) disagreeing with single signature verification. In all of these cases, cofactorless batch verification will exhibit flaky behavior—sometimes accepting and sometimes failing the batch depending on the choice of the random scalars. Note that cofactorless single verification succeeds if and only if $((h \cdot t_A)_{\mathsf{mod}\ L} + t_R)_{\mathsf{mod}\ 8} = 0$. Here h denotes $h = \mathsf{SHA512}(R_1 \| A_1 \| M_1)$, note that h depends on t_A and t_R. Cofactorless batch verification succeeds if and only if $((z_1 \cdot h \cdot t_A)_{\mathsf{mod}\ L} + z_1 \cdot t_R)_{\mathsf{mod}\ 8} = 0$. We assume that single verification (or iterative verification over a batch) is a ground truth, so that batch verification, seen as a "failure detection" procedure, can show false negatives (FN) when it does not reflect an iterated failure or false positives (FP) when it fails a batch where iterated verification would not. The combination that gives false positives (cofactorless single + cofactorless batch) is the most dangerous for applications, since an invalid sequence of signatures might pass the batch verification and be accepted. Moreover those false positives are flaky, meaning that a batch of signatures accepted by one verifier (through batch verification) might be rejected by another verifier that used another set of random scalars. Unfortunately, this combination is proposed in the original paper [5] and is the one most widely implemented (e.g., in Dalek [19] and LibSodium [23] libraries).

---

[4] The incompatibility in semantics between batch verification and cofactorless single verification was known in the form of cryptography community folklore [29], but not laid out precisely.

Table 3. Examples of different combinations of t_A and t_R that cause inconsistency between cofactorless single and batch verifications. FN denotes a false negative case, FP denotes a false positive case, ok denotes no discrepancy.

cofactored		cofactorless		Example conditions							
[1]	[2]	[3]	[4]	t_A	t_R	pk's	R's	[1]+[2]	[1]+[4]	[2]+[3]	[3]+[4]
single	batch	single	batch			order	order				
✓$_1$	✓$_1$	✓$_{1/8}$	✗$_{7/8}$	1	0	mixed	L	ok	FN	ok	FN
✓$_1$	✓$_1$	✗$_{7/8}$	✓$_{1/8}$	1	0	mixed	L	ok	ok	FN	FP
✓$_1$	✓$_1$	✗$_1$	✓$_{1/8}$	0	1	L	mixed	ok	ok	FN	FP
✓$_1$	✓$_1$	✓$_{1/8}$	✗$_{7/8}$	1	1	mixed	mixed	ok	FN	ok	FN
✓$_1$	✓$_1$	✗$_{7/8}$	✓$_{1/8}$	1	1	mixed	mixed	ok	ok	FN	FP

The combinations that give false negatives (cofactorless single + cofactored batch or cofactored single + cofactorless batch) are less devastating, but here the batch verification can only be used as a heuristic and in case of its failure the application will have to downgrade to verifying signatures iteratively to confirm the failure. The only combination that works as expected and where the batch verification can be trusted to conform with iterative verification with overwhelming probability is cofactored single with cofactored batch.

Clearly, inconsistencies yielding false positives or false negatives could mislead developers, and slow the adoption of the scheme in domains that would benefit from the verification performance granted by batch verification.[5]

In summary, an Ed25519 implementation interested in either of:

- serving users which require near-perfect determinism in the behavior of signature verification, such as blockchains,
- batch signature verification and its performance,
- faster signature verification procedures based on linear combinations (e.g., [32]),

would be well-served by at least adding a cofactored verification to their API, if not switching to cofactored verification entirely, similarly to what the NIST FIPS 186-5 suggests.

---

[5] For much of the same reasons, cofactorless verification is incompatible with a method for fast (single) signature verification initially suggested by Antipa et al. [1] and recently made practical by Pornin [32], yielding speedups of about 15% on single signature verification. In essence, this method relies on mutualizing point doublings involved in checking a linear combination of the verification equation using a carefully-chosen scalar. As this check's outcome should not depend on the ability of the scalar to clear small components in the equation, which is only achievable if the verification equation is cofactored.

4   Optimizations

This section presents some optimization tricks for faster canonicity checks and for cofactored verification. Note that many libraries either omit canonicity checks for micro-efficiency reasons or perform a validation logic that fully iterates over the input byte-arrays which is not optimal. However, as there are no secrets involved when verifying a signature, optimized variable-time implementations can be applied; otherwise, if constant-time is required, such optimizations should be used with caution.

Checking for Non-canonical S: Due to the very small probability of the 252-th bit being set, for honestly generated S, a succeed-fast solution can initially check if the four most significant bits of S are unset, and in the rare case when it is set, one can fallback to the exhaustive check of $S < L$.

Listing 1.1. Optimized canonicity validation for S (in Rust)

```rust
fun is_canonical_s (s_bytes: &[u8]) -> bool {
    return
        if s_bytes[31] & 240 == 0 {   true /* succeed fast */ }
        else if s_bytes[31] & 224 != 0 {   false /* fail fast */ }
        else { full_s_canonicity_check (s_bytes) }
}
```

Unfortunately, this optimization trick was only introduced very recently[6,7] and many implementations usually perform the full exhaustive check. Even worse, the original ref10 [33] and all of the libraries that ported that code, perform the"incomplete" fail-fast check (only line#4 in Listing 1.1) which only rejects signatures if any of the first 3 most significant bits are set. The latter implies that non-canonical S values might be accepted, when $S \in [2^{252}, L)$ and as a result this makes the scheme malleable (breaks SUF-CMA security), since an $S < 2^{252} - C$ can be altered to $S' = S + 2^{252} + C$ and still pass the check.

Recall that the order of the base point is $L = 2^{252} + C$, where $C = 2774231$ 7777372353535851937790883648493, is slightly greater than $2^{252} + 2^{124}$ because $C = 2^{124} + 6474669844813699569391024826398135277$ is a 125-bit number. Due to this structure, serialized canonical S values (using a 32-byte array) do always have their first three most significant bits unset, since for canonical S: $S < L$. Along the same lines, for honestly generated signatures, the probability that the fourth most significant bit (252th bit) is set is very small, roughly $1/2^{128}$:

$$\Pr[\text{252-th bit of } S \text{ is set}] = \log_2(1 - (2^{252} - 1)/L) \approx 1/2^{128}$$

Checking for Non-canonical y-coordinates: We present a succeed-fast implementation for validating point canonicity with the minimum effort. The

---

[6] Pull request to Libra: github.com/libra/libra/pull/907, merged Sep 11, 2019.

[7] Pull request to Dalek: github.com/dalek-cryptography/ed25519-dalek/pull/99, merged Dec 5, 2019.

logic is very simple and based on the fact that $2^{255} - 19$ is as 255-bit number, where all of its bits, but the 2nd and 5th less significant bits, are set. That said, the 8 less significant bits correspond to the decimal number 237. Thus, a succeed fast algorithm checking the canonicity of the point could start with an "is less than 237" check on the less significant byte, which will succeed with probability $237/256 = 92.5\%$ and then perform inequality checks ("is not equal to 255") for every next byte, which results to $255/256 = 99.6\%$ probability of success per byte. The above results to an amortized cost of a single byte inequality comparison in the happy path where most of the evaluated points are indeed canonical (see Listing 1.2).

Listing 1.2. Optimized canonicity validation for y-coordinate (in Rust)

```
fun is_canonical_y(bytes: &[u8]) -> bool {
    if bytes[0] < 237 { true }
    else {
        for i in 1..=30 {
            if bytes[i] != 255 { return true }
        }
        (bytes[31] | 128) != 255
    }
}
```

Faster Signature Verification: Note that there is a faster way to evaluate the equation in line #5 of Algorithm 2: first compute $V = SB - R - hA$ and then accept if V is one of 8 small order points (or alternatively compute $8V$ with 3 doublings and check against the neutral element). Similarly, for batch verification, to evaluate the equation on line #4 of Algorithm 3 one can compute $V = (-\sum_i z_i S_i \mod L)B + (\sum_i z_i R_i) + (\sum_i (z_i h_i \mod L)A_i)$ and accept if V is one of 8 small order points.

5 Test Vectors and Analysis of Implementations

We have generated several test vectors to help researchers and implementers manage the complexity of the Ed25519 implementations, beyond the sanity checks present in specification ([20,34]) and the limited set of serialization and malleability checks from project WycheProof [6]. They aim at two goals, a) detecting *specific implementation choices*: for example we strive to detect all combinations of checks on individual components of a signature in vectors [0–4, 6] below, and b) detecting *common implementation mistakes*, which help explain inconsistent behavior occurring in the wild, see vectors [5, 7–9] below.

By running the first set against an implementation, library users will be able to notice at a glance whether that library is using cofactored verification or not, and which security properties from Sect. 3 it provides. They will also know if they can use batch verification soundly, as shown in Sect. 3.2, and if they work in a context where determinism is key, they will able to list the checks that any other library interfacing with their project should match exactly. Yet depending on results, those same users may also discover bugs, so that by providing the second set of vectors, we hope Ed25519 maintainers will also be able to remedy

Table 4. Conditions satisfied by the test vectors.

#	M	σ	S	A's order	R's order	$8(SB) =$ $8R + 8(hA)$	$SB =$ $R + hA$
0	..22b6	..0000	$S = 0$	small	small	✓	✓
1	..2e79	..ac04	$0 < S < L$	small	mixed	✓	✓
2	..b9ab	..260e	$0 < S < L$	mixed	small	✓	✓
3	..2e79	..d009	$0 < S < L$	mixed	mixed	✓	✓
4	..f56c	..1a09	$0 < S < L$	mixed	mixed	✓	✗
5	..f56c	..7405	$0 < S < L$	mixed	L	✓[(1)]	✗
6	..ec40	..a514	$S > L$	L	L	✓	✓
7	..ec40	..8c22	$S \gg L$ [(2)]	L	L	✓	✓
8	..8b41	..5f0f	$0 < S < L$	mixed	small [(3)]	- [(3)]	- [(3)]
9	..8b41	..4908	$0 < S < L$	mixed	small [(3)]	- [(3)]	- [(3)]
10	..155b	..ac04	$0 < S < L$	small [(4)]	mixed	- [(4)]	- [(4)]
11	..c06f	..ac04	$0 < S < L$	small [(4)]	mixed	- [(4)]	- [(4)]

[(1)] #5 fails any cofactored verification that pre-reduces scalar $8h$.

[(2)] #7 fails bitwise tests that $S > L$.

[(3)] #8–9 have a non-canonical R (vector #10 from Table 1); implementations that reduce R before hashing will accept #8 and reject #9, while those that do not will reject #8 and accept #9.

[(4)] #10–11 have a non-canonical A (vector #10 from Table 1); implementations that reduce A before hashing will accept #10 and reject #11, while those that do not will reject #10 and accept #11.

implementation shortcuts and constrain variations in Ed25519 implementations to opinionated but valid approaches.

5.1 Tested Conditions and Bugs

Our test vectors are generated with a HC-128 RNG seeded with decimals of π, and the source code generating them is publicly accessible [15]. The vectors are reproduced in Appendix C. We lay out the conditions satisfied by our vectors in Table 4, following the nomenclature used throughout the paper (public key A, signature $\sigma = (R, S)$, $h = \mathsf{SHA512}(R||A||M)$). As the table lists conditions that each vector verifies simultaneously, readers should be reminded that a verification failure could be attributed to any one of them.

Test vectors 0–3 are made to pass both cofactored and cofactorless verification, vectors 0–2 have small R, A or both, vector 3 only has mixed-order A and R. Vector 4 is made to pass cofactored and fail in cofactorless verification, this vector is the main indicator of what type of verification is used in the implementation (assuming that vector 3 passes which implies that mixed-order points are not checked for). Vector 5 will be rejected in cofactored libraries that erroneously pre-reduce the scalar: compute $(8h \bmod L)A$ instead of $8(hA)$, note that the former might not clear the low order component from A, while the later will always do. Vector 6 or 7 will be accepted in libraries that accept non-canonical S (i.e. $S > L$) or do an incomplete cheaper check. Vectors 8–9 have small R that is serialized in a non-canonical way, libraries that reduce R prior to hashing will accept vector 8 and reject 9, and libraries that do not reduce R for hashing will behave in an oposite way on vectors 8–9. Vectors 10–11 behave in the same way for a public A serialized in a non-canonical way.

SUF-CMA secure libraries should reject non-canonical S, i.e. reject vectors 6–7. Libraries that offer SBS security should reject small order public keys, i.e. reject vectors 0–1. Vector 4 can be used to differentiate between cofactored vs. cofactorless verification.

5.2   Test Results

We have tested a number of major implementations of Ed25519 which we list in Table 5 .

We note that except for Zebra, all tested libraries implement a cofactorless variant of EdDSA (as witnessed by vector 4). That is despite the fact that libraries like Dalek or LibSodium offer batch verification, which, as we have noted in Sect. 3.2, comes with semantics that are not compatible with cofactorless verification.

On the plus side, most libraries do perform the check that a signature's scalar component S is in a canonical form ($S < L$, vectors 6–7), which is essential to prevent malleability issues and is required for SUF-CMA security. The exceptions are ed25519-java, TweetNacl, python-ed25519, ed25519-donna, and ref10, the latter two of which only perform the incomplete fail fast check (as shown in Listing 1.1 line#4), rather than a full check of its size. This explains why ed25519-donna and ref10 reject $S \gg L$ values of vector 7.

Only Libsodium checks for components of small order (vectors 0—2). The absence of this check on the public key, A, (i.e. acceptance of vectors 0–1) could lead to non-binding signatures. No common software library implements a full check for mixed order points (vector 3), which is understandable since this would require an expensive multiplication by the full order of the large subgroup and does not necessarily enhance the security level of the scheme.

The nCipher nShield HSM has a cofactorless implementation, and does not perform a modular reduction on the hash output. In this it follows the precise reading of RFC 8032 referred to above rather than the example code. Vector 2 is accepted because there is no difference between reducing and non-reducing implementations (the scalar multiple of the small-order component happens to be a multiple of 8).

All libraries, except Zebra, reject non-canonical R in the signature (vectors 8–9). The non-canonical A (vectors 10–11) is rejected by BouncyCastle, LibSodium and nCipher nShield, the rest of the libraries accept the non-canonical A (despite the RFC and NIST FIPS mandate its rejection) and all, except ed25519-java, reduce it prior to hashing.

Table 5. Test vector results

Library	0	1	2	3	4	5	6	7	8	9	10	11	SUF-CMA	SBS	cofactored
Algorithm 2	✗	✗	✓	✓	✓	✓	✗	✗	✗	✗	✗	✗	✓	✓	✓
RFC 8032(*) [20]	✓	✓	✓	✓	✓	✓	✗	✗	✗	✗	✗	✗	✓	✗	✓
FIPS 186-5 [34]	✓	✓	✓	✓	✓	✓	✗	✗	✗	✗	✗	✗	✓	✗	✓
BoringSSL	✓	✓	✓	✓	✗	✗	✗	✗	✗	✗	✗	✓	✓	✗	✗
BouncyCastle	✓	✓	✓	✓	✗	✗	✗	✗	✗	✗	✗	✗	✓	✗	✗
CryptoKit	✓	✓	✓	✓	✗	✗	✗	✗	✗	✗	✗	✓	✓	✗	✗
Dalek	✓	✓	✓	✓	✗	✗	✗	✓	✗	✗	✗	✓	✓	✗	✗
ed25519-donna	✓	✓	✓	✓	✗	✗	✓	✗	✗	✗	✗	✓	✗	✗	✗
ed25519-java	✓	✓	✓	✓	✗	✗	✓	✓	✗	✗	✓	✗	✗	✗	✗
Go	✓	✓	✓	✓	✗	✗	✗	✗	✗	✗	✗	✓	✓	✗	✗
LibSodium	✗	✗	✗	✓	✗	✗	✗	✗	✗	✗	✗	✗	✓	✓	✗
nCipher nShield	✗	✗	✓	✗	✗	✗	✗	✗	✗	✗	✗	✗	✓	✓	✓
npm	✓	✓	✓	✓	✗	✗	✗	✗	✗	✗	✗	✓	✓	✗	✗
OpenSSL-3.0	✓	✓	✓	✓	✗	✗	✗	✗	✗	✗	✗	✓	✓	✗	✗
PyCA	✓	✓	✓	✓	✗	✗	✗	✗	✗	✗	✗	✓	✓	✗	✗
python-ed25519	✓	✓	✓	✓	✗	✗	✓	✓	✗	✗	✗	✓	✗	✗	✗
ref10	✓	✓	✓	✓	✗	✗	✓	✗	✗	✗	✗	✓	✗	✗	✗
TweetNaCl.js	✓	✓	✓	✓	✗	✗	✓	✓	✗	✗	✗	✓	✗	✗	✗
Zebra	✓	✓	✓	✓	✓	✓	✗	✗	✗	✓	✓	✓	✓	✗	✓

(*) The cofactored, recommended, version of the RFC 8032 is used.
BoringSSL: version 0.16.5, github.com/briansmith/ring,
BouncyCastle: Java version 1.8.0, www.bouncycastle.org/java.html,
CryptoKit: iOS 13, Apple Swift version 5.3,
Dalek: Version 1.0.0-pre.4, github.com/dalek-cryptography/ed25519-dalek,
ed25519-donna: commit 3a83a4f, github.com/signalapp/libsignal-protocol-c,
ed25519-java: Version 0.3.0, github.com/str4d/ed25519-java,
Go: version 1.11.5 darwin/amd64,
LibSodium: Version 1.0.18, github.com/jedisct1/libsodium,
nCipher nShield: Solo XC High (nC433N) FW 12.60.2, SW 12.50.5,
npm: Version 6.13.4, Node package manager,
OpenSSL-3.0: Version OpenSSL 3.0.0-alpha6-dev, github.com/openssl/openssl,
PyCa: Version 3.1, backed by OpenSSL 1.1.1g, github.com/pyca/cryptography,
python-ed25519: commit d57b8f2c, github.com/warner/python-ed25519,
ref10: from Libsodium version 1.0.18 (ED25519_COMPAT mode),
TweetNaCl.js: version 1.0.3, www.npmjs.com/package/tweetnacl,
Zebra: version 2.1.1, github.com/ZcashFoundation/ed25519-zebra

6   Related Work

6.1   Security Analyses of Ed25519

EdDSA signatures are a variant of Schnorr signatures and inherit the security properties of the latter. Schnorr signatures are compiled from Schnorr's identification protocol [37,38] using the Fiat-Shamir transform [12].

Pointcheval and Stern [30,31] were the first to give a security proof for Schnorr signatures reducing security to the hardness of the discrete logarithm in the Random Oracle model using the celebrated Forking Lemma. However, the reduction had a quadratic loss. It was later shown [28,39] that under a plausible assumption for any algebraic reduction such loss is inevitable, the result was recently extended [13] to show that unconditionally the security of Schnorr signatures can not be tightly based (generically) on any non-trivial non-interactive hardness assumption.

Neven, Smart, and Warinschi [27] gave a proof for Schnorr signatures in the generic group model relying on two concrete properties of the hash function: random-prefix preimage resistance, and random-prefix second-preimage resistance. The generic group model proof combined with the conjectured optimal hash function security by Neven et al. [27] therefore build confidence in the parameter choices of EdDSA and specifically the output length of the hash function.

Most recently, Brendel et al. [8] analyzed the security of three instantiations of EdDSA: the Ed25519-Original [5], the original reference implementation by the authors of the EdDSA paper, the Ed25519-IETF [20], the version standardized by the IETF in RFC 8032 and closely followed by NIST FIPS 186-5 [34], and the implementation used by LibSodium [23], Ed25519-LibSodium. They showed that the strongest notion of security would be achieved by LibSodium library that rejects S not in the set $\{0,\ldots,L-1\}$ and rejects A and R of orders other than L. This variant achieves strong existentially unforgeability (SUF-CMA) and resilience to key substitution attacks, M-S-UEO (slightly weaker than SBS). We observe that to achieve SBS security it is sufficient to reject the public key A of small order which we prove in Theorem 1. Though we rely on the security analysis from [8], we focus on practical aspects of implementing the most secure variant of the scheme correctly. We additionally bring attention to the question of correctness of signatures and the disagreement around this question between different libraries and the standard. We provide test-vectors alongside the way of generating them to check for those inconsistencies.

We additionally observe two errors in the Brendel et al. [8] paper that does not affect the overall merit or proofs of the paper. First, the LibSodium library does not check the full order of the points, rather the library rejects public keys and R components of small order (note that points that pass this check can still have mixed-order $2L, 4L$ or $8L$). This simpler and much cheaper check still preserves the SUF-CMA security with strong binding that Brendel et al. prove. Second, the LibSodium library does not multiply by a cofactor, eight, in the verification equation, and we are only aware of the Zebra library [9,10] of Zcash that does multiply by a cofactor in the verification equation.

6.2   Attacks on Ed25519

In 2017, a vulnerability in the Monero crypto-currency allowed for arbitrary double spending [26] due to the cofactor issue. This issue was mitigated by checking the order of the key image using a full scalar multiplication. Samwel *et al.* [36] showed the feasibility of side-channel attacks on the SHA512 hash function used in EdDSA, and suggest as a protection to add randomness to the output of the hash. Weisbart et al. [40] recently extended these results to show that power analysis of a single trace using convolutional neural networks achieve key recovery on a single trace. In [35] almost 100% key recovery through voltage glitching and electromagnetic fault injection was demostrated. Aranha *et al.* [2] studied the resilience under fault of "hedged" signatures —that hash secret key, message and nonce to derive the per-signature randomness— and discriminate the type of faults mitigated by this practice.

Acknowledgements. The authors would like to thank the reviewers of this paper for comments that greatly improved its contribution. We would also like to thank Yashvanth Kondi and Isis Lovecruft for fruitful discussions on the topic of this paper, and Rob Starkey, Yolan Romailler, Irakliy Khaburzaniya, and Rajath Shanbag for contributing to running our test vectors against EdDSA implementations.

Appendix A   Test Vectors Breaking the Non-repudiation

The test vector in Table 6a attacks the non-repudiation property of Ed25519 signature scheme with a small-order public key and a signature that is valid for two meaningful messages.

Appendix B   Serialized Small Order Points

Table 6b shows 14 possible serializations of small order points. The ordering of the points match the ordering in Table 1 of Sect. 3.

Appendix C   Test Vectors

The test vectors discussed in Sect. 5 are given in little-endian hex-encoded format in Table 6c.

Table 6. Hex-encoded vectors.

```
{"message1"          : "Send 100 USD to Alice",
 "message1 (UTF-8)"  : "53656e6420313030205553442040746f20416c696365",
 "message2"          : "Send 100000 USD to Alice",
 "message2 (UTF-8)"  : "53656e64203130303030205553442040746f20416c696365",
 "pub_key"           : "ecffffffffffffffffffffffffffffffffffffffffffffffffffffffffffff7f",
 "signature"         : "a9d55260f765261eb9b84e106f665e00b867287a761990d7135963ee0a7d59dc\
                        a5bb704786be79fc476f91d3f3f89b03984d8068dcf1bb7dfc6637b45450ac04"}
```

(a) Test vectors breaking non-repudiation

#	Canonical serializations
1	0100000000000000000000000000000000000000000000000000000000000000
2	ECFFFFFFFFFFFFFFFFFFFFFFFFFFFFFFFFFFFFFFFFFFFFFFFFFFFFFFFFFFFFFF7F
3	0000000000000000000000000000000000000000000000000000000000000080
4	0000000000000000000000000000000000000000000000000000000000000000
5	C7176A703D4DD84FBA3C0B760D10670F2A2053FA2C39CCC64EC7FD7792AC037A
6	C7176A703D4DD84FBA3C0B760D10670F2A2053FA2C39CCC64EC7FD7792AC03FA
7	26E8958FC2B227B045C3F489F2EF98F0D5DFAC05D3C63339B13802886D53FC05
8	26E8958FC2B227B045C3F489F2EF98F0D5DFAC05D3C63339B13802886D53FC85

#	Non-canonical serializations
9	0100000000000000000000000000000000000000000000000000000000000080
10	ECFFFFFFFFFFFFFFFFFFFFFFFFFFFFFFFFFFFFFFFFFFFFFFFFFFFFFFFFFFFFFFFF
11	EEFFFFFFFFFFFFFFFFFFFFFFFFFFFFFFFFFFFFFFFFFFFFFFFFFFFFFFFFFFFFFF7F
12	EEFFFFFFFFFFFFFFFFFFFFFFFFFFFFFFFFFFFFFFFFFFFFFFFFFFFFFFFFFFFFFFFF
13	EDFFFFFFFFFFFFFFFFFFFFFFFFFFFFFFFFFFFFFFFFFFFFFFFFFFFFFFFFFFFFFFFF
14	EDFFFFFFFFFFFFFFFFFFFFFFFFFFFFFFFFFFFFFFFFFFFFFFFFFFFFFFFFFFFFFF7F

(b) Full serialization of small order points.

```
[{"message"  : "8c93255d71dcab10e8f379c26200f3c7bd5f09d9bc3068d3ef4edeb4853022b6",
  "pub_key"  : "c7176a703d4dd84fba3c0b760d10670f2a2053fa2c39ccc64ec7fd7792ac03fa",
  "signature": "c7176a703d4dd84fba3c0b760d10670f2a2053fa2c39ccc64ec7fd7792ac037a\
                0000000000000000000000000000000000000000000000000000000000000000"},
 {"message"  : "9bd9f44f4dcc75bd531b56b2cd280b0bb38fc1cd6d1230e14861d861de092e79",
  "pub_key"  : "c7176a703d4dd84fba3c0b760d10670f2a2053fa2c39ccc64ec7fd7792ac03fa",
  "signature": "f7badec5b8abeaf699583992219b7b223f1df3fbbea919844e3f7c554a43dd43\
                a5bb704786be79fc476f91d3f3f89b03984d8068dcf1bb7dfc6637b45450ac04"},
 {"message"  : "aebf3f2601a0c8c5d39cc7d8911642f740b78168218da8471772b35f9d35b9ab",
  "pub_key"  : "f7badec5b8abeaf699583992219b7b223f1df3fbbea919844e3f7c554a43dd43",
  "signature": "c7176a703d4dd84fba3c0b760d10670f2a2053fa2c39ccc64ec7fd7792ac03fa\
                8c4bd45aecaca5b24fb97bc10ac27ac8751a7dfe1baff8b953ec9f5833ca260e"},
 {"message"  : "9bd9f44f4dcc75bd531b56b2cd280b0bb38fc1cd6d1230e14861d861de092e79",
  "pub_key"  : "cdb267ce40c5cd45306fa5d2f29731459387dbf9eb933b7bd5aed9a765b88d4d",
  "signature": "9046a64750444938de19f227bb80485e92b83fdb4b6506c160484c016cc1852f\
                87909e14428a7a1d62e9f22f3d3ad7802db02eb2e688b6c52fcd6648a98bd009"},
 {"message"  : "e47d62c63f830dc7a6851a0b1f33ae4bb2f507fb6cffec4011eaccd55b53f56c",
  "pub_key"  : "cdb267ce40c5cd45306fa5d2f29731459387dbf9eb933b7bd5aed9a765b88d4d",
  "signature": "160a1cb0dc9c0258cd0a7d23e94d8fa878bcb1925f2c64246b2dee1796bed512\
                5ec6bc982a269b723e0668e540911a9a6a58921d6925e434ab10aa7940551a09"},
 {"message"  : "e47d62c63f830dc7a6851a0b1f33ae4bb2f507fb6cffec4011eaccd55b53f56c",
  "pub_key"  : "cdb267ce40c5cd45306fa5d2f29731459387dbf9eb933b7bd5aed9a765b88d4d",
  "signature": "21122a84e0b5fca4052f5b1235c80a537878b38f3142356b2c2384ebad4668b7\
                e40bc836dac0f71076f9abe3a53f9c03c1ceeeddb658d0030494ace586687405"},
 {"message"  : "85e241a07d148b41e47d62c63f830dc7a6851a0b1f33ae4bb2f507fb6cffec40",
  "pub_key"  : "442aad9f089ad9e14647b1ef9099a1ff4798d78589e66f28eca69c11f582a623",
  "signature": "e96f66be976d82e60150baecff9906684aebb1ef181f67a7189ac78ea23b6c0e\
                547f7690a0e2ddcd04d87dbc3490dc19b3b3052f7ff0538cb68afb369ba3a514"},
 {"message"  : "85e241a07d148b41e47d62c63f830dc7a6851a0b1f33ae4bb2f507fb6cffec40",
  "pub_key"  : "442aad9f089ad9e14647b1ef9099a1ff4798d78589e66f28eca69c11f582a623",
  "signature": "8ce5b96c8f26d0ab6c47958c9e68b937104cd36e13c33566acd2fe8d38aa1942\
                7e71f98a4734e74f2f13f06f97c20d58cc3f54b8bd0d272f42b695dd7e89a8c22"},
 {"message"  : "9bedc267423725d473888631ebf45988bad3db83851ee85c85e241a07d148b41",
  "pub_key"  : "f7badec5b8abeaf699583992219b7b223f1df3fbbea919844e3f7c554a43dd43",
  "signature": "ecffffffffffffffffffffffffffffffffffffffffffffffffffffffffffffff\
                03be9678ac102edcd92b0210bb34d7428d12ffc5df5f37e359941266a4e35f0f"},
 {"message"  : "9bedc267423725d473888631ebf45988bad3db83851ee85c85e241a07d148b41",
  "pub_key"  : "f7badec5b8abeaf699583992219b7b223f1df3fbbea919844e3f7c554a43dd43",
  "signature": "ecffffffffffffffffffffffffffffffffffffffffffffffffffffffffffffff\
                ca8c5b64cd208982aa38d4936621a4775aa233aa0505711d8fdcfdaa943d4908"},
 {"message"  : "e96b7021eb39c1a163b6da4e3093dcd3f21387da4cc4572be588fafae23c155b",
  "pub_key"  : "ecffffffffffffffffffffffffffffffffffffffffffffffffffffffffffffff",
  "signature": "a9d55260f765261eb9b84e106f665e00b867287a761990d7135963ee0a7d59dc\
                a5bb704786be79fc476f91d3f3f89b03984d8068dcf1bb7dfc6637b45450ac04"},
 {"message"  : "39a591f5321bbe07fd5a23dc2f39d025d74526615746727ceefd6e82ae65c06f",
  "pub_key"  : "ecffffffffffffffffffffffffffffffffffffffffffffffffffffffffffff7f",
  "signature": "a9d55260f765261eb9b84e106f665e00b867287a761990d7135963ee0a7d59dc\
                a5bb704786be79fc476f91d3f3f89b03984d8068dcf1bb7dfc6637b45450ac04"}]
```

(c) Test vectors in JSON format exercising the cases of § 5

References

1. Antipa, A., Brown, D., Gallant, R., Lambert, R., Struik, R., Vanstone, S.: Accelerated Verification of ECDSA Signatures. In: Preneel, B., Tavares, S. (eds.) SAC 2005. LNCS, vol. 3897, pp. 307–318. Springer, Heidelberg (2006). https://doi.org/10.1007/11693383_21

2. Aranha, D.F., Orlandi, C., Takahashi, A., Zaverucha, G.: Security of hedged Fiat–Shamir signatures under fault attacks. In: Canteaut, A., Ishai, Y. (eds.) EUROCRYPT 2020, Part I. LNCS, vol. 12105, pp. 644–674. Springer, Cham (2020). https://doi.org/10.1007/978-3-030-45721-1_23

3. Barry, N., Losa, G., Mazieres, D., McCaleb, J., Polu, S.: The Stellar Consensus Protocol (SCP). IETF, draft-mazieres-dinrg-scp-05 (2018)

4. Bernstein, D.J., Birkner, P., Joye, M., Lange, T., Peters, C.: Twisted edwards curves. In: Vaudenay, S. (ed.) AFRICACRYPT 2008. LNCS, vol. 5023, pp. 389–405. Springer, Heidelberg (2008). https://doi.org/10.1007/978-3-540-68164-9_26

5. Bernstein, D.J., Duif, N., Lange, T., Schwabe, P., Yang, B.-Y.: High-speed high-security signatures. J Crypt. Eng. **2**, 77–89 (2012)

6. Bleichenbacher, D., Duong, T., Kasper, E., Nguyen, Q.: Project Wycheproof. https://github.com/google/wycheproof

7. Boneh, D., Shen, E., Waters, B.: Strongly unforgeable signatures based on computational Diffie-Hellman. In: Yung, M., Dodis, Y., Kiayias, A., Malkin, T. (eds.) PKC 2006. LNCS, vol. 3958, pp. 229–240. Springer, Heidelberg (2006). https://doi.org/10.1007/11745853_15

8. Brendel, J., Cremers, C., Jackson, D., Zhao, M.: The provable security of ed25519: theory and practice. IACR ePrint **2020**, 823 (2020)

9. de Valence, H.: Zcash-flavored ed25519 for use in zebra. https://github.com/ZcashFoundation/ed25519-zebra, version 2.1.1

10. de Valence, H.: Zip 125: Explicitly defining and modifying ed25519 validation rules (2020). https://github.com/zcash/zips/blob/master/zip-0215.rst

11. Decker, C., Wattenhofer, R.: Bitcoin transaction malleability and MtGox. In: Kutyłowski, M., Vaidya, J. (eds.) ESORICS 2014, Part II. LNCS, vol. 8713, pp. 313–326. Springer, Cham (2014). https://doi.org/10.1007/978-3-319-11212-1_18

12. Fiat, A., Shamir, A.: How to prove yourself: practical solutions to identification and signature problems. In: Odlyzko, A.M. (ed.) CRYPTO 1986. LNCS, vol. 263, pp. 186–194. Springer, Heidelberg (1987). https://doi.org/10.1007/3-540-47721-7_12

13. Fleischhacker, N., Jager, T., Schröder, D.: On tight security proofs for Schnorr signatures. J. Cryptol. **32**(2), 566–599 (2019)

14. Goodman, L.M.: Tezos – a self-amending crypto-ledger. Technical report (2014)

15. Novi Research Group. Ed25519-speccheck. https://github.com/novifinancial/ed25519-speccheck, commit 82d9301

16. Hearn, M.: Corda: A distributed ledger. Corda Technical White Paper (2016)

17. Heninger, N., Durumeric, Z., Wustrow, E., Halderman, J.A.: Mining your Ps and Qs: Detection of widespread weak keys in network devices. In: USENIX Security Symposium (2012)

18. IANIX: Things that use Ed25519. https://ianix.com/pub/ed25519-deployment.html

19. de Valenc, H., Lovecruft, I.A.: ed25519-dalek: Fast and efficient rust implementation of ed25519 key generation, signing, and verification in rust. https://github.com/dalek-cryptography/ed25519-dalek, version 1.0.0-pre.4

20. Josefsson, S., Liusvaara, I.: RFC 8032: Edwards-Curve Digital Signature Algorithm (EdDSA), January 2017
21. Langley, A., Hamburg, M., Turner, S.: RFC 7748: Elliptic Curves for Security, January 2016
22. Libra blockchain. https://github.com/libra/libra
23. LibSodium. https://github.com/jedisct1/libsodium, version 1.0.18
24. Lim, C.H., Lee, P.J.: A key recovery attack on discrete log-based schemes using a prime order subgroup. In: Kaliski, B.S. (ed.) CRYPTO 1997. LNCS, vol. 1294, pp. 249–263. Springer, Heidelberg (1997). https://doi.org/10.1007/BFb0052240
25. Lombrozo, E., Lau, J., Wuille, P.: Segregated Witness. Bitcoin Improvement Proposal 141. Created, 21 December 2015
26. R. luigi1111, "fluffypony" Spagni. Disclosure of a major bug in CryptoNote based currencies (2017)
27. Neven, G., Smart, N.P., Warinschi, B.: Hash function requirements for Schnorr signatures. J. Math. Cryptol. **3**(1), 69–87 (2009)
28. Paillier, P., Vergnaud, D.: Discrete-log-based signatures may not be equivalent to discrete log. In: Roy, B. (ed.) ASIACRYPT 2005. LNCS, vol. 3788, pp. 1–20. Springer, Heidelberg (2005). https://doi.org/10.1007/11593447_1
29. Perrin, T.: Xed25519. email to the Modern Cryptography mailing list (2016)
30. Pointcheval, D., Stern, J.: Security proofs for signature schemes. In: Maurer, U. (ed.) EUROCRYPT 1996. LNCS, vol. 1070, pp. 387–398. Springer, Heidelberg (1996). https://doi.org/10.1007/3-540-68339-9_33
31. Pointcheval, D., Stern, J.: Security arguments for digital signatures and blind signatures. J. Cryptol. **13**(3), 361–396 (2000). https://doi.org/10.1007/s001450010003
32. Pornin, T.: Optimized lattice basis reduction in dimension 2, and fast schnorr and EdDSA signature verification. IACR ePrint 2020/454 (2020)
33. Ref10: the ed25519 software from supercop benchmarking tool. https://bench.cr.yp.to/supercop.html. Accessed 24 Aug 2020
34. Regenscheid, A.: NIST FIPS 186-5 (Draft), Digital Signature Standard (2019)
35. Samwel, N., Batina, L.: Practical fault injection on deterministic signatures: the case of EdDSA. In: Joux, A., Nitaj, A., Rachidi, T. (eds.) AFRICACRYPT 2018. LNCS, vol. 10831, pp. 306–321. Springer, Cham (2018). https://doi.org/10.1007/978-3-319-89339-6_17
36. Samwel, N., Batina, L., Bertoni, G., Daemen, J., Susella, R.: Breaking Ed25519 in WolfSSL. In: Smart, N.P. (ed.) CT-RSA 2018. LNCS, vol. 10808, pp. 1–20. Springer, Cham (2018). https://doi.org/10.1007/978-3-319-76953-0_1
37. Schnorr, C.P.: Efficient identification and signatures for smart cards. In: Quisquater, J.-J., Vandewalle, J. (eds.) EUROCRYPT 1989. LNCS, vol. 434, pp. 688–689. Springer, Heidelberg (1990). https://doi.org/10.1007/3-540-46885-4_68
38. Schnorr, C.P.: Efficient signature generation by smart cards. J. Cryptol. **4**(3), 161–174 (1991). https://doi.org/10.1007/BF00196725
39. Seurin, Y.: On the exact security of Schnorr-type signatures in the random oracle model. In: Pointcheval, D., Johansson, T. (eds.) EUROCRYPT 2012. LNCS, vol. 7237, pp. 554–571. Springer, Heidelberg (2012). https://doi.org/10.1007/978-3-642-29011-4_33

40. Weissbart, L., Picek, S., Batina, L.: One trace is all it takes: Machine learning-based side-channel attack on EdDSA. IACR ePrint 2019/358 (2019)
41. Wuille, P.: Dealing with malleability. Bitcoin Improvement Proposal 62, (2015)
42. Wuille, P.: Strict DER signatures. Bitcoin Improvement Proposal 66 (2015)
43. Zhou, J., Gollmann, D.: Observations on non-repudiation. In: Kim, K., Matsumoto, T. (eds.) ASIACRYPT 1996. LNCS, vol. 1163, pp. 133–144. Springer, Heidelberg (1996). https://doi.org/10.1007/BFb0034842

SoK: Comparison of the Security of Real World RSA Hash-and-Sign Signatures

Saqib A. Kakvi$^{(\boxtimes)}$ (iD)

Bergische Universität Wuppertal, Wuppertal, Germany
kakvi@uni-wuppertal.de

Abstract. In this modern day and age, where the majority of our communication occurs online, digital signatures are more important than ever before. Of the utmost importance are the standardised signatures that are deployed not only across the Internet, but also in everyday devices, such as debit and credit cards. The development of these signatures began in the 1990s and is still an ongoing process to this day. We will focus on RSA-based hash-and-sign signatures, specifically deterministic hash-and-sign signatures. We will give a survey of all standardised deterministic RSA hash-and-signatures, where we explore the history of each one, from inception, to attacks and finally proofs of security. As the security proofs have also appeared over the span of two decades, their statements are not always compatible with one another. To ensure this, we will consider only deterministic standardised signature schemes included in PKCS, ISO, and ANSI standards, as well as the non-standardised Full-Domain Hash, to provide a complete picture.

Keywords: Digital signatures · Random Oracle Model · RSA · Full Domain Hash · Lossy TrapDoor Permutation · PKCS · ANSI · ISO · Standards

1 Introduction

In the early days of the Internet, several practical signature schemes based on the intractability of the RSA problem appeared, both as industry standards and in academic literature. While there was a range of schemes, they were all based on the "hash-and-sign" paradigm, where any message was converted into a "message representative" in the group $\mathbb{Z}_N$ with the use of a hash function(s) and possibly some padding. This was first suggested by Denning [21] and independently by Gordon [27]. The first scheme to follow this blueprint was an industry standard, namely PKCS#1 v1 Signature Scheme with Appendix, which first appeared at the NIST/OSI Implementors' Workshop in 1991. This would later appear publicly in 1998 as the PKCS#1 v1.5 Signature Scheme with Appendix RSASSA-PKCS1-v1_5 [40]. This scheme did not initially have a security proof, and indeed the PKCS#1 standard has seen many attacks, mainly in the form of Bleichenbacher's attacks [8]. In contrast to this, the first scheme proposed

T. van der Merwe et al. (Eds.): SSR 2020, LNCS 12529, pp. 91–113, 2020.
https://doi.org/10.1007/978-3-030-64357-7_5

in academic circles was the Full Domain Hash scheme RSA-FDH of Bellare and Rogaway [2], which had an accompanying security proof, albeit a non-tight one.

While initially disparate, academia and standards did eventually converge with the first provably secure standard being the IEEE P1363-2000 Inter Factorization Signature Scheme with Appendix IFSSA [43] and the ISO/IEC 14888-2:2008 RSA Signature scheme (14888-2 RSA Signature) [31], which is a variant of the Probabilistic Signature Scheme RSA-PSS by Bellare and Rogaway [3,4]. The standardised variant was proven secure by Jonnson [35], the proof itself being based on the proof for the original scheme due to Coron [14]. Ideally, RSASSA-PKCS1-v1_5 would have been replaced with IFSSA, or indeed another provable secure scheme, however, this is not the case. There has been an attempt to replace RSASSA-PKCS1-v1_5 with IFSSA(the scheme is called RSASSA-PSS in the standard), but this has been slow going. IFSSA was suggested as an eventual replacement for RSASSA-PKCS1-v1_5 in PKCS#1 v2.1 [34] in 2003 and was upgraded to a requirement for *new* applications in PKCS#1 v2.2 [49]. However, RSASSA-PKCS1-v1_5 still remains, primarily for the purpose of backwards compatibility.

> "Although no attacks are known against RSASSA-PKCS1-v1_5, in the interest of increased robustness, RSASSA-PSS is REQUIRED in new applications. RSASSA-PKCS1-v1_5 is included only for compatibility with existing applications." [49, Sec. 8]

This is of course not the complete story. After the initial release of the PKCS#1 standard, other standards bodies developed RSA based hash-and-sign signature schemes, with mixed success. The International Organization for Standardization (ISO) developed their own RSA hash-and-sign schemes in the form of the ISO/IEC 9796-2 standard in 1997 [29]. However, this scheme was promptly broken by Coron, Naccache and Stern [16]. The standard was withdrawn and then updated version appeared in 2002 [30], but this was also later broken by Coron, et al. [17]. This standard was also withdrawn and it was then replaced in 2010 [32]. This version remains active and in use and to the best of our knowledge is not vulnerable to known attacks. What is quite interesting is that the vulnerabilities of the ISO/IEC 9796 signatures did not apply to the EMV standard for card payments. The EMV standard uses the ISO/IEC 9796 signatures scheme, but with strictly formatted messages, which meant that the payment ecosystem's security was not affected by this attack.

In addition to the ISO/IEC 9796 signatures being used by EMV payment cards, the American National Standards Institute (ANSI) developed the X9.31 Standard for use in the banking sector [1]. While parts of the X9.31 Standard have been withdrawn, to the best of our knowledge the X9.31 rDSA signature scheme is still valid. This scheme has also been studied in the cryptographic literature, with a proof for the Rabin-Williams variant by Coron [15], as well as appearing in a survey by Menezes [47]. Since this scheme does follow the construction pattern of the other known standards, we include it in our comparison for completeness.

There have also been some strides made forward in the academic side, not only limited to attacks. Coron presented improved proofs for RSA-FDH [12] and the original RSA-PSS [14], as well as showing that these proofs are indeed optimal. The optimality was revisited by Kakvi and Kiltz [38] and shown to hold only when RSA is a Certified TrapDoor Permutation (CTDP) [5,6,25,39]. We say a trapdoor permutation is *certified*, if there is a polynomial time algorithm that verifies that the public evaluation parameters of the trapdoor permutation are well formed i.e. that they do indeed define a permutation. Kakvi and Kiltz exploited the fact that for small prime RSA exponents e, the RSA function is actually a Lossy TrapDoor Permutation (LTDP) [50] under the Φ-Hiding Assumption [9]. This technique laid the groundwork for future proofs of standardised RSA based hash-and-sign signature schemes.

There was also progress more closely related to the standards themselves. Most notably, Coron presented security proofs for 9796-2 Scheme 1 as well as RSASSA-PKCS1-v1_5 with the restriction that $e = 2$, i.e. the Rabin-Williams variant [15]. The caveat is that the output size of the hash function needed to be $2/3$ of the bit length of the modulus N. Much later, Jager, Kakvi and May [33] showed a security proof for RSASSA-PKCS1-v1_5 with the restriction that e be a small prime, using the techniques of Kakvi and Kiltz [38]. This proof also requires a large hash function output, but Jager, Kakvi and May require only $1/2$ of the modulus size, compared to Coron's $2/3$. There is the additional requirement that the modulus must effectively double in bit length and the modulus must have (at least) 3 prime factors[1]. While not explicitly stated, it is clear the proof of Jager, Kakvi and May [38] also applies to the ISO/IEC 9796-2 schemes.

These proofs all crucially consider only the schemes themselves in isolation, and one must ask how close this is to reality. For reasons of economy and efficiency, it is common practice for key material to be shared amongst algorithms. Most notably the EMV standard uses the same RSA key for both signatures and encryption, which was shown to be vulnerable to attack [20]. While strongly suggested against in the PKCS#1 standard, it is common practice to use the same key for both RSASSA-PKCS1-v1_5 and RSASSA-PSS. In contrast to the EMV setting, this was shown to be secure by Kakvi [36], with the same caveats as that of Jager, Kakvi and May [33].

Given that these schemes are widely used in practice and have such a storied history, we feel that it is worth revisiting all the previous schemes and proofs and unifying their notations and security concepts. This will allow for a fair and accurate comparison of the schemes in question. Furthermore, taking a look back at older schemes, their security and how it has developed gives us a good overview of how standardised digital signatures, and the corresponding security proofs, have evolved over the years. We will only look at the deterministic schemes, as they are generally preferable due to the difficulty of generating randomness, especially on constrained devices. Furthermore, there is only one RSA-based ran-

---

[1] The proof is presented with 3 prime factors, but it works for any number co-prime to the modulus where one can compute e^{th} roots, but requires an additional assumption similar to the 2v3PA.

domised digital signature scheme, RSA-PSS, which requires two hash functions, thus making it difficult to compare with the deterministic schemes that use only one.

Finally, we will compare all the schemes in all aspects, namely modulus size, exponent size, number of prime factors and of course security loss, allowing us to give a more complete comparison of parameters. As a small sample, we show the parameters required for each scheme and what the (approximate) effective security is, which we show in Table 1. All the security proofs consider unforgeability in the Random Oracle Model, which we explain in Sect. 2.2 in Fig. 1. The computational assumptions are detailed in Sect. 2.3.

To compute these values, we assume $q_h = 2^{60}$ hash queries and $q_s = 2^{30}$ signature queries. An effective RSA modulus of k bits means that forging a signature is as hard as solving the corresponding problem for a k bit RSA modulus. The equivalent modulus size is computed by first using the equations of Lenstra [44] to calculate the estimated cost of the NFS for that security level. We then take the cost of the NFS and then find the modulus size to the nearest 10 bits that most closely matches it. To compensate for losses that are constants and for losses caused by running time increases, we simply reduce the modulus size by the binary logarithm of the loss factor. We only provide an approximate equivalent key size as there are several factors, such as time-memory trade-offs, that need to be considered for an exact figure and considering these would detract from the main goal. We believe that these figures are accurate enough to illustrate the security of each scheme. We provide a more comprehensive comparison in Tables 2, 3, 4, 5. We provide a comparison of all schemes in Tables 6.

Table 1. Parameter sizes and security for deterministic RSA based hash-and-sign schemes with a 1024 bit modulus

Scheme	Proof	Assumption	No. prime factors	Exponent e	$|\mathtt{H}()|$	Equiv. modulus
RSASSA-PKCS1-v1_5	[15]	Factoring	2	2	$\geqslant 623$	≈ 560
	[33]	RSA	3	Arbitrary	$\geqslant 512$	≈ 280
	[33]	Lossines	3	Prime $\leqslant 2^{256}$	$\geqslant 512$	≈ 511
9796-2 Scheme 1	[15]	Factoring	2	2	$\geqslant 623$	≈ 552
	[33]	RSA	3	Arbitrary	$\geqslant 512$	≈ 273
	[33]	Lossines	3	Prime $\leqslant 2^{256}$	$\geqslant 512$	≈ 504
X9.31 rDSA	[15]	Factoring	2	2	$\geqslant 623$	≈ 544
	[33]	RSA	3	Arbitrary	$\geqslant 512$	≈ 265
	[33]	Lossines	3	Prime $\leqslant 2^{256}$	$\geqslant 512$	≈ 497

We now recall the definitions of signature schemes and the relevant computational assumptions. We then present a brief discussion of the known attacks.

After that we present each scheme and recall the security theorem(s) for each scheme. We conclude with an overview of all the schemes.

2 Preliminaries

2.1 Notations and Conventions

We denote our security parameter as $\lambda \in \mathbb{N}$, which determines our key sizes. For all $n \in \mathbb{N}$, we denote by 1^n the n-bit string of all ones and by 0^n the n-bit string of all zeroes. We denote the concatenation of two bitstrings x and y as $x||y$. For any set S, we use $x \in_R S$ to indicate that we choose x uniformly random from S. All algorithms may be randomised. For any algorithm A, we define $x \leftarrow_\$ A(a_1, \ldots, a_n)$ as the execution of A with inputs $a_1, \ldots, a_n$ and fresh randomness and then assigning the output to x. For deterministic algorithms, we drop the \$ from the arrow. We denote the set of prime numbers by $\mathbb{P}$ and we denote the subset of κ-bit primes as $\mathbb{P}[\kappa]$. Similarly, we denote the set of κ-bit integers as $\mathbb{Z}[\kappa]$. We denote by $\mathbb{Z}_N^*$ the multiplicative group modulo $N \in \mathbb{N}$. For any $a, b \in \mathbb{Z}$, with $a < b$ we denote the set $\{a, a+1, \ldots, b-1, b\}$ with $[\![a, b]\!]$. For any $n \in \mathbb{N}$ and for any $a \in \mathbb{N}[\kappa]$, with $\kappa < n$, we denote by $\langle a \rangle_n$ the binary representation of a padded to n bits, i.e. $\langle a \rangle_n = 0^{n-\kappa}||a$. For any bit string x of sufficient length, we denote by $\texttt{MSBs}(x, n)$ the n most significant (leading) bits of x and $\texttt{LSBs}(x, n)$ the n least significant (trailing) bits of x.

2.2 Signature Schemes

We first recall the standard definition of a signature scheme, as well as its security.

Definition 1. *A digital signature scheme* Sig *with message space* $\mathbb{M}$ *and signature space* $\mathbb{S}$ *is defined as a triple of probabilistic polynomial time (PPT) algorithms* Sig = (KeyGen, Sign, Verify):

- KeyGen *takes as an input the unary representation of our security parameter* 1^λ *and outputs a signing key* sk *and verification key* pk.
- Sign *takes as input a signing key* sk, *message* $m \in \mathbb{M}$ *and outputs a signature* $\sigma \in \mathbb{S}$.
- Verify *is a deterministic algorithm, which on input of a public key and a message-signature pair* $(m, \sigma) \in \mathbb{M} \times \mathbb{S}$ *outputs 1 (accept) or 0 (reject).*

We say Sig *is correct if for any* $\lambda \in \mathbb{N}$, *all* $(pk, sk) \leftarrow_\$ KeyGen(1^\lambda)$, *all* $m \in \mathbb{M}$, *and all* $\sigma \leftarrow_\$ Sign(sk, m)$ *we have that*

$$\Pr[\texttt{Verify}(pk, m, \sigma) = 1] = 1.$$

For signature security, we consider the standard notion of *UnForgeability under adaptive Chosen Message Attack* [26] *in the Random Oracle Model* [2] (UF-CMA(ROM)). The security experiment is presented in Fig. 1. It must be

Game UF-CMA(ROM)

Initialize(1^λ)
$(\mathsf{pk}, \mathsf{sk}) \leftarrow_\$ \mathsf{Sig}.\mathsf{KeyGen}(1^\lambda)$
return pk

Hash(m)
if $(m, \cdot) \in \mathcal{H}$
  fetch $(m, y) \in \mathcal{H}$
  return y
else
  $y \in_R \{0,1\}^\ell;$
  $\mathcal{H} \leftarrow \mathcal{H} \cup \{(m, y)\}$
  return y

Sign(m)
$\mathcal{M} \leftarrow \mathcal{M} \cup \{m\}$
return $\sigma \leftarrow_\$ \mathsf{Sig}.\mathsf{Sign}(sk, m)$

Finalize(m^*, σ^*)
if $\mathsf{Sig}.\mathsf{Verify}(\mathsf{pk}, m^*, \sigma^*) == 1 \wedge m^* \notin \mathcal{M}$
  return 1
else
  return 0

Fig. 1. UF-CMA security game in the Random Oracle Model

noted that all hash function calls are replaced with a call to the random oracle. In the case where we have multiple hash functions, we have multiple oracles. All the security statements we discuss in this paper are with respect to UF-CMA(ROM).

We say that Sig is $(t, \varepsilon, q_h, q_s)$-UF-CMA(ROM) secure if for any forger $\mathcal{F}$ running in time at most t, making at most q_h hash queries and making at most q_s signature queries, we have:

$$\mathbf{Adv}_{\mathcal{F},\mathsf{Sig}}^{\mathsf{UF\text{-}CMA(ROM)}} = \Pr \begin{bmatrix} 1 \leftarrow \mathbf{Finalize}(m^*, \sigma^*); \\ (m^*, \sigma^*) \leftarrow \mathcal{F}^{\mathbf{Hash}(\cdot), \mathbf{Sign}(\cdot)}(\mathsf{pk}) \\ \mathsf{pk} \leftarrow_\$ \mathbf{Initialize}(1^\lambda) \end{bmatrix} \leqslant \varepsilon$$

2.3 Computational Assumptions

We now recall the computation assumptions that were used in the proofs of the security statements that we will discuss, namely the RSA Assumption k-RSA$[\lambda]$, φ-Hiding Assumption k-$\varPhi$HA$[\lambda]$, the Factoring Assumption FACT$[\lambda]$ and the 2 vs 3 Primes Assumption 2v3PA. Note that all assumptions have additional parameters k, which is the number of prime factors in our modulus, and λ, which is the bit-size of the modulus. The number of prime factors does play a role in some of the proofs, so we include it in all the theorem statements for consistency.

We begin by presenting the RSA Assumption, which essentially states that given a modulus N, and exponent e and a random $y \in \mathbb{Z}_N^*$, it is hard to compute an eth root of y modulo N, equivalently, it is hard to find x such that x^e mod $N = y$.

Definition 2 (RSA Assumption [51]**).** *The RSA Assumption, denoted by* k-$RSA[\lambda]$, *states that given* (N, e, x^e) *it is hard to compute* x, *where* N *is a* λ-*bit number and is the product of* k *distinct random prime numbers* $p_i \in \mathbb{P}$, *for* $i \in [\![1, k]\!]$, *for* k *constant,* $e \in \mathbb{Z}^*_{\varphi(N)}$, *and* $x \in_R \mathbb{Z}_N$. k-$RSA[\lambda]$ *is said to be* (t, ε)-*hard, if for all adversaries* $\mathcal{A}$ *running in time at most* t, *we have*

$$\mathbf{Adv}^{k\text{-}RSA[\lambda]}_{\mathcal{A}} = \Pr\left[x = \mathcal{A}(N, e, x^e \bmod N)\right] \leqslant \varepsilon.$$

Next, we discuss the φ-Hiding Assumption by Cachin et al. [9], which essentially states that given a modulus N and a sufficiently small exponent e, it is hard to decide if $e | \varphi(N)$ or not. In this case sufficiently small means that $e < N^{\frac{1}{4}}$, as for larger exponents, Kakvi, Kiltz and May. [39] show how to decide this using Coppersmith's method [10]. Note that when $\gcd(e_{los}, \varphi(N)) = e_{los}$, the RSA function $x^{e_{los}} \bmod N$ is exactly e_{los}-to-1, i.e. it is said to be e_{los}-*regular lossy* as defined by Kakvi and Kiltz [38].

Definition 3 (The φ-**Hiding Assumption.** [9]**).** *The* φ-*Hiding Assumption, denoted by* k-$\Phi HA[\lambda]$, *states that it is hard to distinguish between* (N, e_{inj}) *and* (N, e_{los}), *where* N *is a* λ-*bit number and is the product of* k *distinct random prime numbers* $p_i \in \mathbb{P}$, *for* $i \in [\![1, k]\!]$, *for* k *constant, and* $e_{inj}, e_{los} \in \mathbb{P}$ *and* and $3 < e_{inj}, e_{los}, \leqslant N^{\frac{1}{4}}$, *with* $\gcd(e_{inj}, \varphi(N)) = 1$ *and* $\gcd(e_{los}, \varphi(N)) = e_{los}$, *where* φ *is the Euler Totient function.* k-$\Phi HA[\lambda]$ *is said to be* (t, ε)-*hard, if for all distinguishers* $\mathcal{D}$ *running in time at most* t, *we have:*

$$\mathbf{Adv}^{k\text{-}\Phi HA[\lambda]}_{\mathcal{D}} = \Pr\left[1 \leftarrow \mathcal{D}(N, e_{inj})\right] - \Pr\left[1 \leftarrow \mathcal{D}(N, e_{los})\right] \leqslant \varepsilon$$

Now we mention the strongest assumption we need, namely the Factoring assumption Factoring. While both RSA and ΦHA imply Factoring, it is also conjectured that ΦHA is equivalent to Factoring. Additionally, the problem of finding quadratic residues modulo N is known to be equivalent to Factoring.

Definition 4 (Factoring Assumption). *The Factoring Assumption, denoted by* k-$FACT[\lambda]$, *states that given* N, *which is a* λ-*bit number and is the product of* k *distinct random prime numbers* $p_i \in \mathbb{P}$, *for* $i \in [\![1, k]\!]$, *for* k *constant, it is hard to compute the factors of* N, $p_1, \ldots, p_k$. k-$FACT[\lambda]$ *is said to be* (t, ε)-*hard, if for all adversaries* $\mathcal{A}$ *running in time at most* t, *we have*

$$\mathbf{Adv}^{k\text{-}FACT[\lambda]}_{\mathcal{A}} = \Pr\left[(p_1, \ldots, p_k) = \mathcal{A}(N)\right] \leqslant \varepsilon.$$

The final assumption that we need to recall is the 2 vs 3 primes assumption 2v3PA. This assumption essentially states that you cannot decide if a given modulus has 2 or 3 prime factors. This assumption has never formally been studied and is simply widely believed to hold. This is needed to bring any proof that requires a 3 prime factor modulus to the standard case of a 2 prime factor modulus.

Definition 5 (2v3PA Assumption). *The 2 vs. 3 Primes Assumption, denoted by* 2v3PA[λ], *states that it is hard to distinguish between N_2 and N_3, where N_2, N_3 are λ-bit numbers, where $N_2 = p_1 p_2$ is the product of 2 distinct random prime numbers $p_1, p_2 \in \mathbb{P}$ and $N_3 = q_1 q_2 q_3$ is the product of 3 distinct random prime numbers $q_1, q_2, q_3 \in \mathbb{P}$.* 2v3PA[$\lambda$] *is said to be (t, ε)-hard, if for all distinguishers $\mathcal{D}$ running in time at most t, we have:*

$$\mathbf{Adv}_{\mathcal{D}}^{\Phi HA} = \Pr\left[1 \leftarrow \mathcal{D}(N_2)\right] - \Pr\left[1 \leftarrow \mathcal{D}(N_3)\right] \leqslant \varepsilon$$

3   Attacks

Here we briefly discuss the known attacks on standardised RSA hash-and-sign signatures. Even before the development of the standardised signatures, there had been general cryptanalysis of the RSA primitive. One of the first general RSA attacks was due to Davida [18], which was later generalised by Desmedt and Odlyzko [22]. Indeed, the most general attacks on RSA-based system are so-called "Coppersmiths attacks" as they are based on the initial results of Coppersmith [10] based on the LLL algorithm [45]. This has since been an active research area and we refer the reader to May's survey for further details [46].

Following this, attacks were found on more concrete settings by Gordon [27] and DeJonge and Chaum [19]. The latter attacks were extended by Girault and Misarsky [23,48]. For a more technical overview of the attacks, we refer the reader to the invited survey of Misarsky [48].

Based on this, Denning [21] and Gordon [27] independently suggested what would become the hash-and-sign paradigm. This knowledge was taken on board during the design of the PKCS#1 signatures [42], as well as the ISO 9796 signatures [28]. One would hope that this would result in secure and robust schemes. This, however, proved not to be the case, as demonstrated by Bleichenbacher's "million message attack" for PKCS#1 v1.5 encryption [7], which used the malleability of RSA to transform a valid ciphertext into a new (possibly invalid) ciphertexts. These new ciphertexts were sent to the server, whose responses could be used to eventually decrypt the original ciphertext. In some circumstances, the attack can also be extended to PKCS#1 v1.5 signatures. Also of note are the attacks on ISO/IEC 9796 by Coron, Naccache and Stern [16] and Coron et al. [17].

4   Full-Domain Hash

We start by looking at the RSA Full-Domain Hash signature scheme RSA-FDH. While it is not included in any of the standards, it still bears investigation, as the proof methodologies developed for it have led to proof methodologies for all the other schemes. RSA-FDH was first introduced by Bellare and Rogaway [2] and while they did have a security proof, it was a non-tight one. This was then improved by Coron [12] who showed a better, but still non-tight proof. Coron's proof has a security loss that depends on the number of signing queries q_s, as opposed to the number of hash queries q_h, which is generally much larger. Additionally, Coron showed that this proof was actually optimal by means of a meta-reduction [12], removing any hope of a tight proof.

However, Kakvi and Kiltz [38] noticed that the meta-reduction crucially requires that the RSA public key (N, e) be a CTDP [5,6]. We say a TDP is *certified*, if there is a polynomial time algorithm that verifies that the public evaluation parameters of the trapdoor permutation are well formed i.e. that they do indeed define a permutation. This is not the case for RSA if the exponent e is a small prime. In particular, if $e \leqslant N^{1/4}$ then this defines an LTDP [50] under the φ-Hiding Assumption [9]. Furthermore, Kakvi, Kiltz and May [39] showed that for large prime exponents e, i.e. $e \geqslant N^{1/4}$, one can check if an RSA key does indeed define a permutation in polynomial time. Additionally, Goldberg et al. showed an efficient non-interactive method to certify an RSA public key [25]. We recall the RSA-FDH scheme in Fig. 2 and then present the proofs.

Scheme RSA-FDH

KeyGen(1^λ)
$p, q \in_R \mathbb{P}[\lambda/2]$
$N = pq$
$\varphi(N) = (p-1)(q-1)$
$e \in_R \mathbb{Z}_N^*, \gcd(e, \varphi(N)) = 1$
pick hash function $\mathtt{H} : \{0,1\}^* \rightarrow \{0,1\}^\lambda$
return $(\mathsf{pk} = (N, e, \mathtt{H}), \mathsf{sk} = (p, q))$
Sign(sk, m)
$y \leftarrow \mathtt{H}(m)$
return $\sigma = y^{1/e} \mod N$
Verify(pk, m, σ)
$y' = \sigma^e \mod N$
$z = \mathtt{H}(m)$
if $(z == y')$
return 1
else
return 0

Fig. 2. RSA Full-Domain Hash RSA-FDH

The original proof of Bellare and Rogaway [2] was simply to guess which message would be forged and program the random oracle to give a solution to the RSA problem. This is achieved by setting the hash value of the selected message to be the RSA target value y. This works with probability $1/q_h$, where q_h is the number of hash function queries made by the adversary.

Theorem 1 (Bellare-Rogaway [2]). *Assume that 2-RSA[λ] is (t', ε')-hard. Then for any (q_h, q_s), RSA–FDH is $(t, \varepsilon, q_h, q_s)$-*UF-CMA* secure in the Random Oracle Model, where*

$$\varepsilon' = \frac{\varepsilon}{q_h} \cdot$$
$$t' = t + (q_h + q_s + 1) \cdot \mathcal{O}(\lambda^3).$$

Coron [12] improved this by embedding the RSA target value y into multiple hash values. The drawback to this was that the reduction cannot simulate a signature for any message whose hash value had y embedded in it. Therefore, the proportion must be chosen carefully. The analysis by Coron showed that an optimal choice yielded a loss of q_s, where q_s is the number of signature queries.

Theorem 2 (Coron [12]). *Assume that 2-RSA[λ] is (t', ε')-hard. Then for any (q_h, q_s), RSA–FDH is $(t, \varepsilon, q_h, q_s)$-*UF-CMA* secure in the Random Oracle Model, where*

$$\varepsilon' = \frac{\varepsilon}{q_s} \cdot \left(1 - \frac{1}{q_s + 1}\right)^{q_s + 1} \approx \frac{\varepsilon}{q_s}$$
$$t' = t + \mathcal{O}(q_h \cdot \lambda^3).$$

Kakvi and Kiltz [38] later revisited Coron's optimality result and observed that this only holds for the case when RSA is a CTDP [5,6]. This is only possible for RSA if the exponent is a large prime (or a product thereof) [39], or if we provide some additional information [25]. Kakvi and Kiltz leveraged the fact that RSA is a lossy permutation for small prime e and were able to show a tight proof in this case.

Theorem 3 (Kakvi-Kiltz [38]). *Assume 2-ΦHA[λ] is (t', ε')-hard and gives an η-regular lossy trapdoor function. Then, for any (q_h, q_s), we have that RSA–FDH is $(t, \varepsilon, q_h, q_s)$-*UF-CMA* secure in the Random Oracle Model, where*

$$\varepsilon = \left(\frac{2\eta - 1}{\eta - 1}\right) \cdot \varepsilon'$$
$$t = t' + \mathcal{O}(q_h \cdot \lambda^3)$$

We now compare these security statements and their effect on parameter selection in Table 2, concretely for the case of 1024 bit moduli. We present these in a similar manner to that of Table 1, but we drop some of the less relevant parameters. Here we also provide the size of the modulus used in the reduction, but this does not directly correspond to the security of the scheme, i.e. the scheme is not necessarily as secure as the assumption. The scheme is as secure as the assumption with a modulus of bit length given in the "Equiv. modulus" column. To compute these values we have taken $q_h = 2^{60}, q_s = 2^{30}$. As with Table 1, the key sizes are approximate due to the complexity of computing exact key sizes.

Table 2. Security of RSA-FDH with a 1024-bit modulus

Scheme	Proof methodology	Assumption	Exponent e	Equiv. modulus
RSA-FDH	Bellare-Rogaway	2-RSA[1024]	Arbitrary	≈ 250
	Coron	2-RSA[1024]	Arbitrary	≈ 560
	Kakvi-Kiltz	2-ΦHA[1024]	Prime $\leqslant 2^{256}$	≈ 1023

5 Public-Key Cryptography Standards #1

We will now look at the PKCS#1 signature scheme, which was one of the first standardised hash-and-sign signature schemes. The PKCS#1 version 1 actually predates Full-Domain Hash and hence the idea of a larger hash function was not considered at first. The scheme was first made public with version 1.5 [40], which is why the scheme is most commonly referred to as PKCS#1 v1.5. The standard was updated to version 2.0 [41] in short order to include RSA-OAEP as a replacement for the encryption algorithm due Bleichenbacher's "million message attack" [7].

While the signatures schemes were not affected by this, the consensus was that RSASSA-PKCS1-v1_5 needed to be replaced with a secure signature scheme. The natural candidate in RSASSA-PSS was added in version 2.1 [34]. However, at this point it was a recommendation and not a requirement. This was further changed in version 2.2 [49], where it was required for all *new* applications. The main reason for this was that a large number of systems had implemented RSASSA-PKCS1-v1_5 in *hardware*, in particular in middleware, which proved problematic to upgrade[2].

While no real attacks were found against RSASSA-PKCS1-v1_5, the lack of security proof was of some concern. The only known proof was that of Coron [15], but that was for the Rabin-Williams variant and required a larger hash function output than the norm. This has since been improved somewhat by Jager, Kakvi and May [33], who showed a proof for the small-exponent RSA case, but still required a large hash function output, albeit smaller than that of Coron [15]. We now recall (a generalised variant of) RSASSA-PKCS1-v1_5 in Fig. 3 and then we recall the security theorems.

The first statement of security was by Coron [15] for the Rabin-Williams variant, i.e. with $e = 2$, which is secure based on the factoring assumption. Coron's theorem statements was quite general and in indeed it extended to the ANSI X9.31 rDSA signatures directly. Coron considered signatures of the form $\sigma = (\gamma \cdot \text{H}(m) + f(m))^{1/2}$, i.e. scheme with (potentially) message-dependent padding. Coron gave the security of these schemes in Theorem 4.

Theorem 4 (Coron [15]). *Assume that* 2-*FACT*$[\lambda]$ *is* (t', ε')-*hard. Then for any* (q_h, q_s), *any partial domain hash signature scheme i.e.,*

---

[2] cf. https://www.ietf.org/mail-archive/web/tls/current/msg19360.html.

Scheme RSASSA-PKCS1-v1_5

```
KeyGen(1^λ, k, (λ₁, ..., λₖ), ℓ)
for i ∈ ⟦1, k⟧
    pᵢ ∈_R ℙ[λᵢ]
next i
N = ∏ᵢ₌₁ᵏ pᵢ
φ(N) = ∏ᵢ₌₁ᵏ (pᵢ − 1)
e ∈_R ℤ*_N, gcd(e, φ(N)) = 1
pick hash function H : M → {0,1}ℓ
Look-up α-bit ID_H for H
ν = λ − ℓ − α − 23
PAD = 0¹⁵||1ⁿ||0⁸||ID_H
return (pk = (N, e, PAD, H), sk = (p, q))


Sign(sk, m)
z ← H(m)
y = PAD||z
return σ = y^(1/e) mod N


Verify(pk, m, σ)
y' = σ^e mod N
z ← H(m)
if (PAD||z == y')
    return 1
else
    return 0
```

Fig. 3. RSA PKCS#1 v1.5 Signature RSASSA-PKCS1-v1_5

$\sigma = (\gamma \cdot H(m) + f(m))^{1/2}$, *is* $(t, \varepsilon, q_h, q_s)$*-UF-CMA secure in the Random Oracle Model, where*

$$\varepsilon' = \frac{\varepsilon - 32(q_h + q_s + 1)(\ell - \frac{2\lambda}{3})(\gamma \cdot 2^{\frac{3}{13}(\ell - \frac{2\lambda}{3})})}{8q_s}$$

$$t' = t + \gamma \left(\ell - \frac{2\lambda}{3}\right)(q_h + q_s + 1) \cdot \mathcal{O}(\lambda^3).$$

For RSASSA-PKCS1-v1_5 we can see that $\gamma = 1$ and $f(m) = \text{PAD} \times 2^\ell$. If we set $\ell = \frac{2\lambda}{3} + 1$, we get the following Theorem.

Theorem 5 (Coron [15]). *Assume that 2-FACT[λ] is* (t', ε')*-hard. Then for any* (q_h, q_s), *RSASSA-PKCS1-v1_5 with e=2 is* $(t, \varepsilon, q_h, q_s)$*-UF-CMA secure in the Random Oracle Model, where*

$$\varepsilon' = \frac{\varepsilon - 32(q_h + q_s + 1)(2^{\frac{3}{13}})}{8q_s} \approx \frac{\varepsilon}{8q_s} - \frac{4q_h}{q_s}$$

$$t' = t + \mathcal{O}(q_h \cdot \lambda^3).$$

For many years, this remained the only known proof for RSASSA-PKCS1-v1_5, or any variant thereof, until the proof of Jager, Kakvi and May [33]. The main technical hurdle was that the fixed padding and relatively small size of the hash function meant that signatures could not be simulated in polynomial time. Jager, Kakvi and May overcame this with their novel Encode algorithm to allow simulation of signatures in polynomial time. Using this, combined with the proof techniques for RSA-FDH of Coron [12, 13] and Kakvi and Kiltz [37, 38], they presented theorems with similar bounds.

The drawback, however, is that the Encode algorithm requires the bit size of the modulus to be doubled, by multiplying it with a prime of the same size. That is to say, if we wish to reduce the security of 2-ΦHA[λ] or 2-RSA[λ], we need a 2λ-bit modulus in our key, with the additional λ-bits made up by a third prime factor. Therefore they proved security for keys where $N = pqr$, i.e. is the product of three primes. Under the assumption that 3-prime moduli are indistinguishable from 2-prime moduli, these results can be brought back to the case $N = pq$. We now present the results of Jager, Kakvi and May [33].

Theorem 6 (Jager-Kakvi-May [33]). *Assume that 2-RSA[λ] is (t', ε')-hard. Then for any (q_h, q_s), RSASSA-PKCS1-v1_5 is $(t, \varepsilon, q_h, q_s)$-UF-CMA secure in the Random Oracle Model, where*

$$\varepsilon' = \frac{\varepsilon}{q_s} \cdot \left(1 - \frac{1}{q_s + 1}\right)^{q_s+1} \approx \frac{\varepsilon}{q_s} \cdot exp(-1)$$
$$t' = t + \mathcal{O}(q_h \cdot \lambda^4).$$

Theorem 7 (Jager-Kakvi-May [33]). *Assume 2-ΦHA[λ] is (t', ε')-hard and gives an η-regular lossy trapdoor function. Then, for any (q_h, q_s), RSASSA-PKCS1-v1_5 is $(t, \varepsilon, q_h, q_s)$-UF-CMA secure in the Random Oracle Model, where*

$$\varepsilon = \left(\frac{2\eta - 1}{\eta - 1}\right) \cdot \varepsilon'$$
$$t = t' + \mathcal{O}(q_h \cdot \lambda^4)$$

We now compare these security statements and their effect on parameter selection in Table 3, concretely for the case of 1024 bit moduli. We present these in a similar manner to that of Table 1. Here we also provide the size of the modulus used in the reduction, but this does not directly correspond to the security of the scheme, i.e. the scheme is not necessarily as secure as the assumption. The scheme is as secure as the assumption with a modulus of bit length given in the "Equiv. modulus" column. To compute these values we have taken $q_h = 2^{60}, q_s = 2^{30}$. As with Table 1, the key sizes are approximate due to the complexity of computing exact key sizes.

6   International Organization for Standardization 9796-2

We will now look at the ISO/IEC 9796-2:2010 signature scheme, which is one of the most widely deployed schemes. This scheme is used in the EMV

Table 3. Parameter sizes and security for `RSASSA-PKCS1-v1_5` with a 1024 bit modulus

Scheme	Proof methodology	Assumption	No. prime factors	Exponent e	$|\mathtt{H}()|$	Equiv. modulus
`RSASSA-PKCS1-v1_5`	Coron	2-FACT[1024]	2	2	$\geqslant 623$	≈ 560
	Jager-Kakvi-May	2-RSA[512]	3	Arbitrary	$\geqslant 512$	≈ 280
		+ 2v3PA[1024]	2	Arbitrary	$\geqslant 512$	≈ 280
	Jager-Kakvi-May	2-ΦHA[512]	3	Prime $\leqslant 2^{256}$	$\geqslant 512$	≈ 511
		+ 2v3PA[1024]	2	Prime $\leqslant 2^{256}$	$\geqslant 512$	≈ 511

payment system for so-called "chip and pin" cards. According to EMVCo. There are around 9,893,000,000 (9.8 billion) EMV cards in circulation as of Q4 2019, making up 63.8% of cards issued globally[3]. Despite this huge usage, the signatures are known to be vulnerable to some attacks and indeed the ISO/IEC 9796 standard has had several iterations of breaks and fixes. It is worth noting that while the scheme has been broken, the EMV implementation is not vulnerable. The reason for this is that the attacks require signatures on some specially crafted messages, which exploit the multiplicative property of RSA, but are incompatible with the EMV standard. Messages in the EMV standard have a very fixed format and include some identifiers and serial numbers, as well as the date. Thus, it is very unlikely that an honest EMV endpoint would sign the messages required for the attack to be successful. An equivalent way of looking at this would be to say that the attacks only work on larger message spaces than the messages space used by the EMV protocol.

The very first version, the ISO/IEC 9796-1 was very quickly broken and is no longer in use, so we will not discuss in great detail, but instead refer the reader to the articles by Coppersmith, Halevi and Jutla [11] and Girault and Misarsky [24] for further details. It is for this reason that the ISO/IEC 9796-1 standard was replaced by the first version of the ISO/IEC 9796-2 standard in 1997 [29]. This version was also vulnerable to attack, specifically the attacks due to Coron, Naccache and Stern [16]. The standard was then further updated in 2002 to combat these attacks [30], but eventually would fall to the attacks of Coron et al. [17]. Finally, the standard was updated to its current form, that is the ISO/IEC 9796-2:2010 [32], which is what we will focus on, particularly Scheme 1.

The ISO/IEC 9796-2 Scheme 1 is a deterministic scheme with message recovery. In particular it has two modes, namely full message recovery, which works for messages that are sufficiently small, and partially message recovery for larger messages. When signing, the starting bits of the message representative indicate if we are using full or partial recovery. For partial recovery, the message representative begins with 0x6A, and for full message recovery it begins with 0x4A. This is then followed by the message portion that is recoverable, padded up with zeros, if needed, which is followed by the hash of the complete message. The signatures then end with 0xBC. We recall the (generalised) scheme with

---

[3] cf. https://www.emvco.com/about/deployment-statistics.

partial recovery 9796-2 Scheme 1(PR) in Fig. 4a and the (generalised) scheme with full recovery 9796-2 Scheme 1(FR) in Fig. 4b.

Scheme 9796-2 Scheme 1(PR)

$\underline{\textbf{KeyGen}(1^\lambda, k, (\lambda_1, \ldots, \lambda_k), \ell)}$
for $i \in [\![1, k]\!]$
$\quad p_i \in_R \mathbb{P}[\lambda_i]$
next i
$N = \prod_{i=1}^{k} p_i$
$\varphi(N) = \prod_{i=1}^{k} (p_i - 1)$
$e \in_R \mathbb{Z}_N^*, \gcd(e, \varphi(N)) = 1$
pick hash function $\mathrm{H} : \{0,1\}^* \to \{0,1\}^\ell$
$\mathrm{PAD}_L = 1101010, \mathrm{PAD}_R = 10111100$
return $(\mathrm{pk} = (N, e, \mathrm{PAD}_L, \mathrm{PAD}_R, \mathrm{H}), \mathrm{sk} = (p, q))$

$\underline{\textbf{Sign}(\mathrm{sk}, m)}$
$z \leftarrow \mathrm{H}(m)$
$\nu = \lambda - \ell - 16$
$m_1 = \mathrm{MSBs}(m, \nu)$
$y = \mathrm{PAD}_L || m_1 || z || \mathrm{PAD}_R$
return $\sigma = y^{1/e} \mod N$

$\underline{\textbf{Verify}(\mathrm{pk}, m_2, \sigma)}$
$y' = \sigma^e \mod N$
interpret $y = \mathrm{PAD}_L || m_1 || z || \mathrm{PAD}_R$
if $(\mathrm{H}(m_1 || m_2) == z)$
$\quad$ return 1
else
$\quad$ return 0

Scheme 9796-2 Scheme 1(FR)

$\underline{\textbf{KeyGen}(1^\lambda, k, (\lambda_1, \ldots, \lambda_k), \ell)}$
for $i \in [\![1, k]\!]$
$\quad p_i \in_R \mathbb{P}[\lambda_i]$
next i
$N = \prod_{i=1}^{k} p_i$
$\varphi(N) = \prod_{i=1}^{k} (p_i - 1)$
$e \in_R \mathbb{Z}_N^*, \gcd(e, \varphi(N)) = 1$
pick hash function $\mathrm{H} : \{0,1\}^* \to \{0,1\}^\ell$
$\mathrm{PAD}_L = 1101010, \mathrm{PAD}_R = 10111100$
return $(\mathrm{pk} = (N, e, \mathrm{PAD}_L, \mathrm{PAD}_R, \mathrm{H}), \mathrm{sk} = (p, q))$

$\underline{\textbf{Sign}(\mathrm{sk}, m)}$
$z \leftarrow \mathrm{H}(m)$
$\nu = \lambda - \ell - 16$
$m_1 = \mathrm{MSBs}(m, \nu)$
$y = \mathrm{PAD}_L || m_1 || z || \mathrm{PAD}_R$
return $\sigma = y^{1/e} \mod N$

$\underline{\textbf{Verify}(\mathrm{pk}, m_2, \sigma)}$
$y' = \sigma^e \mod N$
interpret $y = \mathrm{PAD}_L || m_1 || z || \mathrm{PAD}_R$
if $(\mathrm{H}(m_1 || m_2) == z)$
$\quad$ return 1
else
$\quad$ return 0

(a) ISO/IEC RSA Signature with Partial Message Recovery 9796-2 Scheme 1(PR)

(b) ISO/IEC RSA Signature with Full Message Recovery 9796-2 Scheme 1(FR)

Fig. 4. The two versions of the ISO/IEC 9796-2 Scheme 1

While the two schemes are distinct, the proofs work identically for both. Therefore, we will simply present the theorems for the scheme as whole and not for each case individually. We first present the Rabin-Williams proof by Coron [15]. Recall that Theorem 4 was stated for schemes of the form $\sigma = (\gamma \cdot \mathrm{H}(m) + f(m))^{1/2}$. Here we can see that for 9796-2 Scheme 1, we have $\gamma = 2^8$ and $f(m) = \mathrm{PAD}_L || \mathrm{MSBs}(m, \nu) \times 2^{\ell+8} + \mathrm{PAD}_R$. If we set $l = \frac{2\lambda}{3} + 1$, we see that we get the following Theorem.

Theorem 8 (Coron [15]). *Assume that 2-FACT$[\lambda]$ is (t', ε')-hard. Then for any (q_h, q_s), 9796-2 Scheme 1 is $(t, \varepsilon, q_h, q_s)$-UF-CMA secure in the Random Oracle Model, where*

$$\varepsilon' = \frac{\varepsilon - 32(q_h + q_s + 1) \cdot 2^8 \cdot 2^{\frac{3}{13}}}{8q_s} \approx \frac{\varepsilon}{8q_s} - \frac{1024 \cdot q_h}{q_s}$$
$$t' = t + 2^8 \cdot \mathcal{O}(q_h \cdot \lambda^3).$$

Although Jager, Kakvi and May did not explicitly prove the security of 9796-2 Scheme 1, the scheme fits almost perfectly into their setting. If we use the repeated Encode method of Kakvi [36], then we can adapt the proof accordingly and we get similar bounds, with the similar 3-prime requirement as in Theorems 6 and 7. We now present the Theorems for 9796-2 Scheme 1.

Theorem 9 (Jager-Kakvi-May [33]). *Assume that 2-RSA[λ] is (t', ε')-hard. Then for any (q_h, q_s), 9796-2 Scheme 1 is $(t, \varepsilon, q_h, q_s)$-UF-CMA secure in the Random Oracle Model, where*

$$\varepsilon' = \frac{\varepsilon}{q_s} \cdot \left(1 - \frac{1}{q_s + 1}\right)^{q_s + 1} \approx \frac{\varepsilon}{q_s} \cdot exp(-1)$$
$$t' = t + 2^7 \cdot \mathcal{O}(q_h \cdot \lambda^4).$$

Theorem 10 (Jager-Kakvi-May [33]). *Assume 2-ΦHA[λ] is (t', ε')-hard and gives an η-regular lossy trapdoor function. Then, for any (q_h, q_s), 9796-2 Scheme 1 is $(t, \varepsilon, q_h, q_s)$-UF-CMA secure in the Random Oracle Model, where*

$$\varepsilon = \left(\frac{2\eta - 1}{\eta - 1}\right) \cdot \varepsilon'$$
$$t = t' + 2^7 \cdot \mathcal{O}(q_h \cdot \lambda^4)$$

We now compare these security results and their effect on parameter selection in Table 3, concretely for the case of 1024 bit moduli. We present these in a similar manner to that of Table 1. Here we also provide the size of the modulus used in the reduction, but this does not directly correspond to the security of the scheme, i.e. the scheme is not necessarily as secure as the assumption. The scheme is as secure as the assumption with a modulus of bit length given in the "Equiv. modulus" column. To compute these values we have taken $q_h = 2^{60}, q_s = 2^{30}$. As with Table 1, the key sizes are approximate due to the complexity of computing exact key sizes.

Table 4. Parameter sizes and security for 9796-2 Scheme 1 with a 1024 bit modulus

Scheme	Proof methodology	Assumption	No. prime factors	Exponent e	$|H()|$	Equiv. modulus
ISO 9769-2 Scheme 1	Coron	2-FACT[1024]	2	2	$\geqslant 623$	≈ 552
	Jager-Kakvi-May	2-RSA[512]	3	Arbitrary	$\geqslant 512$	≈ 273
		+ 2v3PA[1024]	2	Arbitrary	$\geqslant 512$	≈ 273
	Jager-Kakvi-May	2-ΦHA[512]	3	Prime $\leqslant 2^{256}$	$\geqslant 512$	≈ 504
		+ 2v3PA[1024]	2	Prime $\leqslant 2^{256}$	$\geqslant 512$	≈ 504

7   American National Standards Institute X9.31 Signatures

We now look at the final deterministic hash-and-sign signature on our list, namely, the ANSI X9.31 signatures [1]. While these signatures were standardised at a similar time to the others, and follows a similar construction philosophy, there is scant mention of them in the academic literature. To the best of our knowledge, the signature were only ever investigated by Coron [15] and Menezes [47]. While parts of the standard have been withdrawn, specifically those related to the generation of random numbers, to the best of our knowledge the signature is still valid. We now recall the (generalised) scheme in Fig. 5.

Scheme X9.31 rDSA

KeyGen$(1^\lambda, k, (\lambda_1, \dots, \lambda_k), \ell)$
for $i \in [\![1, k]\!]$
$\quad p_i \in_R \mathbb{P}[\lambda_i]$
next i
$N = \prod_{i=1}^k p_i$
$\varphi(N) = \prod_{i=1}^k (p_i - 1)$
$e \in_R \mathbb{Z}_N^*, \gcd(e, \varphi(N)) = 1$
pick hash function $\mathtt{H} : \mathbb{M} \to \{0,1\}^\ell$
Look-up 16-bit $\mathtt{ID_H}$ for $\mathtt{H}$
$\nu = (\lambda - \ell - 24)/4$
$\mathtt{PAD} = 0110\|\|(1011)^\nu\|\|1010$
return $(\mathsf{pk} = (N, e, \mathtt{PAD}, \mathtt{ID_H}, \mathtt{H}), \mathsf{sk} = (p, q))$
Sign(sk, m)
$z \leftarrow \mathtt{H}(m)$
$y = \mathtt{PAD}\|\|z\|\|\mathtt{ID_H}$
return $\sigma = y^{1/e} \mod N$
Verify(pk, m, σ)
$y' = \sigma^e \mod N$
$z \leftarrow \mathtt{H}(m)$
if $(\mathtt{PAD}\|\|z == y')$
$\quad$ return 1
else
$\quad$ return 0

Fig. 5. American National Standards Institute X9.31 rDSA

As we can see the scheme is very similar to RSASSA-PKCS1-v1_5, with two small differences. Firstly, the padding string is 0x6B...BA and not 0x0F...F0, but this makes no difference for the proofs, as they are for both for arbitrary padding. Secondly, the (fixed-length) hash function identifier is after the hash as opposed to before it. Although both proofs can deal with this, it does affect the security differently. In the case of Jager, Kakvi and May [33], if we adapt the proof using the repeated Encode sampling method of Kakvi [36], we get this loss appearing only in the runtime of our reduction. On the other hand, in the proof of Coron [15] this factor only appears in the both the running time and the success probability, as if we express X9.31 rDSA in terms of Theorem 4, we have $\gamma = 2^{16}$ (and $f(m) = \mathtt{PAD} \times 2^{\ell+16} + \mathtt{ID_H}$). As in the previous proofs, we set $\ell = \frac{2\lambda}{3} + 1$. We now present the theorems for the security of X9.31 rDSA.

Theorem 11 (Coron [15]). *Assume that 2-FACT[λ] is (t', ε')-hard. Then for any (q_h, q_s), X9.31 rDSA is $(t, \varepsilon, q_h, q_s)$-UF-CMA secure in the Random Oracle Model, where*

$$\varepsilon' = \frac{\varepsilon - 32(q_h + q_s + 1) \cdot 2^{16} \cdot 2^{\frac{3}{13}}}{8q_s} \approx \frac{\varepsilon}{8q_s} - \frac{2^{18} \cdot q_h}{q_s}$$

$$t' = t + 2^{16} \cdot \mathcal{O}(q_h \cdot \lambda^3).$$

Theorem 12 (Jager-Kakvi-May [33]). *Assume that 2-RSA[λ] is (t', ε')-hard. Then for any (q_h, q_s), X9.31 rDSA is $(t, \varepsilon, q_h, q_s)$-UF-CMA secure in the Random Oracle Model, where*

$$\varepsilon' = \frac{\varepsilon}{q_s} \cdot \left(1 - \frac{1}{q_s + 1}\right)^{q_s+1} \approx \frac{\varepsilon}{q_s} \cdot exp(-1)$$

$$t' = t + 2^{15} \cdot \mathcal{O}(q_h \cdot \lambda^4).$$

Theorem 13 (Jager-Kakvi-May [33]). *Assume 2-ΦHA[λ] is (t', ε')-hard and gives an η-regular lossy trapdoor function. Then, for any (q_h, q_s), X9.31 rDSA is $(t, \varepsilon, q_h, q_s)$-UF-CMA secure in the Random Oracle Model, where*

$$\varepsilon = \left(\frac{2\eta - 1}{\eta - 1}\right) \cdot \varepsilon'$$

$$t = t' + 2^{15} \cdot \mathcal{O}(q_h \cdot \lambda^4)$$

We now compare these proofs and their effect on parameter selection in Table 5, concretely for the case of 1024 bit moduli. We present these in a similar manner the that of Table 1. Here we also provide the size of the modulus used in the reduction, but this does not directly correspond to the security of the scheme, i.e. the scheme is not necessarily as secure as the assumption. The scheme is as secure as the assumption with a modulus of bit length given in the "Equiv. modulus" column. To compute these values we have taken $q_h = 2^{60}, q_s = 2^{30}$. As with Table 1, the key sizes are approximate due to the complexity of computing exact key sizes.

8   Comparison

Having now examined all the schemes, we now present a complete comparison. Unlike in the case of Tables 2, 3, 4, 5, we do not take any concrete figures, but

Table 5. Parameter sizes and security for X9.31 rDSA with a 1024 bit modulus

Scheme	Proof methodology	Assumption	No. prime factors	Exponent e	$|\mathrm{H}()|$	Equiv. modulus
X9.31 rDSA	Coron	2-FACT[1024]	2	2	$\geqslant 623$	≈ 544
	Jager-Kakvi-May	2-RSA[512]	3	Arbitrary	$\geqslant 512$	≈ 265
		+ 2v3PA[1024]	2	Arbitrary	$\geqslant 512$	≈ 265
	Jager-Kakvi-May	2-ΦHA[512]	3	Prime $\leqslant 2^{256}$	$\geqslant 512$	≈ 497
		+ 2v3PA[1024]	2	Prime $\leqslant 2^{256}$	$\geqslant 512$	≈ 497

Table 6. Comparison of the security of the RSA hash-and-sign signatures

Scheme	Proof methodology	Assumption	No. prime factors	Exponent e	$|\mathrm{H}()|$	Security loss
RSA-FDH	Bellare-Rogaway	2-RSA[λ]	2	Arbitrary	λ	q_h
	Coron	2-RSA[λ]	2	Arbitrary	λ	q_s
	Kakvi-Kiltz	2-ΦHA[λ]	2	Prime $\leqslant 2^{\lambda/4}$	λ	$o(1)$
RSASSA-PKCS1-v1_5	Coron	2-FACT[λ]	2	2	$\geqslant 2\lambda/3$	q_s
	Jager-Kakvi-May	2-RSA[$\lambda/2$]	3	Arbitrary	$\geqslant \lambda/2$	q_s
		+ 2v3PA[λ]	2	Arbitrary	$\geqslant \lambda/2$	q_s
	Jager-Kakvi-May	2-ΦHA[$\lambda/2$]	3	Prime $\leqslant 2^{\lambda/4}$	$\geqslant \lambda/2$	$o(1)$
		+ 2v3PA[λ]	2	Prime $\leqslant 2^{\lambda/4}$	$\geqslant \lambda/2$	$o(1)$
ISO 9769-2 Scheme 1	Coron	2-FACT[λ]	2	2	$\geqslant 2\lambda/3$	q_s
	Jager-Kakvi-May	2-RSA[$\lambda/2$]	3	Arbitrary	$\geqslant \lambda/2$	q_s
		+ 2v3PA[λ]	2	Arbitrary	$\geqslant \lambda/2$	q_s
	Jager-Kakvi-May	2-ΦHA[$\lambda/2$]	3	Prime $\leqslant 2^{\lambda/4}$	$\geqslant \lambda/2$	$o(1)$
		+ 2v3PA[λ]	2	Prime $\leqslant 2^{\lambda/4}$	$\geqslant \lambda/2$	$o(1)$
X9.31 rDSA	Coron	2-FACT[λ]	2	2	$\geqslant 2\lambda/3$	q_s
	Jager-Kakvi-May	2-RSA[$\lambda/2$]	3	Arbitrary	$\geqslant \lambda/2$	q_s
		+ 2v3PA[λ]	2	Arbitrary	$\geqslant \lambda/2$	q_s
	Jager-Kakvi-May	2-ΦHA[$\lambda/2$]	3	Prime $\leqslant 2^{\lambda/4}$	$\geqslant \lambda/2$	$o(1)$
		+ 2v3PA[λ]	2	Prime $\leqslant 2^{\lambda/4}$	$\geqslant \lambda/2$	$o(1)$

we instead use the parameters, to allow for a more general comparison. We first compare all our signatures in Table 6.

As we can see from the tables above, there is a wide variety of schemes and proofs, each with advantages and disadvantages, with no clear best or worst scheme. While it would be ideal to be able to state with certainty that one scheme is superior to others, the variety of parameter choices mean that one would have to select the scheme best suited for their purposes. This decision would be based on the specific use case and the factors therein e.g. hardware or communication constraints. For example, if we have a device with constrained storage, we would want to keep the key size as low as possible, which would mean we would have to avoid any schemes proven using the Jager-Kakvi-May methodology. On the other hand if storage is not an issue, but we have computational constraints, then one might consider picking the scheme that requires the smallest hash function. In which case, the schemes proven with the Jager-Kakvi-May methodology would be good candidates. Furthermore, in a system where we do not expect a large number of signatures, a loss of q_s might lead to acceptable parameters. It remains an open question to get a tight, parameter preserving proof for a deterministic standardised signature.

Acknowledgements. The authors would like to thanks the anonymous reviewers of SSR 2020 for their insightful comments. We would also like to thank Cathy Meadows and Ruqayya Shaheed for their editorial comments.

References

1. ANSI: Digital signatures using reversible public key cryptography for the financial services industry (rDSA). Technical report X9.31, American National Standards Institute, New York, New York, USA (1998)
2. Bellare, M., Rogaway, P.: Random oracles are practical: a paradigm for designing efficient protocols. In: Denning, D.E., Pyle, R., Ganesan, R., Sandhu, R.S., Ashby, V. (eds.) ACM CCS 93, pp. 62–73. ACM Press (1993). https://doi.org/10.1145/168588.168596
3. Bellare, M., Rogaway, P.: The exact security of digital signatures-how to sign with RSA and Rabin. In: Maurer, U. (ed.) EUROCRYPT 1996. LNCS, vol. 1070, pp. 399–416. Springer, Heidelberg (1996). https://doi.org/10.1007/3-540-68339-9_34
4. Bellare, M., Rogaway, P.: PSS: provably secure encoding method for digital signatures. Submission to IEEE P1363 Working Group (1998)
5. Bellare, M., Yung, M.: Certifying cryptographic tools: the case of trapdoor permutations. In: Brickell, E.F. (ed.) CRYPTO 1992. LNCS, vol. 740, pp. 442–460. Springer, Heidelberg (1993). https://doi.org/10.1007/3-540-48071-4_31
6. Bellare, M., Yung, M.: Certifying permutations: noninteractive zero-knowledge based on any trapdoor permutation. J. Cryptol. **9**(3), 149–166 (1996). https://doi.org/10.1007/BF00208000
7. Bleichenbacher, D.: Generating ElGamal signatures without knowing the secret key. In: Maurer, U. (ed.) EUROCRYPT 1996. LNCS, vol. 1070, pp. 10–18. Springer, Heidelberg (1996). https://doi.org/10.1007/3-540-68339-9_2
8. Bleichenbacher, D.: Chosen ciphertext attacks against protocols based on the RSA encryption standard PKCS #1. In: Krawczyk, H. (ed.) CRYPTO 1998. LNCS, vol. 1462, pp. 1–12. Springer, Heidelberg (1998). https://doi.org/10.1007/BFb0055716
9. Cachin, C., Micali, S., Stadler, M.: Computationally private information retrieval with polylogarithmic communication. In: Stern, J. (ed.) EUROCRYPT 1999. LNCS, vol. 1592, pp. 402–414. Springer, Heidelberg (1999). https://doi.org/10.1007/3-540-48910-X_28
10. Coppersmith, D.: Small solutions to polynomial equations, and low exponent RSA vulnerabilities. J. Cryptol. **10**(4), 233–260 (1997). https://doi.org/10.1007/s001459900030
11. Coppersmith, D., Halevi, S., Jutla, C.: ISO 9796-1 and the new forgery strategy (working draft). Submission to IEEE P1363 Working Group (1999)

12. Coron, J.-S.: On the exact security of full domain hash. In: Bellare, M. (ed.) CRYPTO 2000. LNCS, vol. 1880, pp. 229–235. Springer, Heidelberg (2000). https://doi.org/10.1007/3-540-44598-6_14
13. Coron, J.S.: Optimal security proofs for PSS and other signature schemes. Cryptology ePrint Archive, Report 2001/062 (2001). http://eprint.iacr.org/2001/062
14. Coron, J.-S.: Optimal security proofs for PSS and other signature schemes. In: Knudsen, L.R. (ed.) EUROCRYPT 2002. LNCS, vol. 2332, pp. 272–287. Springer, Heidelberg (2002). https://doi.org/10.1007/3-540-46035-7_18
15. Coron, J.-S.: Security proof for partial-domain hash signature schemes. In: Yung, M. (ed.) CRYPTO 2002. LNCS, vol. 2442, pp. 613–626. Springer, Heidelberg (2002). https://doi.org/10.1007/3-540-45708-9_39
16. Coron, J.-S., Naccache, D., Stern, J.P.: On the security of RSA padding. In: Wiener, M. (ed.) CRYPTO 1999. LNCS, vol. 1666, pp. 1–18. Springer, Heidelberg (1999). https://doi.org/10.1007/3-540-48405-1_1
17. Coron, J.S., Naccache, D., Tibouchi, M., Weinmann, R.P.: Practical cryptanalysis of ISO 9796-2 and EMV signatures. J. Cryptol. 29(3), 632–656 (2016). https://doi.org/10.1007/s00145-015-9205-5
18. Davida, G.I.: Chosen signature cryptanalysis of the RSA (MIT) public key cryptosystem. University of Wisconsin, Milwaukee, Technical report (1982)
19. de Jonge, W., Chaum, D.: Attacks on some RSA signatures. In: Williams, H.C. (ed.) CRYPTO 1985. LNCS, vol. 218, pp. 18–27. Springer, Heidelberg (1986). https://doi.org/10.1007/3-540-39799-X_3
20. Degabriele, J.P., Lehmann, A., Paterson, K.G., Smart, N.P., Strefler, M.: On the joint security of encryption and signature in EMV. In: Dunkelman, O. (ed.) CT-RSA 2012. LNCS, vol. 7178, pp. 116–135. Springer, Heidelberg (2012). https://doi.org/10.1007/978-3-642-27954-6_8
21. Denning, D.E.: Digital signatures with RSA and other public-key cryptosystems. Commun. ACM 27(4), 388–392 (1984). https://doi.org/10.1145/358027.358052
22. Desmedt, Y., Odlyzko, A.M.: A chosen text attack on the RSA cryptosystem and some discrete logarithm schemes. In: Williams, H.C. (ed.) CRYPTO 1985. LNCS, vol. 218, pp. 516–522. Springer, Heidelberg (1986). https://doi.org/10.1007/3-540-39799-X_40
23. Girault, M., Misarsky, J.-F.: Selective forgery of RSA signatures using redundancy. In: Fumy, W. (ed.) EUROCRYPT 1997. LNCS, vol. 1233, pp. 495–507. Springer, Heidelberg (1997). https://doi.org/10.1007/3-540-69053-0_34
24. Girault, M., Misarsky, J.-F.: Cryptanalysis of countermeasures proposed for repairing ISO 9796-1. In: Preneel, B. (ed.) EUROCRYPT 2000. LNCS, vol. 1807, pp. 81–90. Springer, Heidelberg (2000). https://doi.org/10.1007/3-540-45539-6_6
25. Goldberg, S., Reyzin, L., Sagga, O., Baldimtsi, F.: Efficient noninteractive certification of RSA moduli and beyond. In: Galbraith, S.D., Moriai, S. (eds.) ASIACRYPT 2019. LNCS, vol. 11923, pp. 700–727. Springer, Cham (2019). https://doi.org/10.1007/978-3-030-34618-8_24
26. Goldwasser, S., Micali, S., Rivest, R.L.: A digital signature scheme secure against adaptive chosen-message attacks. SIAM J. Comput. 17(2), 281–308 (1988)
27. Gordon, J.A.: How to forge RSA key certificates. Electron. Lett. 21(9), 377–379 (1985). https://doi.org/10.1049/el:19850269
28. Guillou, L.C., Quisquater, J.-J., Walker, M., Landrock, P., Shaer, C.: Precautions taken against various potential attacks. In: Damgård, I.B. (ed.) EUROCRYPT 1990. LNCS, vol. 473, pp. 465–473. Springer, Heidelberg (1991). https://doi.org/10.1007/3-540-46877-3_42

29. ISO: Information technology - security techniques - digital signature schemes giving message recovery - part 2: Mechanisms using a hash-function. ISO 9796–2:1997, International Organization for Standardization, Geneva, Switzerland (1997). https://www.iso.org/standard/28232.html (WITHDRAWN)

30. ISO: Information technology - security techniques - digital signature schemes giving message recovery - part 2: Integer factorization based mechanisms. ISO 9796–2:2002, International Organization for Standardization, Geneva, Switzerland (2002). https://www.iso.org/standard/35455.html (WITHDRAWN)

31. ISO: Information technology - security techniques - digital signatures with appendix - part 2: Integer factorization based mechanisms. ISO 14888–2:2008, International Organization for Standardization, Geneva, Switzerland (2008). https://www.iso.org/standard/44227.html

32. ISO: Information technology - security techniques - digital signature schemes giving message recovery - part 2: Integer factorization based mechanisms. ISO 9796–2:2010, International Organization for Standardization, Geneva, Switzerland (2010). https://www.iso.org/standard/54788.html

33. Jager, T., Kakvi, S.A., May, A.: On the security of the PKCS#1 v1.5 signature scheme. In: Lie, D., Mannan, M., Backes, M., Wang, X. (eds.) ACM CCS 2018, pp. 1195–1208. ACM Press (2018). https://doi.org/10.1145/3243734.3243798

34. Jonsson, J., Kaliski, B.: Public-Key Cryptography Standards (PKCS) #1: RSA Cryptography Specifications Version 2.1. RFC 3447 (Informational), February 2003. Obsoleted by RFC 8017. https://doi.org/10.17487/RFC3447, https://www.rfc-editor.org/rfc/rfc3447.txt

35. Jonsson, J.: Security proofs for the RSA-PSS signature scheme and its variants. Cryptology ePrint Archive, Report 2001/053 (2001). http://eprint.iacr.org/2001/053

36. Kakvi, S.A.: On the security of RSA-PSS in the wild. In: Mehrnezhad, M., van der Merwe, T., Hao, F. (eds.) Proceedings of the 5th ACM Workshop on Security Standardisation Research Workshop, London, UK, 11 November 2019, pp. 23–34. ACM (2019). https://doi.org/10.1145/3338500.3360333

37. Kakvi, S.A., Kiltz, E.: Optimal security proofs for full domain hash, revisited. In: Pointcheval, D., Johansson, T. (eds.) EUROCRYPT 2012. LNCS, vol. 7237, pp. 537–553. Springer, Heidelberg (2012). https://doi.org/10.1007/978-3-642-29011-4_32

38. Kakvi, S.A., Kiltz, E.: Optimal security proofs for full domain hash, revisited. J. Cryptol. **31**(1), 276–306 (2018). https://doi.org/10.1007/s00145-017-9257-9

39. Kakvi, S.A., Kiltz, E., May, A.: Certifying RSA. In: Wang, X., Sako, K. (eds.) ASIACRYPT 2012. LNCS, vol. 7658, pp. 404–414. Springer, Heidelberg (2012). https://doi.org/10.1007/978-3-642-34961-4_25

40. Kaliski, B.: PKCS #1: RSA Encryption Version 1.5. RFC 2313 (Informational), March 1998. 10.17487/RFC2313, obsoleted by RFC 2437. https://www.rfc-editor.org/rfc/rfc2313.txt

41. Kaliski, B., Staddon, J.: PKCS #1: RSA Cryptography Specifications Version 2.0. RFC 2437 (Informational), October 1998. 10.17487/RFC2437, obsoleted by RFC 3447. https://www.rfc-editor.org/rfc/rfc2437.txt

42. Kaliski, B.: From PKC to PKI: Reflections on standardizing the RSA algorithm (2019). https://youtu.be/sqsDKjPaJVg

43. Kaliski, B. (ed.): IEEE standard specifications for public-key cryptography. IEEE Std 1363–2000, pp. 1–228, August 2000. https://doi.org/10.1109/IEEESTD.2000.92292, https://ieeexplore.ieee.org/servlet/opac?punumber=7168

44. Lenstra, A.K.: Unbelievable security *matching AES security using public key systems*. In: Boyd, C. (ed.) ASIACRYPT 2001. LNCS, vol. 2248, pp. 67–86. Springer, Heidelberg (2001). https://doi.org/10.1007/3-540-45682-1_5
45. Lenstra, A.K., Lenstra, H.W., Lovász, L.: Factoring polynomials with rational coefficients. Math. Ann. **261**(4), 5150–534 (1982). https://doi.org/10.1007/BF01457454
46. May, A.: Using LLL-reduction for solving RSA and factorization problems. In: Nguyen, P., Vallée, B. (eds.) The LLL Algorithm. Information Security and Cryptography, pp. 315–348. Springer, Heidelberg (2010). https://doi.org/10.1007/978-3-642-02295-1_10
47. Menezes, A.: Evaluation of security level of cryptography: RSA signature schemes (2002). http://citeseerx.ist.psu.edu/viewdoc/download?doi=10.1.1.612.1271&rep=rep1&type=pdf
48. Misarsky, J.-F.Ç.: A multiplicative attack using LLL algorithm on RSA signatures with redundancy. In: Kaliski, B.S. (ed.) CRYPTO 1997. LNCS, vol. 1294, pp. 221–234. Springer, Heidelberg (1997). https://doi.org/10.1007/BFb0052238
49. Moriarty, K. (ed.), Kaliski, B., Jonsson, J., Rusch, A.: PKCS #1: RSA Cryptography Specifications Version 2.2. RFC 8017 (Informational), November 2016. 10.17487/RFC8017, https://www.rfc-editor.org/rfc/rfc8017.txt
50. Peikert, C., Waters, B.: Lossy trapdoor functions and their applications. In: Ladner, R.E., Dwork, C. (eds.) 40th ACM STOC, pp. 187–196. ACM Press (2008). https://doi.org/10.1145/1374376.1374406
51. Rivest, R.L., Shamir, A., Adleman, L.M.: A method for obtaining digital signatures and public-key cryptosystems. Commun. Assoc. Comput. Mach. **21**(2), 120–126 (1978)

The Vacuity of the Open Source Security Testing Methodology Manual

Martin R. Albrecht$^{(\boxtimes)}$ and Rikke Bjerg Jensen$^{(\boxtimes)}$

Information Security Group, Royal Holloway, University of London, London, UK
{martin.albrecht,rikke.jensen}@rhul.ac.uk

Abstract. The Open Source Security Testing Methodology Manual (OSSTMM) provides a "scientific methodology for the accurate characterization of operational security" [Her10, p.13]. It is extensively referenced in writings aimed at security testing professionals such as textbooks, standards and academic papers. In this work we offer a fundamental critique of OSSTMM and argue that it fails to deliver on its promise of actual security. Our contribution is threefold and builds on a textual critique of this methodology. First, OSSTMM's central principle is that security can be understood as a quantity of which an entity has more or less. We show why this is wrong and how OSSTMM's unified security score, the rav, is an empty abstraction. Second, OSSTMM disregards risk by replacing it with a trust metric which confuses multiple definitions of trust and, as a result, produces a meaningless score. Finally, OSSTMM has been hailed for its attention to human security. Yet it understands all human agency as a security threat that needs to be constantly monitored and controlled. Thus, we argue that OSSTMM is neither fit for purpose nor can it be salvaged, and it should be abandoned by security professionals.

1 Introduction

Penetration testing textbooks advise their readers to follow a pre-established methodology. For example, Johansen et al. write: "A penetration testing methodology defines a roadmap, with practical ideas and proven practices that can be followed to assess the true security posture of a network, application, system, or any combination thereof" [JAHA16]. Similarly, Duffy notes: "The biggest benefit of using a methodology is that it allows assessors to evaluate an environment holistically and consistently" and "when standard exploits do not work, testers can have tunnel vision; sticking to a methodology will prevent that" [Duf15, pp.5-6]. Penetration testing methodologies are therefore seen to enable a systematic assessment of an organisation's security.

However, the use of a penetration testing methodology contains within it a tension. On the one hand, it ought to provide a complete coverage of the target, thus enabling a better understanding of its security; deciding on a methodology before engagement should enable a better understanding of the object afterwards. On the other hand, fixing the steps and tests performed to understand

T. van der Merwe et al. (Eds.): SSR 2020, LNCS 12529, pp. 114–147, 2020.
https://doi.org/10.1007/978-3-030-64357-7_6

the security of a target before engaging with it, may subvert the understanding of it. The methodology may simply not be adequate for the object under consideration. For example, if a methodology does not cover IPv6, attack vectors via IPv6 will be missed unless the tester deviates from the methodology under their own initiative. Similarly, vulnerabilities involving, say, SCTP traffic are unlikely to be captured, since methodologies typically focus on TCP and UDP.

This tension is, for example, identified by Wilhelm when he writes: "What we need in our industry is a repeatable process that allows for verifiable findings, but which also allows for a high degree of flexibility on the part of the pentest analyst to perform 'outside-the-box' attacks and inquiries against the target systems and networks" [Wil13, p.76]. Similarly, Stuttard and Pinto emphasise: "Following all the steps in this methodology will not guarantee that you discover all the vulnerabilities within a given application. However, it will provide you with a good level of assurance that you have probed all the necessary regions of the application's attack surface and have found as many issues as possible given the resources available to you" [SP11].

This tension does not invalidate the utility of penetration testing methodologies in many scenarios as the tested objects tend to exhibit a large level of similarity, permitting presumptions to be made about the objects under consideration. It does, however, caution against claims of actual security, i.e. a full understanding of the object under consideration, when the object was not, in fact, studied in its own right but through the lens of a predecided methodology. The standardised nature of such methodologies also questions their ability to yield reliable results about an organisation's total security posture.

Significantly, however, this limitation of penetration testing methodologies is not necessarily acknowledged by the methodologies themselves. In particular, the Open Source Security Testing Methodology Manual (OSSTMM), which we consider in this work, promises an accurate understanding of security – what it terms "Actual Security" – as the result of the application of its scientific methodology:

> The primary purpose of this manual is to provide a scientific methodology for the accurate characterization of operational security (OpSec) through examination and correlation of test results in a consistent and reliable way. [Her10, Introduction, p.13]

OSSTMM. The methodology was first introduced in 2000. The current version is 3.0 and was released in 2010 by the Institute for Security and Open Methodologies (ISECOM). There is also a draft version 4.0, but it seems to be hardly considered, plausibly due to the fact that it is only available to ISECOM members.

OSSTMM is structured similarly to other security testing methodologies. It introduces its basic premises, notions and processes in chapters one to six. This is followed by five chapters on particular areas, each discussing concrete tests. The methodology finishes with pointers on compliance, reporting, expected outcomes and the licence. OSSTMM opens its Introduction with:

The Open Source Security Testing Methodology Manual (OSSTMM) provides a methodology for a thorough security test, herein referred to as
an OSSTMM audit. An OSSTMM audit is an accurate *measurement* of
security at an operational level that is *void of assumptions* and anecdotal
evidence. [Her10, Introduction, p.11, emphasis added]

With this, the authors announce OSSTMM's two out of three core contributions to security testing which distinguish it from other methodologies: its
security metrics (Chapter 4) and its trust analysis (Chapter 5).

First, OSSTMM defines a unified security *score* – the rav – to be measured
which ought to express the deviation from perfect security:

The rav is a scale measurement of an attack surface, the amount of uncon-
trolled interactions with a target, which is calculated by the quantitative
balance between porosity, limitations, and controls. In this scale, 100 rav
(also sometimes shown as 100% rav) is perfect balance and anything less
is too few controls and therefore a greater attack surface. More than 100
rav shows more controls than are necessary which itself may be a problem
as controls often add interactions within a scope as well as complexity and
maintenance issues. [Her10, Ch.1, p.22]

Second, for the avoidance of bias and reliance on assumptions, OSSTMM
defines security independent of risk, the environment and threats:

However, to remove bias from security metrics and provide a more fair
assessment we removed the use of risk. Risk itself is heavily biased and
often highly variable depending on the environment, assets, threats, and
many more factors. [Her10, Ch.1, p.28]

To avoid the pitfalls it associates with risk, OSSTMM proposes quantifiable, fact
based *trust* metrics:

Our intention is to eventually eliminate the use of risk in areas of security
which have no set price value of an asset (like with people, personal privacy,
and even fluctuating markets) in favor of trust metrics which are based
completely on facts. [Her10, Instructions, p.2]

The third major contribution of OSSTMM is its "holistic" [Her10, Ch.4, p.68]
approach to security. That is, OSSTMM applies this metric and its methodology
to a comprehensive variety of areas, including, and in contrast to other such
methodologies, to *Human Security* (Chapter 7):

This is a methodology to test the operational security of physical locations,
human interactions, and all forms of communications such as wireless,
wired, analog, and digital. [Her10, Instructions, p.2]

This contribution is often highlighted in the literature, in e.g. [PR10]
OSSTMM is recognised for being the first methodology "to include human factors in the tests, taking into account the established fact that humans may be
very dangerous for the system".[1]

---

[1] The seminal work criticising this notion is [AS99], see Section 5.1.

OSSTMM's Impact. ISECOM offers various certifications for security professionals, such as OPST (OSSTMM Professional Security Tester), OPSE (OSSTMM Professional Security Expert) and CTA (Certified Trust Analyst), and for organisations, infrastructure and products, such as STAR (Security Test Audit Report) and the OSSTMM Seal of Approval. Furthermore, ISECOM has several related projects that build on OSSTMM, such as SCARE (Source Code Analysis Risk Evaluation) which applies the rav to source code analysis, HSM (Home Security Methodology and Vacation Guide) which applies the rav to securing a home, HHS (Hacker Highschool) which teaches security awareness to teenagers based on OSSTMM, and BPP (The Bad People Project) which is a security and safety awareness programme for children and parents based on OSSTMM's rav and trust metrics. These projects further emphasise the centrality of the rav, trust and human interactions, i.e. the aspects of OSSTMM focused on in this work, to the ISECOM mission.

Beyond these affiliated projects, it is difficult to assess how widely OSSTMM is used. However, in a 2015 survey [KBM15], 10 out of 32 penetration testing providers cite OSSTMM as an influence for their own methodology.[2] Furthermore, CREST's *A guide for running an effective Penetration Testing programme* refers to OSSTMM as an authoritative source for a "standard penetration testing methodolog[y]" and notes its comprehensiveness [Cre17]. NIST Special Publication 800-115 calls it a "widely used assessment methodology" [SSCO08] and the PCI Penetration Testing Guidance for the PCI Data Security Standard (PCI DSS) lists it as one of five "industry-accepted methodologies" [Cou15]. A similar note is struck in [Sha14]: "There are not many standards in use today for assessments and pen tests: PTES, OSSTMM, etc."[3]; in [HHM+14] Holik et al. refer to OSSTMM as "heavily reputable in penetration testers community"; in [PR10] Prandini and Ramilli go further and refer to OSSTMM as "the de-facto standard for security testers" and in [FML+14] the authors refer to it as one of "the two most important standards in cyber-security". OSSTMM is referenced in many textbooks on penetration testing, e.g. [Wil13, Off14, Duf15, JAHA16, McP17], is the methodology of choice in "Hacking Exposed Linux" [ISE08], and is used in [Sch09] for Information Assurance testing and certification by the US Defense Information Systems Agency (DISA). Several academic works reference and build on OSSTMM, e.g. [CZCG05, CCZC05, FMP+15, dJ16, CK16, TFS+18]. Overall, OSSTMM has more than 150 citations according to Google Scholar as of Summer 2020.

Contributions. In this work, we investigate if the Open Source Security Testing Methodology Manual delivers on what it promises with a particular focus on its main contributions. As a consequence, we offer a fundamental critique of this

---

[2] For context, 16 mentioned OWASP generally but only three mentioned the OWASP testing guide, PTES was mentioned by six providers, three providers mentioned NIST SP 800-115.

[3] See Sect. 5.1 for a discussion of other security testing methodologies.

methodology. We do so by addressing its three main contributions, OSSTMM's raisons d'être, in turn.

First, OSSTMM's central premise and promise is that security across many areas can be understood as a *quantity* of which an entity has more or less. In Sect. 2, we explain and demonstrate why this is incorrect and show how OSSTMM fails to deliver on its promise of bringing security to the fore by supplanting an understanding of its object with a method that disregards it. The end result of this process, the rav, is a number that can be readily calculated but conveys little about the security of the considered object.

Second, OSSTMM's Trust definition, which is essential to the methodology and intended to replace risk, not only shares the shortcomings of the rav, but also collapses under its own contradictions on inspection. In particular, OSSTMM's attempt to identify sociological, psychological and technical notions of trust produces nonsensical claims and meaningless metrics, as we explain in Sect. 3.

Third, this leads us to question OSSTMM's decision to treat all areas of security the same in Sect. 4. This decision, combined with the resolve to disregard any notion of risk or threat, leads OSSTMM to conceptualise *all* human agency as a security threat. This results in a Human Security testing approach treating all employees effectively as potential insurgents and testing procedures that test the "requirements to incite fear, revolt, violence, and chaos" [Her10, Ch.7, p.110].

Our critique of OSSTMM's core components invalidates its intended function. Overall, we find that OSSTMM imposes its abstractions against the reality they are designed to model, producing an understanding of security that is empty at best and outright harmful when Human Security is concerned. As such, our conclusion is that OSSTMM's approach to security (testing) cannot be salvaged and the use of OSSTMM should be abandoned by practitioners. We discuss this further and set out broader lessons in Sect. 5.

Method. While information security research routinely features critiques of security technologies in the form of "attack papers", analogues of such works for policies, frameworks and conceptions are largely absent from its core venues. This work is a textual critique of OSSTMM based on a close reading of the methodology and pursues two purposes. First, immediately, to show that OSSTMM is inadequate as a security testing methodology, despite being referenced routinely in the security testing literature. Second, more mediated, to show that the *ideas* at the core of OSSTMM are wrong. As we show in Sect. 5, these ideas are not OSSTMM's privilege. It is for this reason that we chose the form of a textual critique over alternative approaches such as empirical studies to the effectiveness of OSSTMM in practice.

2   The Rav

The central concept in OSSTMM is its security score – the *rav* – as illustrated by ISECOM's "OSSTMM Seal of Approval":

This seal defines an operational state of security, safety, trust, and privacy. The successfully evaluated products, services, and processes carry their visible certification seal and rav score. This allows a purchaser to see precisely the amount and type of change in security that the evaluated solutions present. It removes the guesswork from procurement and allows one to find and compare alternative solutions. [Her10, Introduction, p.16]

2.1   Health Analogy

OSSTMM illustrates its approach with an analogy to health in its chapter on Operational Security Metrics. Since this analogy provides a succinct summary, we also start there.

Imagine a machine exists that can audit all the cells in a human body. This machine works by monitoring the cells in their environment and even prodding each cell in a way it can react to better categorize its purpose. We could then see what various cells do and how they contribute to the overall make-up of the human body. Some cells make up tissue walls like skin cells do. Some, like white blood cells, provide authentication and attack other cells which are on its "bad" list. Then some cells are foreigners, like bacteria which have entered at some point and thrived. The machine would classify all the cells that make up the person, a defined scope, rather than say which are "bad" or "good". [Her10, Ch.4, p.64]

The starting point of the thought experiment is the ability to audit every cell in a human body. While the analogy appeals to an atomic view of health – cells – initially the audit is not atomic. That is, the hypothetical machine observes cells "in their environment" as part of the human body. Yet, this perspective is immediately abandoned:

By counting the cells the machine can tell mostly how well the person as an organism works (health) and how well they fit into their current environment. It can also determine which cells are broken, which are superfluous, and of which type more might be required for the person to be more efficient, prepared for the unexpected, or for any number of specific requirements. Since the cells are dividing and dying all the time, the machine must also make regular tests and chart the person's ability to improve or at least maintain homeostasis. [Her10, Ch.4, p.64]

OSSTMM moves from understanding cells in their environment to *counting* them. This transition is premised on the fact that these different parts of the body are all called "cells" which gives the impression that they share the same unit and the premise that they can be *added up* to understand a person's health. Furthermore, this is premised on the idea that health is a *totally ordered set*. Finally, note that OSSTMM here promises to make "the person [...] more efficient [...] for any number of specific requirements" by exclusively considering the inner workings of the body without any reference to for what *purpose* said person ought to be made more efficient. We shall see below that these ideas shape OSSTMM's consideration of security.

2.2 Introducing the Rav

Having introduced the key ideas of its security metric, OSSTMM is ready to introduce its security score: the rav.

> Unfortunately there is no such machine for counting all cells in a human body. However it does exist for security. Analysts can count and verify the operations of targets in a scope as if it is a super-organism. They record its interactions and the controls surrounding those interactions. They classify them by operation, resources, processes, and limitations. Those numbers the Analysts generate are combined so that controls add to operational security and limitations take away from it. Even the value of the limitations, how badly each type of problem hurts, is also not arbitrary because it's based on the combination of security and controls within that particular scope. So a bad problem in a protective environment will provide less overall exposure than one in a less controlled environment. [Her10, Ch.4, p.64]

As it does for health, OSSTMM considers security – Actual Security in OSSTMM terms – to be *one* ranking in which an entity scores higher or lower, a totally ordered set. It is, perhaps, common to say "System A is more secure than System B because System A has Advanced Cyber Thread Analysis Blockchain Technology^{TM}". However, is a system with a local privilege escalation bug that requires physical access more or less secure *per se* than a server vulnerable to a Denial of Service attack from an IoT botnet? Is a person using a menstruation app to avoid pregnancy that is running on a phone to which their partner has access more or less secure than a server running the stable release of Debian GNU/Linux patched four days ago? These questions make no sense. What we mean by security depends on the object and the threats we are considering.[4]

OSSTMM computes its rav score from "Porosity" (also referred to as "OpSec"), "Controls" and "Limitations".

Porosity. To establish Actual Security, OSSTMM starts by considering the porosity of the target, where each "pore" is either "Visibility", "Access", or "Trust". For example, a server with ports 22, 80 and 443 open, would have an Access of three. Since porosity is always considered as a negative for security, the minimal rav in this example would be −3 (up to some normalisation).

---

[4] Indeed, in e.g. cryptography where quantitative statements of security are abound in the form of advantages and computational complexities, these are always related to specific security goals and attacker capabilities. For example, any cryptographic textbook will distinguish between the collision resistance and preimage resistance of a cryptographic hash function and will shy away from unifying those into one score.

The minimum rav is made by the calculation of porosity which are the holes in the scope. The problem with security metrics is generally in the determination of the assessors to count what they can't possibly really know. This problem does not exist in the rav. You get what you know from what is there for a particular vector and you make no assumptions surrounding what is not there. You count all that which is visible and interactive outside of the scope and allows for unauthenticated interaction between other targets in the scope. That becomes the porosity. This porosity value makes the first of 3 parts of the final rav value. [Her10, Ch.4, p.67]

We will return to porosity, with a focus on Trust, in Sect. 3. For now, note that OSSTMM's critique of other security metrics is that they aim to count what they cannot possibly know. That indeed sounds like something worth avoiding. Presumably, though, those metrics wish to include a certain bit of information – which they nevertheless do not have – because it is *relevant*. Thus, there is a dilemma: we need information which we do not have. OSSTMM resolves this dilemma by discarding what it needs to know in order to simply count what is known. The task – understanding the security of the object at hand – is replaced by a counting method whose appeal is merely that it is *feasible*. It is one thing to give an account of what you know, it is another thing entirely to claim that whatever you are able to observe from your vantage point is the correct understanding of the object, when you *know* it is not.

Controls. Next, OSSTMM identifies control classes, all of which are always to be acknowledged in all domains, or "channels", that OSSTMM considers: Human, Physical, Wireless, Telecommunications, and Data Network Security. Thus, from the perspective of OSSTMM, these different domains share a high level of similarity. Here, the argument relies on homographs. We illustrate this using the control class "Integrity":

Count each instance for Access or Trust in the scope which can assure that the interaction process and Access to assets has finality and cannot be corrupted, stopped, continued, redirected, or reversed without it being known to the parties involved. Integrity is a change control process. In COMSEC data networks, encryption or a file hash can provide the Integrity control over the change of the file in transit.[5] In HUMSEC, segregation of duties and other corruption-reduction mechanisms provide Integrity control. Assuring integrity in personnel requires that two or more people are required for a single process to assure oversight of that process.

---

[5] It is worth noting that neither cryptographic mechanism described here provides integrity protection: for example, CBC mode encryption and textbook RSA are famously malleable, e.g. [AP13, Ble98], and hash functions are public functions operating on public data so an adversary can simply recompute the hash after message modification. The authors should have recommended a message authentication code or a digital signature.

This includes that no master Access to the whole process exists. There can be no person with full access and no master key to all doors. [Her10, Ch.4, p.70]

The COMSEC example in the above quote refers to the integrity of messages, i.e. the prevention of message modification by someone other than the sender. The recommended controls are intended to ensure that whatever message the sender intended to send is indeed received. The HUMSEC example, however, is concerned with distrust in the sender. It recommends "corruption-reduction mechanisms" to hedge against the originators of actions. Thus, the two controls are aimed at different threats: the first aims to ensure an honest actor's messages are not corrupted in flight, the second aims to ensure an actor itself is not corrupt.[6] The only relation is that the words "integrity" and "corruption" are used in both cases. We see that the identification is merely facilitated by their identical linguistic features and not by their distinct meanings. The control classes identified by OSSTMM are anything but self-evident. Yet, OSSTMM does not justify them.

Overall OSSTMM defines ten such control classes – "authentication", "indemnification", "subjugation", "continuity", "resilience", "non-repudiation", "confidentiality", "privacy", "integrity", and "alarm" [Her10, p.72-75]. The controls from all the classes are then *added up* with weights $1/10$ for each class.

The next part is to account for the controls in place per target. This means going target by target and determining where any of the 10 controls are in place such as Authentication, Subjugation, Non-repudiation, etc. Each control is valued as 10% of a pore since each provides $1/10$th of the total controls needed to prevent all attack types. This is because having all 10 controls for each pore is functionally the same as closing the pore provided the controls have no limitations. [Her10, Ch.4, p.67]

For example,[7] two such controls would be "log file is in place" and "authentication is required" and we would obtain

$$1/10 \times \text{"log file is in place"} + 1/10 \times \text{"authentication is required"}.$$

At this point, the reader may think of the above expression as a formulaic way of saying "one log file is in place and authentication is required". However, as OSSTMM explains above, this is meant to be a weighted sum where each summand is "valued" at $1/10$, i.e. as far as OSSTMM is concerned, the sum of a log file and "authentication required" is meaningful in a mathematical sense. This reasoning presumes that all controls are the same in some quantifiable way. The authors of OSSTMM explain:

---

[6] An analogous cryptographic control would be the use of secret sharing and secure multiparty computation techniques.

[7] We give a full worked example of a rav calculation in Appendix A.

It is difficult to work with relative or inconsistent measurements like choosing a specific hue of yellow to paint a room, starting work at sunrise, having the right flavor of strawberry for a milkshake, or preparing for the next threat to affect your organization's profits because the factors have many variables which are biased or frequently changing between people, regions, customs, and locations. For this reason, many professions attempt to standardize such things like flavors, colors, and work hours. This is done through reductionism, a process of finding the elements of such things and building them up from there by quantifying those elements. This way, colors become frequencies, work hours become hours and minutes, flavors become chemical compounds, and an attack surface becomes porosity, controls, and limitations. The only real problem with operational metrics is the requirement for knowing how to properly apply the metric for it to be useful. [Her10, Ch.4, p.62]

OSSTMM claims to have identified "the elements" of a log file and the requirement for authentication. However, while e.g. adding up the frequencies of colours indeed produces a new colour (frequency), i.e. colours have a quantitative side to them that permits addition, this does not hold true for log files and authentication requirements.

One log file and one authentication requirement is not the same as one log file and a message authentication code; log files, message authentication codes and (user) authentication requirements are different and protect against different threats. Thus, there are no inherent weights when adding these things that are not reducible to the same dimension.

Even assuming that "having all 10 controls for each pore is functionally the same as closing the pore provided the controls have no limitations", this does not imply adding up (a subset of) ten controls to obtain a score since each of the specific controls needs to be in place. OSSTMM's appeal to the diversity of the controls does not produce the posited identity. Rather, the sentence merely implies that the ten classes should sum to one (or whatever stands in for "all good") when they are all in place. The weights are irrelevant when all control classes are in place since they are designed to sum to one in this case, but matter for when a particular control class is missing, i.e. they are meant to encode the importance attributed to this particular lack. This, in turn, will depend on what is being protected and the nature of the threat under consideration. It is not at all clear that adding an authentication requirement closes a pore to the same extent as adding a log file documenting access after the fact does. The *choice* 1/10 "authentication required" and 1/10 "log file" is as much a choice as $\sqrt{2\pi/e}$ "authentication required" and 1/10 "log file". OSSTMM is not "void of assumptions" [Her10, Introduction, p.11].

Limitations. To complete the rav, limitations are considered:

The third part of the rav is accounting for the limitations found in the protection and the controls. These are also known as "vulnerabilities".

The value of these limitations comes from the porosity and established controls themselves. [Her10, Ch.4, p.67]

To make this concrete, too, we may think of this operation of adding up several "buffer overflows" with, say, one "CR/LF escape".

Sums. With all components in place, the rav can be calculated.

> With all counts completed, the rav is basically subtracting porosity and limitations from the controls. This is most easily done with the rav spreadsheet calculator. [Her10, Ch.4, p.67]

Thus, OSSTMM goes beyond the idea of security as a ranking and considers security to possess an additive structure.[8] Enabling encryption "adds to" security, having a telnet port open permitting root login "takes away" security.[9] Mathematics also speaks of "adding" and "taking away", when referring to addition and subtraction over, say, the Integers, and *thus*, so OSSTMM's leap, we shall add and subtract open ports and authentication:

$$c_0 \times \log \text{file} + c_1 \times \text{auth.} - c_2 \times \text{open port} - c_3 \times \text{buf. overfl.},$$

where c_i are some weights.[10] These sums can further be extended to not only cover the moments of an IT system but across all areas considered by OSSTMM:

> One important requirement in applying the rav is that Actual Security can only be calculated per scope. A change in channel, vector, or index is a new scope and a new calculation for Actual Security. However, once calculated, multiple scopes can be combined together in aggregate to create one Actual Security that represents a fuller vision of the operational security [of] all scopes. For example, a test can be made of Internet-facing servers from both the Internet side and from within the perimeter network where the servers reside. That is 2 vectors. Assume that, the Internet vector is indexed by IP address and contains 50 targets. The intranet vector is indexed by MAC address and is made of 100 targets because less controls exist internally to allow for more collaborative interaction between systems. Once each test is completed and the rav is counted they can be combined into one calculation of 150 targets as well as the sums of each limitations and controls. This will give a final Actual Security metric which

---

[8] These are not equivalent. The letters in the alphabet are ordered but this does not endow them with an addition rule. The integers modulo some prime p have an addition (multiplication, division) rule but do not possess a natural ordering.

[9] "Those numbers the Analysts generate are combined so that controls add to operational security and limitations take away from it" [Her10, Ch.4, p.64].

[10] These weights are not always constants. In particular, limitations are weighted according to their class and porosity. Thus, the actual expression is more complex than given here for illustration purposes.

is more complete for that perimeter network than either test would provide alone. It would also be possible to add the analysis from physical security, wireless, telecommunications, and human security tests in the same way. Such combinations are possible to create a better understanding of the total security in a holistic way. [Her10, Ch.4, p.68]

In other words, OSSTMM not only adds and subtracts ports and log files but also doors (Physical Security), "whispering or using hand signals" [Her10, Ch.4, p.74] or "a cultural bias" [Her10, Ch.4, p.76] (Human Security). The computation continues for a few more steps to produce the final rav value (see Appendix A for a more detailed example). However, already at this stage this score is an arbitrary choice produced by eradicating the differences between the features considered in order to combine them using some chosen weights. As its opening gambit OSSTMM promises the reader the avoidance of "general best practices, anecdotal evidence, or superstitions" [Her10, p.1], but the answer OSSTMM gives as to the "Actual Security" of the studied object is vacuous and is based on category mistakes and unsubstantiated choices.

Remark 1. While it is possible to construct examples where an OSSTMM score contradicts an expert's verdict on security, since e.g. all controls are weighted the same, being vacuous does not mean that the score must commonly and strikingly disagree with the reality it subsumes. Consider the following hypothetical example: if the rav score for, say, an unpatched Windows 7 system exposing SMB on the Internet were to be lower than for, say, an up-to-date copy of OpenBSD in the default configuration, no one would question the security of the latter in favour of the former. Rather, if this was the case, the rav would change. In contrast, if we were to rethink the security of a patched OpenBSD and an unpatched Windows 7, it would be because we had learned something new about these systems. Echoing Kay [Kay09], the rav tells us nothing that we have not previously told the rav. It does, however, obscure what we tell it. The rav score itself is not useful to an engineer tasked with improving it: the engineer would have to return to the data that was used to compute it to understand which security controls were missing and where. The sentence "telnet is open" contains more information than whatever numerical value OSSTMM assigns to it.

3   Trust

As mentioned above, in OSSTMM terms, Access, Visibility and Trust make up Porosity (also referred to as OpSec), and security is defined as the separation of a threat and an asset. While Access is roughly what you would expect – the ability to interact with the asset – Visibility is "a means of calculating opportunity" [Her10, Introduction, p.23]. From this perspective, an asset needs to be visible to be targeted.

For OSSTMM, Trust is a core component of security testing and, unlike e.g. Access and Visibility, requires its own separate analysis, which is why OSSTMM dedicates the whole of Chapter 5 to it. This attention to Trust is chiefly motivated by ISECOM's ambition to replace considerations of risk with trust metrics, as discussed in our introduction. Thus, examining Trust in OSSTMM is examining one of its key tenets. The centrality of this notion to ISECOM's mission is underlined by ISECOM offering certification specifically for its Trust analysis:

> The Certified Trust Analyst proves a candidate has the skills and knowledge to efficiently evaluate the trust properties[11] of any person, place, thing, system, or process and make accurate and efficient trust decisions. [Her10, Introduction, p.15]

Whether applied to a person, an object or a process, Trust has a numerical value – zero or more Trusts – that determines "Trust", the unit of analysis.

3.1   What Trust?

In what follows, we use "Trust" to denote the concept of trust as defined in OSSTMM and "trust" for its wider conceptions, such as the diverging notions of trust in computer science and the social sciences, as outlined in our discussion of related work in Sect. 5.1. Critically, this distinction and the plurality of trust definitions are not recognised by OSSTMM. Rather, in order for its trust analysis to capture what it needs it to capture, OSSTMM collapses multiple trust definitions, making its understanding and application of trust nonsensical. While OSSTMM maintains that "people [. . .] misuse trust as a concept" [Her10, Ch.5, p.87], we show how this statement directly applies to OSSTMM. We identify and discuss this below by showing how OSSTMM needs to appeal to understandings of trust within computer science as well as sociological and behavioural notions of trust in order to facilitate its trust analysis.

Computer Science. The Trust unit in OSSTMM is better understood as modelling the need to trust. Trust is always measured as a negative in OSSTMM, a person with a Trust score of five, for example, is understood to be a riskier proposition than someone with a Trust/need-to-trust score of, say, two (the same goes for any other object):

> Where security is like a wall that separates threats from assets, trust is a hole in that wall. [Her10, Ch.5, p.87]

Trust in OSSTMM terms is couched in an understanding of trust as a risk of exploitation and as a vulnerability. This notion of trust is not necessarily controversial from a computer science perspective. For example, this mirrors the notion of trust in cryptography where constructions not relying on a trusted third party are considered preferable to ones that do. Indeed, cryptographic protocols can be characterised as emulating a trusted third party by mutually distrustful parties.[12]

---

[11] We discuss OSSTMM's ten trust properties in Sect. 3.2.

[12] As Goldreich writes: "A general framework for casting (m-party) cryptographic (protocol) problems consists of specifying a random process that maps m inputs to m

Sociological. More specifically, OSSTMM defines Trust as Internal Access.

> In operational security, Trust is merely a contributor to porosity, just another interaction to control. It differs from Access (the other form of interaction), in how it relates to other targets within the scope. So where Access is interaction between two sides of a vector into and out of the scope, Trust is measured as the interactions between targets within the scope. [Her10, Ch.5. p.87]

This notion of trust assumes interaction and thus relies on relations between objects within the environment. Recalling that OSSTMM also attempts to model Human Security, it thus models human interactions which are social in nature. Put differently, access – internal or not – is (also) social. Thus, we observe that OSSTMM relies on a sociological conception of trust precisely because it insists that Trust is understood as Internal Access.

However, trust, regardless of disciplinary grounding, is fundamentally different from access and it needs to be recognised as such.[13] It is therefore not only unhelpful to employ the two terms in similar ways, as done here by OSSTMM, it also obfuscates both the cognitive and emotional aspects that make up trust interactions [LW85]. Furthermore, OSSTMM's Trust metric assumes that trust relations do not exist outside the environment as this is simply considered as Access by OSSTMM. Thus, why label Internal Access as Trust? If Trust is simply another form of Access, shaped by different types of interactions, why not declare it as such?

Behavioural. On the same page, OSSTMM introduces a third definition:

> Trust is a decision. While some people claim it is an emotion, like love, or a feeling, like pain, its clearly a complex quality we humans are born with. Unlike an emotion or a feeling, we can choose to trust or not to trust someone or something even if it feels wrong to do so. It appears that we are capable to rationalize in a way to supersede how we feel about trusting a target. [Her10, Ch.5, p.87]

Here, OSSTMM posits trust as either an emotion/feeling or a decision, in order to then reject the former in favour of the latter.[14] OSSTMM is interested

---

outputs. The inputs to the process are to be thought of as local inputs of m parties, and the m outputs are their corresponding (desired) local outputs. The random process describes the desired functionality. That is, if the m parties were to trust each other (or trust some external party), then they could each send their local input to the trusted party, who would compute the outcome of the process and send to each party the corresponding output. A pivotal question in the area of cryptographic protocols is the extent to which this (imaginary) trusted party can be 'emulated' by the mutually distrustful parties themselves." [Gol04].

[13] For example, the cryptographic literature would not refer to interactions, typically modelled as oracle access, in a cryptographic protocol as "trust".

[14] We may note a category mistake in the initial dichotomy being offered: trust is a content of thought – what we think – whereas an emotion is a form – how it appears.

in this conclusion because it wants to posit that trust is an object of reason or rationality: trust is open to reflection.[15] This is not controversial. However, declaring trust as an atomic decision is. Since OSSTMM insists that Trust is Internal Access, and given its appeal to Human Security, it requires a broader understanding of trust; an understanding that acknowledges the contextual and the "environment" in which trust interactions emerge and take form. Within these environments, trust does not exist in isolation, in the same way that trust-decisions are not made in a vacuum. Rather, here, trust is a key building block of the (social) environment in which interactions take place – hence, OSSTMM's notion that trust is *solely* a choice is deceptive in this context.

This is also evident in the wider social sciences where, for example, in psychological terms, a person's self-efficacy is critical to any understanding of how an individual makes security decisions [Ban82]. From a sociological perspective, societal structures and interpersonal relations influence how people make security decisions [WC03]. From an organisational perspective, workplace culture as well as formal and informal policies influence security decisions [VNVS10, DG14]. Exemplified by these works, trust decisions, like security, are deeply interwoven into human relations and contextual settings.

3.2   Trust Properties

Countable. However, these objections are moot when we recall that OSSTMM simply defined Trust as Internal Access. Yet, so is OSSTMM's discussion above: "While some people claim *internal access* is an emotion, like love, or a feeling, like pain, it is clearly a complex quality we humans are born with" makes no sense. OSSTMM wants both: to redefine Trust as Internal Access *as well as* maintaining this redefinition captures the notion of trust as a human capacity. This confusion is meant to enable OSSTMM to make trust quantifiable for the rav:

> This means we can quantify it by applying a logical process. It also means we can assign trust values to objects and processes as well as people based on these values. This brings new power to those who can analyze trust and make decisions based on that analysis. [Her10, Ch.5, p.87]

This does not mean that at all. As far as OSSTMM is concerned, to rationally understand an object, to reason about it, means to quantify it; a leap OSSTMM simply asserts here. This is like saying to reason about OSSTMM we should count, say, its number of pages, words, characters, revisions and so on. Or, since OSSTMM appeals to mathematics, this is like saying we understand the ring $\mathbb{Z}_{7681}[x]/(x^{256} + 1)$ when we know it has 7681^{256} elements.

However, since this line of enquiry would take us away from the object at hand, we abandon it here.

[15] This is why OSSTMM can afford to contradict itself by re-admitting trust emotions one sentence later. It is not actually invested in the either-or question but that the former can override the latter.

Properties. To compute Trust, OSSTMM proposes ten Trust Properties [Her10, Ch.5, p.90]. These range from seemingly calculable notions such as size and value to more evasive ones such as symmetry and consistency:[16]

> The Trust Properties are the quantifiable, objective elements which are used to create trust. We can say these properties are what we would say give us "reason to trust".[17] These properties are to be made into baseline rules based on the target and situation which we are verifying. During research, many potential Trust Properties were discovered which are commonly in use and even official, government and industry regulations recommend [sic.], however they failed logic tests and were discarded from our set of properties leaving only ten. [Her10, Ch.5, p.88]

As this paragraph exemplifies, all Trust Properties identified in the methodology are treated as quantifiable and unbiased. However, at no point does OSSTMM attempt to explain from where these Trust Properties have emerged – or which properties were excluded – except that they were discovered "during research" and either passed or failed "logic tests". Which and whose research, and what logic, we do not know. One could say that we are being asked to *blindly trust* the methodology, which OSSTMM, ironically, tells us should be avoided. While we might accept that a property such as *size* is addable and comprises quantifiable elements, other properties hold no calculable features – claiming that they do renders the methodology increasingly futile. To this end, let us take a closer look at one of the Trust Properties identified by OSSTMM: *consistency* – which is defined as the "historical evidence of compromise or corruption of the target" [Her10, Ch.5, p.90].

Rules. In order to make this Trust Property (like all ten Trust Properties) calculable, OSSTMM introduces Trust Rules [Her10, Ch.5, p.91]. This, it claims, translates properties into rules through a series of questions which will produce unbiased numbers as answers.

> Using the trust properties allows us to create only quantifiable rules, not "soft" rules that can either substantiate the trust level nor disrupt it with a biased, emotional weight. However, the properties on their own are useless if they cannot become quantifiable properties, objective, or understandable by the common person not necessarily involved in the security field. [Her10, Ch.5, p.91]

OSSTMM gives an example which concerns making better hiring decisions. Here, humans (as the potential new hires) are the target, meaning that a series of human qualities are assessed; framed within the ten Trust Properties and

---

[16] The ten Trust Properties identified by OSSTMM are: Size, Symmetry, Visibility, Subjugation, Consistency, Integrity, Offsets, Value, Components, Porosity.

[17] As we shall see below, these are actually reasons *not* to trust, i.e. a high score in one of the Trust Properties implies a high need to trust.

measured using the Trust Rules. Thus, let us return to the Trust Property *consistency* to explore how OSSTMM translates this into a Trust Rule that can be used in the hiring of new staff:

5. *Consistency*:

5.1. The total number of months which the applicant has not been employed divided by the total number of months the applicant has been on the workforce and eligible for employment.

5.2. The total number of criminal offenses known divided by the current age less eighteen years (or the legal age of an adult in your region) of the applicant.

5.3. The number of neutral or negative references from past employers divided by the total number of past employers.

5.4. Record the average of these results. [Her10, Ch.5, p.93]

These questions introduce several uncertainties and unknowns. For example, calculating the number of criminal offences "known" naturally ignores potentially unknown criminal offences, but more importantly, it ignores what the offences were, when they happened and how they might influence the work of the applicant.[18] Moreover, assessing whether a reference is "neutral" or "negative" requires individual interpretation and qualitative judgement, which is not accounted for in OSSTMM. So, while these calculations *can* be done – i.e. they are feasible – and will result in a number, what this number tells us is unclear at best. Similarly, every object of calculation is chosen to be weighted exactly the same, one neutral reference per past employer and one criminal offence per year are treated the same and carry the same value. Finally, why the average number, instead of, say, the median or the max, of the answers to these questions is equally obscure.[19]

In summary, in OSSTMM's Trust Properties and Rules, the category mistake we have encountered when discussing the rav, i.e. assigning – without justification – quantities to qualitative data, reappears.

3.3   Risks and Threats

As discussed in the introduction, the reason OSSTMM gives for introducing its trust metric is to avoid risk analysis, which OSSTMM maintains "speculates" and "derives opinions" [Her10, Ch.3, p.53]:

The fundamental difference between doing a risk analysis versus a security analysis is that in security analysis you never analyze the threat. [Her10, Ch.5. p.53]

---

[18] Many legal systems distinguish between criminal convictions such as felonies and misdemeanours. Similarly, the nature of an offence is taken into account by e.g. the Solictors Regulation Authority in England and Wales https://www.sra.org.uk/solicitors/handbook/suitabilitytest/part2/content.page.

[19] For example, taking the computer science perspective of trust, one would expect the max i.e. worst-case security, not average-case: one vulnerability suffices to subvert security goals.

Threats, in any form or shape, do therefore not form part of Actual Security. This is perhaps not surprising given OSSTMM's sole focus on what can be observed and the assertion that the existence, timing and direction of a threat can only be assumed and not known.

In OSSTMM terms, then, doing away with considerations of threats allows for the creation of "Perfect Security, the exact balance of security and controls with operations and limitations" [Her10, Ch.1, p.20]. This invites the question of what standard it has to judge this balance as perfect. OSSTMM posits a balance of controls (adding security) with operations (taking away security) or a balance of *means* to achieve security in light of functionality requirements, without discussing the *end* that is pursued by these means, i.e. against what security ought to be achieved. OSSTMM's balance is not a relation between the object and the environment but exists purely within the object by definition:

> In reality, "perfect" is a subjective concept and what may not be perfect for one person may indeed be perfect for another. Within the context of this manual, "perfect" means a perfectly balanced equation when calculating the attack surface consisting of OpSec and Limitations against Controls. [Her10, Ch.3, p.55]

The balanced equation is attained when each access has all ten, unlimited controls since, as we noted above, "having all 10 controls for each pore is functionally the same as closing the pore provided the controls have no limitations" [Her10, Ch.4, p.67]. Thus, in any field, OSSTMM's security goal is achieved when no conceivable threat has any access to the asset under protection, all pores are "functionally" closed. OSSTMM's security is perfectly balanced when all controls that OSSTMM can think of are in place without limitations, i.e. when no degree of freedom exists beyond these totally encompassing controls.[20] In Data Network Security this approach may lead to "interactions within a scope as well as complexity and maintenance issues" [Her10, Ch.1, p.22]. In Human Security, it develops a whole different impact to be reckoned with.

4 Human Security

Recall that one of the key features of OSSTMM is that it employs one single security testing methodology for all five channels identified in the document: Human (Chapter 7), Physical (Chapter 8), Wireless (Chapter 9), Telecommunications (Chapter 10), and Data Network Security (Chapter 11). Thus, it produces a methodology that can, in principle, be applied to anything or anyone amongst those irrespective of the object under consideration. To do this, the same 17 "Testing Modules"[21] are employed for each of the five channels; meaning that

---

[20] Note that this is a worst-case notion of security, in contrast to the average-case notion used when applying the Trust Rules.

[21] Posture Review, Logistics, Active Detection Verification, Visibility Audit, Access Verification, Trust Verification, Controls Verification, Process Verification, Training

the methodology determines which aspects of each channel matter in security terms. As a result, and as we highlight in the introduction, OSSTMM considers itself a "holistic" methodology and has been recognised for its "comprehensive" approach to security testing [Cre17]. Particularly its attention to Human Security separates it from other methodologies (see Sect. 5.1).

OSSTMM's treatment of trust gives a first account of how it conceptualises human interactions. For example, in the hiring process of new employees, OSSTMM suggests the following Trust Rule under the heading "Porosity":

> The number of employees living in the same community as the applicant divided by the total number [of] people in the community. [Her10, Ch.5, p.93]

An employee at age 50 with one prior conviction for fraud is the same security liability (1/32) as an employee living in a town of 5,000 people together with 156 other employees. That is, an employee living in a small town with many other employees of the same organisation is considered a possible "hole in [the] wall", i.e. a security threat. This might seem counter-intuitive, when starting from a perspective of, say, social cohesion, but is consequential in OSSTMM's logic. These small-town employees have social relations with other employees outside the control of the employer, i.e. they engage in processes outside the control of it. In OSSTMM's perspective on human agency and relations, they appear as potential threats. It thus laments that social norms prevent the security enthusiast from treating people accordingly:

> Unfortunately, while using more controls works with objects and processes, it may not work between people. Many times social norms consider controls beyond simple authentication like matching a face or voice with an identity to be offensive to the person to be trusted. Society often requires us to be more trusting as individuals in order to benefit society as a whole and sometimes at the expense of everyone's individual protection. [Her10, Ch.5, p.87]

When OSSTMM rhetorically takes the standpoint of the individual's protection that is being undermined by "society as a whole", it practically takes the standpoint of an uninhibited authority against the individuals under its command. To this imagined authority any moment merely out of reach of surveillance and control is to the detriment of an organisation's security, which, we recall, makes no reference to threats. Using the same example as above, OSSTMM demonstrates this in another Trust Rule:

> The number of hours per day the applicant will be working alone, unassisted, unmonitored divided by the number of working hours. [Her10, Ch.5, p.92]

Verification, Configuration Verification, Property Verification, Segregation Review, Exposure Verification, Competitive Intelligence Scouting, Quarantine Verification, Privileges Audit, Survivability Validation, and Alert and Log Review [Her10, Ch.6].

This view of human agency, as something that needs to be controlled, is also evident throughout Chapter 7 on Human Security Testing. Here, OSSTMM takes a more pro-active approach and, for example, suggests to test Trust as:

In Terrorem. Test and document the depth of requirements to incite fear, revolt, violence, and chaos, through the disruption of personnel and the use of rumor or other psychological abuse. [Her10, Ch.7, p.110]

How OSSTMM proposes to carry out these tests is unaccounted for. How it can be done without breaking ethical guidelines and legal frameworks remains unanswered.

OSSTMM's proposition to target people through psychological means, including "fear", "rumor", and "abuse" to test the level to which they can be trusted is reminiscent of modern counterinsurgency operations, which, compared with traditional military campaigns, rely as much on psychological means as on physical action. A quick search through a few military counterinsurgency field manuals and doctrines, such as [Arm09, AC10, MOD15], demonstrates these similarities by identifying the need to influence individual perceptions through "aggressive" information operations [AC10, p.152] aiming "to influence, disrupt, corrupt, or usurp the decision making TAs [target audiences] to create a desired effect to support achievement of an objective" [oD14, p.x].

This standpoint of requiring counterinsurgency-like techniques to test the resilience of an organisation paired with a desire for total control over human (inter)actions is no accident but the consequence of two of OSSTMM's key tenets: first, Human Security is treated identically to all other areas of security; humans are treated as objects, just like computers, buildings and so on. Second, security is defined without any regard to risk or threat.

While, as discussed above, perfect security is conceptualised as a balance of operations and controls, this balance itself has no reference to any threat. Hence, OSSTMM contains no notion of proportionality; whether a control measure is justified in light of a threat or not cannot be determined given OSSTMM's rejection of threats altogether. To illustrate this consider the legal category of proportionality first developed by High State Administrative Courts in Germany to review actions of the police, i.e. the Security State [Hir81].[22] It is part of European Human Rights law under the European Convention of Human Rights (ECHR) and in UK Human Rights law it is interpreted as follows: "it is necessary to determine (1) whether the objective of the measure is sufficiently important to justify the limitation of a protected right, (2) whether the measure is rationally connected to the objective, (3) whether a less intrusive measure could have been used without unacceptably compromising the achievement of the objective, and (4) whether, balancing the severity of the measure's effects on the rights of the persons to whom it applies against the importance of the objective, to the extent

---

[22] Also in military campaigns, from where OSSTMM appears to borrow some of its language and approach, proportionality is a legal obligation and according to one US Field Manual "requires that the advantage gained by a military operation not be exceeded by the collateral harm" [AC10, p.247].

that the measure will contribute to its achievement, the former outweighs the latter" [UKS13].

In contrast, OSSTMM, while referencing human rights as a consideration "to assure a safe, high quality test" [Her10, Ch.7, p.105], is conceptually incapable of "balancing the severity of the measure's effects on [the rights of] the persons to whom it applies against the importance of the objective".[23]

OSSTMM does not see people as a strength in security terms but holds an increasingly criticised view of humans in the security loop (see e.g. [PSF14]), one where humans are always perceived as the "weakest link" rather than as the subject of security. Instead, OSSTMM anticipates that people will "make mistakes, forget tasks, and purposefully abandon tasks" [Her10, Ch.2, p.33], and it aims to eradicate these "traits" by reducing the human to an object whose interactions should be monitored, controlled and restricted. It does so by developing a methodology that replaces the notion of people as subjects of security with one where people are understood solely as objects of security. It models human agency as a wild-card to be controlled:

> Unfortunately, how we interact is just based on a collection of biases we accumulate during life, which are subjected to the emotional or bio-chemical state we are under when we have them. [Her10, Ch.14, p.204]

This position contradicts most writings in security studies which recognise the human as a critical security actor, e.g. [BWDW98] and explored further below in Sect. 5.1. The rejection of human agency is not only a problem in academic terms. By not seeing the human as a key security actor, capable of doing the securing, security itself is weakened. OSSTMM chooses to frame human agency as a problem, rather than as a potential solution. This view does not stop with those being tested. Indeed, OSSTMM's suspicion of human agency also applies to those doing the testing:

> We are, after all, only human. Most often though our opinions are limited and restricted to a small scope we know as "our little world". We apply them everywhere because they make life easier. But when we take them with us and try to adhere them to larger, different, more complicated series and types of interactions, we will likely make mistakes. What may make perfect sense to us based on our experiences may not make any sense at all outside of "our little world". So what we need is a better, less biased way of looking at the bigger, more dynamic, less personal, world beyond ourselves. [Her10, Ch.14, p.204]

OSSTMM's methodology for studying human security eliminates the human from security: both in the form of the recognising subject – the tester – whose verdicts it fundamentally distrusts as biased and replaces with a score with little meaning, and in the form of recognised subjects – the tested – whose agency is a "hole in [the] wall". In OSSTMM's view, the human mind is a security threat.

---

[23] This is not a claim about OSSTMM's legality but ought to explain that its heavy-handed approach to human security is a logical consequence of its conception of security.

5 Discussion

We have reviewed OSSTMM's main contributions to the field of security testing. In Sect. 2, we observed that OSSTMM commits a type error by treating categorical values that are specific to different domains as ordinal values that apply across a wide range of domains. As a consequence it presents a security score using homographs and unmotivated choices which has little relation to the object being measured. In Sect. 3, we observed that OSSTMM's notion of Trust confuses and identifies different notions of trust, producing nonsensical claims. This lack of clarity serves to create a unified Trust score to replace considerations of risk and threats, producing a notion of security that is internal to the object being studied, independent of attacker goals or capabilities. Finally, in Sect. 4, we criticised the effects of OSSTMM's approach to identify Human Security with other areas of security, disregarding the subjectivity of the objects under consideration. This produces an approach to security testing that alienates those who are relied on to do the securing, which ultimately weakens security itself.

In summary, we found none of OSSTMM's key contributions to survive under scrutiny and that the flaws identified in OSSTMM render it incorrect. These flaws, however, are an artefact of OSSTMM's ambition to be "scientific", which it characterises as "not [being] about believing or relying on your experience, no matter how vast, but on knowing facts we can build upon" [Her10, Ch.3, p.53]. In OSSTMM's view this means quantifying its data.[24] As we have shown, to square this circle OSSTMM has to rely on unmotivated choices and assertions throughout. OSSTMM does not provide justification or evidence to ground its methodology, rendering it unscientific on its own terms. We conclude that the serious flaws identified in our analysis make the methodology futile. Thus, we suggest that security professionals abandon the use of OSSTMM as a guide to security testing.

Remark 2. It might be objected that OSSTMM has utility despite the flaws identified in this work. Indeed, in addition to its conceptualisation of security, it – like any other security testing guideline – also does advise a security tester to scan, say, port 80 on each host in a network using a TCP SYN scan, which is sound advice. We remark, however, that the flaws we identified invalidate OSSTMM's key concepts, as expressed by ISECOM itself and others, i.e. OSSTMM in its own right. Put differently, removing what makes OSSTMM OSSTMM from OSSTMM might result in a functional, albeit by now somewhat outdated, security testing checklist.

5.1 Related Work

OSSTMM's claim that it is a "holistic" security testing methodology that covers both technological and human security, with a scoring system that captures trust

---

[24] "It appears that we are capable to rationalize in a way to supersede how we feel about trusting a target. This means we can quantify it by applying a logical process" [Her10, Ch.5, p.87].

as well as access and visibility, necessitates engagement with a diverse set of literatures and bodies of work.

Security Metrics. A growing number of works focus on the use of security metrics and the benefits of such metrics to organisations, e.g. [KH06, Pay06, Jaq07, Hay10, BH11, Bra14, Cam14], while only a small body of writings offers critical reflections on such claims and on the wide use of metrics to satisfy security assessments. For example, in an overview of security metrics Ahmed [Ahm16, p.108] writes: "They [security metrics] do not provide any help in measuring or monitoring the effectiveness of controls. Instead they measure the existence of controls". Moreover, Kaur and Jones [KJ08, p.45] note the tension embedded in security metrics: "It is difficult to have one metrics [sic.] that covers all types of devices. To be effective the level of detail and granularity needed is high. However, to have a large scope and cover all manner of devices requires a general metrics [sic.] which will not meet all security challenges". Recently, CERT/CC published a critique of the widely used Common Vulnerability Scoring System (CVSS) [SHH+18] where the authors note the data type error committed by CVSS by treating ordinal values as interval values, the difficulty of assigning a single score irrespective of differing requirements and suggest "the way to fix this problem is to skip converting qualitative measurements to numbers". Hence, while security metrics and standardised forms of assessing the robustness of an organisation's security posture are widely used and generally accepted, some criticisms, albeit a small selection, do exist.

Metrics. Beyond information security, the pitfalls of translating qualitative statements into quantities (which may then be algebraically manipulated) are a subject of active debate in the social, psychological and clinical sciences, see e.g. [KUM96, PS13] and the references therein. These discussions testify to the need for critical engagement with the methods of evaluation before offering conclusive findings. This is also evident in economics, where e.g. Kay criticises the "modern curse of bogus quantification" [Kay11] and points out that the "index [...] is not telling us anything we have not already told the index [...]" [Kay09]. Such critiques thus warn against relying on metrics for a complete understanding of the objects under evaluation.

Trust. Measuring trust is a key component of OSSTMM. Yet, as evidenced in our critique and exemplified by a broad range of literature, trust is not a monolithic concept. It carries multiple meanings depending on perspective, purpose and disciplinary grounding. Within the social and behavioural sciences, disciplines such as sociology, (social) psychology and behavioural economics disagree on trust definitions and methodological approaches, see e.g. [BNH10, Coo05, CLH09, Kra99, RS08, Har04, Har13], which in turn differ from notions of trust in computer science, e.g. [BFL96, LN10, GW11]. A common understanding of trust does therefore not exist. This is epitomised by Mollering [Mol06] when outlining three schools of thought on trust: trust as reason, trust as routine and trust as reflexive. More specifically, for (social) psychologists, e.g. [BV04, DF11], the notion of trust as a rational choice – as a decision – dominates, whilst behavioural economic understandings of trust focus on averting negative outcomes of opportunism and to limit the risk of exploitation [Lin00, Tul08]. These positions rely heavily on individualistic and psychological positions put forward by experimental and quantitative researchers, and they contrast with the notion of trust as a "sociological reality" where "[t]rust in everyday life is a mix of feelings and rational thinking" [LW85]. While sociology defines trust in relation to social processes and relations, behavioural notions of trust founded in psychology or behavioural economics take an individualistic approach.

While some seminal writings have placed trust at the centre of sociological theorising [Luh79, Bar83], most computer security perspectives on humans largely ignore this branch of trust research – trust as a social construction – and, instead, conceptualise trust in line with psychology and behavioural economics [LN10, BFL96, Col09] as their primary aim is usability, e.g. [BCL15, CJL+13, KOB+08, RSM03, RSM05, RSM07, Tad10]. This therefore also leads to a reductive and individualistic view of trust, and the mistaken assumption that trust and *trusted* in computer science carry the same meaning as in the social sciences. For example, Camp et al. [CNM01, p.96] note: "trusted in the social sciences has exactly the same meaning of trusted in computer science [...] that which is trusted is trusted exactly because if it fails there is a loss". This not only assumes a common understanding of "trusted" in social and computer science, but also within the social sciences themselves; an assumption that is invalidated by the works cited above. From this non-exhaustive, yet, multi-perspective discussion on trust, it is evident that no single definition exists and that each distinct definition of trust serves its own specific purpose.

Human Agency. As we have seen, applying its security tests to humans is a key aspect of OSSTMM; an aspect that also distinguishes it from other security testing methodologies, see e.g. [PR10]. Critically, however, humans have agency which means that they have the capacity to act independently or collectively upon their environment, to influence their surroundings and to make choices. The notion of human agency has also received increased attention in scholarly writings pertaining to organisational consequences of technological advancements, e.g. [FP03, SO04, BR05]. In this body of literature, the notion of an "agentic turn" describes the increased agency of actors in relation to the organisation. From this perspective, security processes and technologies are shaped as much by the humans that use them as by their material objects.

However, Pfleeger and Caputo [PC12] note that while a key aspect of improving information security involves understanding human behaviour, most efforts "focus primarily on incorporating new technological approaches in products and processes". Similarly, Sasse and Flechais [SF05] argue that a secure system is a sociotechnical system based on an understanding of human behaviours to "prevent users from being the 'weakest link'". This is a view that was already cemented in Adams and Sasse's seminal work. It showed that a lack of under-standing of users resulted in an absence of user-centred design in security mech-anisms [AS99], which led users to both intentionally and unintentionally circum-vent such mechanisms (see also later work, e.g. [CJL+13, FC12, Wol17]). Such writings evidence the critical need to recognise and understand human agency in security terms, rather than treating humans as passive objects that need security to be done *to* them.

Security Testing Methodologies. OSSTMM is one of a handful of established penetration testing methodologies, standards and guidances such as [RBD+06, SSCO08, Cou15, NKR+12, MM14]. Most of these documents focus on technical steps to be carried out by the tester [RBD+06, MM14], while some focus more on pre- and post-engagement [Cou15] or provide a combination of both [NKR+12]. Besides OSSTMM no methodology lays any claim to being scientific or attempts to capture such a broad range of areas in which security could be consid-ered.[25] Indeed, typically these methodologies focus on network- and infrastruc-ture penetration testing, while specialised methodologies for web applications exist [MM14], i.e. the focus in other documents is considerably narrower than in OSSTMM. These methodologies are largely compatible by exhibiting a signifi-cant level of similarity in suggesting variants of a stepped discovery, enumeration and exploitation approach. It is worth noting, however, that regardless of this similarity some methodologies are incompatible. For example, the popular Pene-tration Testing Execution Standard [NKR+12] and OSSTMM are incompatible. The former prominently features threat modelling, whereas the latter insists on disregarding threats.

Academic treatments of OSSTMM or penetration testing methodologies as objects of study only come in the form of comparisons of various methodologies, either in the preliminaries of academic works to justify their particular choice of methodology or as publications in their own right, e.g. [Sha14, SJ15, KCSK15]. However, these comparisons restrict their attention to high-level features, such as the level of detail or what is and is not covered, as well as the genealogies of the different versions. To our knowledge, prior to this work no work existed in the literature that conceptually examines penetration testing methodologies on whether they deliver on what they promise.

---

[25] "Therefore, with version 3, the OSSTMM encompasses tests from all channels – Human, Physical, Wireless, Telecommunications, and Data Networks. This also makes it a perfectly suited for testing cloud computing, virtual infrastructures, mes-saging middleware, mobile communication infrastructures, high-security locations, human resources, trusted computing, and any logical processes which all cover multi-ple channels and require a different kind of security test." [Her10, Introduction, p.11].

5.2 Future Work

This work provokes the question of whether broader lessons can be drawn from it. While OSSTMM might be unsuitable for interrogating security, do its failings point to broader issues that should be addressed?

On the one hand, other standard security testing methodologies, such as PTES [NKR+12] or OWASP [MM14], avoid many of the issues which we criticise in this work. They do not define scores, they do not posit new notions of trust and they do not focus on human and social aspects of security. On the other hand, some of the issues we highlight in OSSTMM are more general.

Scores. While OSSTMM expresses the methodological dogma that scientific knowledge equals quantification particularly crudely this is not its privilege.[26] Rather, this conviction is common across information security, as exemplified, for example, in CVSS which claims to score security vulnerabilities by a single magnitude. Moreover, the somewhat bad reputation of security testing as a "tickbox exercise" speaks of the same limitation: counting rather than understanding. Echoing the critique of CVSS in [SHH+18], we thus suggest, too, that security professionals "skip converting qualitative measurements to numbers". The healthy debates in other disciplines (see Sect. 5.1) provide material for a debate within information security to examine the correctness and utility of assigning numerical values to various pieces of data.

Social. A mistake we criticise in OSSTMM is the failure to recognise that the moments of a social organisation are different from the moments of a computer network. This, too, is no privilege of OSSTMM as can be easily verified by the prevalence of mantras along the lines of "humans/people/users are the weakest link". This standpoint, which is as prevalent as it is wrong [AS99,PSF14], offers the curious indictment that people fail to integrate into a piece of technology that does not work for them. In the context of security testing this standpoint has a home under the heading of "social engineering" and its most visible expression: routine but ineffective phishing simulations [KS12]. It is worth noting, though, that even when the focus is exclusively on technology, not engaging with the social relations that this technology ought to serve may produce undesirable results, for example leading to designs of technological controls with draconian effects where less invasive means would have been adequate [DG10].

---

[26] Perhaps the most prominent quote in this spirit is attributed to Lord Kelvin: "When you can measure what you are speaking about, and express it in numbers, you know something about it; when you cannot measure it, when you cannot express it in numbers, your knowledge is of a meager and unsatisfactory kind; it may be the beginning of knowledge, but you have scarcely, in your thoughts, advanced to the stage of science.".

More broadly, the tendency of information security to rely on psychology, dominated by individualistic and behavioural perspectives and quantitative approaches to understanding social and human aspects of security [BCL15, CJL+13, FC12], may represent an obstacle. Alternative methodological approaches from the social sciences, particularly from sociology and even anthropology, such as semi-structured interviews, participant-led focus groups and ethnography offer promising avenues to deeply understand the security practices and needs in an organisation, see e.g. [GRF15].

A   A Synthetic Toy Example

In the following, we symbolically work through OSSTMM's calculation [Her10, Section 4.4] of the rav using a synthetic toy example of one host in a network providing a remote login service. To keep expressions compact we also do not model all the accesses, trusts and controls typically found in such a scenario. OSSTMM starts from the scope's Visibility P_V, Access P_A and Trust P_T. In our case, one host is visible $P_V = 1h$ which responds on one port $P_A = 1p$ (and on the IP layer, which we do not model here). In the interest of compactness, we will also assume $P_T = 0$. OSSTMM defines Operational Security as $OpSec_{sum} = P_V + P_A + P_T = 1h + 1p$. From this, OSSTMM computes the Operational Security base value

$$OpSec_{base} = \log^2 (1 + 100h + 100p).$$

Considering a logarithm is motivated in [Her10, Section 1.5] and [Her10, Section 4.1] but the particular choice of $\log^2(\cdot)$ is not motivated, the additive factor 1 is motivated to obtain zero in case of no attack surface. OSSTMM defines control meta classes $A = \{Au, Id, Re, Su, Ct\}$ and $B = \{NR, It, Pr, Cf, Al\}$, see Sect. 2. We assume only authentication LC_{Au} is enforced via a login $LC_{Au} = 1\ell$. In OSSTMM's terms the sum of loss controls in this example is thus

$$LC_{sum} \sum_{\lambda \in A \cup B} LC_\lambda = 1\ell.$$

Let $\lambda \in A \cup B$ be any control type. Then, OSSTMM further defines Missing Controls as

$$MC_\lambda = \max (OpSec_{sum} - LC_\lambda, 0)$$

and the sum of these missing controls as $MC_{sum} = \sum_{\lambda \in A \cup B} MC_\lambda$. True Controls are then defined as

$$TC_\lambda = OpSec_{sum} - TC_\lambda = OpSec_{sum} - \max (OpSec_{sum} - LC_\lambda, 0)$$
$$= \min (LC_\lambda, OpSec_{sum})$$

In our case, we would have to decide if $1h + 1p > 1\ell$, i.e. if one active host added to one port is greater than a login being applied. OSSTMM considers all formal variables as equal to the integer 1, suggesting the inequality does not hold in OSSTMM's model. The idea of this check is you cannot miss less than zero controls. OSSTMM does not motivate why controls are not normalised by $1/10$ here in contrast to other formulas. Following along, we obtain the True Controls base TC_{base} and the Full Controls base FC_{base}:

$$
\begin{aligned}
TC_{base} &= \log^2 \left(1 + 100 \times (OpSec_{sum} - MC_{sum}/10)\right) \\
&= \log^2 \left(10\ell + 1\right) \\
&= \log^2 \left(1 + 10 \times LC_{sum}\right) \\
&= FC_{base}
\end{aligned}
$$

$$
\begin{aligned}
SecLim_{sum} &= (L_V \times (OpSec_{sum} + MC_{sum})/OpSec_{sum}) + (L_W \times (OpSec_{sum} + MC_A)/OpSec_{sum}) \\
&\quad + (L_C \times (OpSec_{sum} + MC_B)/OpSec_{sum}) \\
&\quad + (L_E \times ((P_V + P_A) \times MC_{vg} + L_V + L_W + L_C)/OpSec_{sum}) \\
&\quad + (L_A \times (P_T \times MC_{vg} + L_V + L_W + L_C)/OpSec_{sum}) \\
&= \frac{(11\,h - \ell + 11\,p)^2}{(h+p)^2} + \frac{\left(10\,h - \ell + 10\,p + \frac{10\,(11\,h - \ell + 11\,p)}{h+p} + \frac{10\,(6\,h - \ell + 6\,p)}{h+p} + 60\right)^2}{100\,(h+p)^2} \\
&\quad + \frac{(6\,h - \ell + 6\,p)^2}{(h+p)^2} + \frac{\left(\frac{11\,h - \ell + 11\,p}{h+p} + \frac{6\,h - \ell + 6\,p}{h+p} + 6\right)^2}{(h+p)^2} + 36
\end{aligned}
$$

Fig. 1. Security limitations

These expressions are then combined into various Limitations Formula encoding vulnerabilities L_V, weaknesses L_W, concerns L_C, exposures L_E, anomalies L_A which are then combined to obtain the Security Limitations sum as given Figure 1 where $MC_{vg} = MC_{sum}/(10 \times OpSec_{sum})$. As before, $SecLim_{base}$ is defined as $\log^2(1 + 100 \times SecLim_{sum})$. Finally, Actual Security, the "true state of security as a hash of all three sections" [Her10, p.85] is defined as

$$
\begin{aligned}
ActSec &= 100 + FC_{base} - OpSec_{base} - \log(1 + 100 \times SecLim_{sum}) \\
&\quad - 1/100 \times OpSec_{base} \times (FC_{base} - \log(1 + 100 \times SecLim_{sum})) \\
&\quad + 1/100 \times FC_{base} \times \log(1 + 100 \times SecLim_{sum}).
\end{aligned}
$$

Expanding this formula for our toy example produces Figure 2. To compute the numerical rav value OSSTMM evaluates this expression at one for all formal variables. In our example, this gives a value of ≈ -12. The reader is invited to compare information provided by the symbolic or numerical Actual Security to the information provided by our initial informal description of the toy example. We stress that while the methodology, for example, forces the analyst to recognise that our login service provides no confidentiality ($LC_{Cf} = 0$ in OSSTMM terms), this does not distinguish OSSTMM from other security testing methodologies. Rather, OSSTMM's key procedure is the rav computation producing Figure 2.

$$ActSec = \log\left(\frac{19401\,h^4}{h^4 + 4\,h^3 p + 6\,h^2 p^2 + 4\,h p^3 + p^4} - \frac{3420\,h^3\ell}{h^4 + 4\,h^3 p + 6\,h^2 p^2 + 4\,h p^3 + p^4}\right.$$

$$+ \frac{201\,h^2\ell^2}{h^4 + 4\,h^3 p + 6\,h^2 p^2 + 4\,h p^3 + p^4} + \frac{77604\,h^3 p}{h^4 + 4\,h^3 p + 6\,h^2 p^2 + 4\,h p^3 + p^4}$$

$$- \frac{10260\,h^2\ell p}{h^4 + 4\,h^3 p + 6\,h^2 p^2 + 4\,h p^3 + p^4} + \frac{402\,h\ell^2 p}{h^4 + 4\,h^3 p + 6\,h^2 p^2 + 4\,h p^3 + p^4}$$

$$+ \frac{116406\,h^2 p^2}{h^4 + 4\,h^3 p + 6\,h^2 p^2 + 4\,h p^3 + p^4} - \frac{10260\,h\ell p^2}{h^4 + 4\,h^3 p + 6\,h^2 p^2 + 4\,h p^3 + p^4}$$

$$+ \frac{201\,\ell^2 p^2}{h^4 + 4\,h^3 p + 6\,h^2 p^2 + 4\,h p^3 + p^4} + \frac{77604\,h p^3}{h^4 + 4\,h^3 p + 6\,h^2 p^2 + 4\,h p^3 + p^4}$$

$$- \frac{3420\,\ell p^3}{h^4 + 4\,h^3 p + 6\,h^2 p^2 + 4\,h p^3 + p^4} + \frac{19401\,p^4}{h^4 + 4\,h^3 p + 6\,h^2 p^2 + 4\,h p^3 + p^4}$$

$$+ \frac{4600\,h^3}{h^4 + 4\,h^3 p + 6\,h^2 p^2 + 4\,h p^3 + p^4} - \frac{860\,h^2\ell}{h^4 + 4\,h^3 p + 6\,h^2 p^2 + 4\,h p^3 + p^4}$$

$$+ \frac{40\,h\ell^2}{h^4 + 4\,h^3 p + 6\,h^2 p^2 + 4\,h p^3 + p^4} + \frac{13800\,h^2 p}{h^4 + 4\,h^3 p + 6\,h^2 p^2 + 4\,h p^3 + p^4}$$

$$- \frac{1720\,h\ell p}{h^4 + 4\,h^3 p + 6\,h^2 p^2 + 4\,h p^3 + p^4} + \frac{40\,\ell^2 p}{h^4 + 4\,h^3 p + 6\,h^2 p^2 + 4\,h p^3 + p^4}$$

$$+ \frac{13800\,h p^2}{h^4 + 4\,h^3 p + 6\,h^2 p^2 + 4\,h p^3 + p^4} - \frac{860\,\ell p^2}{h^4 + 4\,h^3 p + 6\,h^2 p^2 + 4\,h p^3 + p^4}$$

$$+ \frac{4600\,p^3}{h^4 + 4\,h^3 p + 6\,h^2 p^2 + 4\,h p^3 + p^4} + \frac{105800\,h^2}{h^4 + 4\,h^3 p + 6\,h^2 p^2 + 4\,h p^3 + p^4}$$

$$- \frac{18400\,h\ell}{h^4 + 4\,h^3 p + 6\,h^2 p^2 + 4\,h p^3 + p^4} + \frac{800\,\ell^2}{h^4 + 4\,h^3 p + 6\,h^2 p^2 + 4\,h p^3 + p^4}$$

$$+ \frac{211600\,h p}{h^4 + 4\,h^3 p + 6\,h^2 p^2 + 4\,h p^3 + p^4} - \frac{18400\,\ell p}{h^4 + 4\,h^3 p + 6\,h^2 p^2 + 4\,h p^3 + p^4}$$

$$\left.+ \frac{105800\,p^2}{h^4 + 4\,h^3 p + 6\,h^2 p^2 + 4\,h p^3 + p^4}\right)^2$$

$$\cdot\left(\frac{1}{100}\log\left(100\,h + 100\,p + 1\right)^2 - \frac{1}{100}\log\left(10\,\ell + 1\right)^2 - 1\right)$$

$$- \frac{1}{100}\left(\log\left(10\,\ell + 1\right)^2 + 100\right)\log\left(100\,h + 100\,p + 1\right)^2 + \log\left(10\,\ell + 1\right)^2 + 100$$

Fig. 2. Actual security

References

[AC10] US Army and US Marine Corps. Counterinsurgency Field Manual. Number 3–24. Cosimo Inc. (2010)

[Ahm16] Ahmed, R.K.A.: Security metrics and the risks: an overview. IJCTT **41**(4), 106–112 (2016)

[AP13] AlFardan, N.J., Paterson, K.G.: Lucky thirteen: breaking the TLS and DTLS record protocols. In: 2013 IEEE Symposium on Security and Privacy, pp. 526–540. IEEE Computer Society (2013)

[Arm09] British Army: British Army Field Manual Volume 1 Part 10: Countering Insurgency. Ministry of Defence (2009)

[AS99] Anne Adams and Martina Angela Sasse: Users are not the enemy. Commun. ACM **42**(12), 40–46 (1999)

[Ban82] Bandura, A.: Self-efficacy mechanism in human agency. Am. Psychol. **37**(2), 122 (1982)

[Bar83] Barber, B.: The Logic and Limits of Trust. Rutgers University Press (1983)

[BCL15] Blythe, J.M., Coventry, L., Little, L.: Unpacking security policy compliance: the motivators and barriers of employees' security behaviors. In: Eleventh Symposium On Usable Privacy and Security (SOUPS 2015), pp. 103–122 (2015)

[BFL96] Blaze, M., Feigenbaum, J., Lacy, J.: Decentralized trust management. In: Proceedings 1996 IEEE Symposium on Security and Privacy, pp. 164–173. IEEE (1996)

[BH11] Breier, J., Hudec, L.: Risk analysis supported by information security metrics. In: Proceedings of the 12th International Conference on Computer Systems and Technologies, pp. 393–398. ACM (2011)

[Ble98] Bleichenbacher, D.: Chosen ciphertext attacks against protocols based on the RSA encryption standard PKCS #1. In: Krawczyk, H. (ed.) CRYPTO 1998. LNCS, vol. 1462, pp. 1–12. Springer, Heidelberg (1998). https://doi.org/10.1007/BFb0055716

[BNH10] Ben-Ner, A., Halldorsson, F.: Trusting and trustworthiness: what are they, how to measure them, and what affects them. J. Econ. Psychol. 31(1), 64–79 (2010)

[BR05] Boudreau, M.-C., Robey, D.: Enacting integrated information technology: a human agency perspective. Organ. Sci. 16(1), 3–18 (2005)

[Bra14] Brazil, J.: Security metrics to manage change. Netw. Secur. 2014(10), 5–7 (2014)

[BV04] Bierhoff, H.-W., Vornefeld, B.: The social psychology of trust with applications in the internet. Analyse Kritik 26(1), 48–62 (2004)

[BWDW98] Buzan, B., Wæver, O., De Wilde, J.: Security: A New Framework for Analysis. Lynne Rienner Publishers (1998)

[Cam14] Campbell, G.: Measures and Metrics in Corporate Security. Elsevier (2014)

[CCZC05] Corral, G., Cadenas, X., Zaballos, A., Teres Cadenas, M.: A distributed vulnerability detection system for WLANs. In: Imre, S., Crowcroft, J. (eds.) 1st International ICST Conference on Wireless Internet, WICON, pp. 86–93. IEEE (2005)

[CJL+13] Crossler, R.E., Johnston, A.C., Lowry, P.B., Hu, Q., Warkentin, M., Baskerville, R.: Future directions for behavioral information security research. Comput. Secur. 32, 90–101 (2013)

[CK16] Caselli, M., Kargl, F.: A security assessment methodology for critical infrastructures. In: Panayiotou, C.G.G., Ellinas, G., Kyriakides, E., Polycarpou, M.M.M. (eds.) CRITIS 2014. LNCS, vol. 8985, pp. 332–343. Springer, Cham (2016). https://doi.org/10.1007/978-3-319-31664-2_34

[CLH09] Cook, K.S., Levi, M., Hardin, R.: Whom Can We Trust? How Groups, Networks, and Institutions Make Trust Possible. Russell Sage Foundation (2009)

[CNM01] Camp, L.J., Nissenbaum, H., McGrath, C.: Trust: a collision of paradigms. In: Syverson, P. (ed.) FC 2001. LNCS, vol. 2339, pp. 91–105. Springer, Heidelberg (2002). https://doi.org/10.1007/3-540-46088-8_10

[Col09] Colwill, C.: Human factors in information security: the insider threat-who can you trust these days? Inf. Secur. Tech. Rep. 14(4), 186–196 (2009)

[Coo05] Cook, K.S.: Networks, norms, and trust: the social psychology of social capital 2004 cooley mead award address. Soc. Psychol. Q., 4–14 (2005)

[Cou15] Penetration Test Guidance Special Interest Group PCI Security Standards Council. PCI Penetration Testing Guidance, March 2015. https://www.pcisecuritystandards.org/documents/Penetration_Testing_Guidance_March_2015.pdf

[Cre17] Creasey, J.: A guide for running an effective penetration testing programme. Technical report, CREST (2017)

[CZCG05] Corral, G., Zaballos, A., Cadenas, X., Grane, A.: A distributed vulnerability detection system for an intranet. In: Proceedings 39th Annual 2005 International Carnahan Conference on Security Technology. IEEE (2005)

[DF11] Dunning, D., and Detlef Fetchenhauer: Understanding the psychology of trust. Psychology Press (2011)

[DG10] Danezis, G., Gürses, S.: A critical review of 10 years of privacy technology. In: Proceedings of Surveillance Cultures: A Global Surveillance Society, pp. 1–16 (2010)

[DG14] D'Arcy, J., Greene, G.: Security culture and the employment relationship as drivers of employees' security compliance. Inf. Manag. Comput. Secur. **22**(5), 474–489 (2014)

[dJ16] de Jiménez, R.E.L.: Pentesting on web applications using ethical hacking. In: 2016 IEEE 36th Central American and Panama Convention, pp. 1–6, November 2016

[Duf15] Duffy, C.: Learning Penetration Testing with Python. Packt Publishing Ltd. (2015)

[FC12] Furnell, S., Clarke, N.: Power to the people? The evolving recognition of human aspects of security. Comput. Secur. **31**(8), 983–988 (2012)

[FML+14] Fiaschetti, A.: Control architecture to provide E2E security in interconnected systems: the (new) SHIELD approach. In: Advances in Information Science and Applications - Volume II (2014)

[FMP+15] Fiaschetti, A., Morgagni, A., Panfili, M., Lanna, A., Mignanti, S.: Attack-surface metrics, OSSTMM and common criteria based approach to "composable security" in complex systems. WSEAS Trans. Syst. **14** (2015)

[FP03] Feldman, M.S., Pentland, B.T.: Reconceptualizing organizational routines as a source of flexibility and change. Adm. Sci. Q. **48**(1), 94–118 (2003)

[Gol04] Goldreich, O.: The Foundations of Cryptography, vol. 2. Cambridge University Press, Basic Applications (2004)

[GRF15] Greig, A., Renaud, K., Flowerday, S.: An ethnographic study to assess the enactment of information security culture in a retail store. In: 2015 World Congress on Internet Security (WorldCIS), pp. 61–66. IEEE (2015)

[GW11] Gligor, V., Wing, J.M.: Towards a theory of trust in networks of humans and computers. In: Christianson, B., Crispo, B., Malcolm, J., Stajano, F. (eds.) Security Protocols 2011. LNCS, vol. 7114, pp. 223–242. Springer, Heidelberg (2011). https://doi.org/10.1007/978-3-642-25867-1_22

[Har04] Hardin, R.: Trust & Trustworthiness. Russell Sage Foundation (2004)

[Har13] Hardin, R.: Government without trust. J. Trust Res. **3**(1), 32–52 (2013)

[Hay10] Hayden, L.: IT Security Metrics: A Practical Framework for Measuring Security & Protecting Data. McGraw-Hill Education Group (2010)

[Her10] Herzog, P.: The Open Source Security Testing Methodology Manual, vol. 3 (2010)

[HHM+14] Holik, F., Horalek, J., Marik, O., Neradova, S., Zitta, S.: Effective penetration testing with Metasploit framework and methodologies. In: 2014 IEEE 15th International Symposium on Computational Intelligence and Informatics (CINTI), November 2014

[Hir81]   Hirschberg, L.: Der Grundsatz der Verhältnismäßigkeit, Schwarz (1981)

[ISE08]   ISECOM: Hacking Exposed Linux: Linux Security Secrets & Solutions. McGraw-Hill (2008)

[JAHA16] Johansen, G., Allen, L., Heriyanto, T., Ali, S.: Kali Linux 2 - Assuring Security by Penetration Testing. Packt Publishing Ltd. (2016)

[Jaq07]   Jaquith, A.: Security Metrics: Replacing Fear, Uncertainty, and Doubt. Pearson Education (2007)

[Kay09]   Kay, J.: Do Not Discount What You Cannot Measure. Financial Times, 22 September 2009

[Kay11]   Kay, J.: Obliquity: Why Our Goals Are Best Achieved Indirectly. Profile Books (2011)

[KBM15]   Knowles, W., Baron, A., McGarr, T.: Analysis and recommendations for standardisation in penetration testing and vulnerability assessment: penetration testing market survey. Technical report, BSI (2015)

[KCSK15] Kang, Y.-S., Cho, H.-H., Shin, Y., Kim, J.-B.: Comparative study of penetration test methods. Adv. Sci. Technol. Lett. **87**, 34–37 (2015)

[KH06]   Kovacich, G.L., Halibozek, E.P.: Security Metrics Management: How to Measure the Costs and Benefits of Security. Butterworth-Heinemann (2006)

[KJ08]   Kaur, M., Jones, A.: Security metrics-a critical analysis of current methods. In: Australian Information Warfare and Security Conference. School of Computer and Information Science, Edith Cowan University, Perth, Western Australia (2008)

[KOB+08] Kindberg, T., O'Neill, E., Bevan, C., Kostakos, V., Fraser, D.S., Jay, T.: Measuring trust in WI-FI hotspots. In: Proceedings of the SIGCHI Conference on Human Factors in Computing Systems, pp. 173–182 (2008)

[Kra99]   Kramer, R.M.: Trust and distrust in organizations: emerging perspectives, enduring questions. Ann. Rev. Psychol. **50**(1), 569–598 (1999)

[KS12]   Kirlappos, I., Sasse, M.A.: Security education against phishing: a modest proposal for a major rethink. IEEE Secur. Priv. Mag. **10**(2), 24–32 (2012)

[KUM96]   Kuzon, W., Urbanchek, M., McCabe, S.: The seven deadly sins of statistical analysis. Ann. Plast. Surg. **37**, 265–272 (1996)

[Lin00]   Lindenberg, S.: It takes both trust and lack of mistrust: the workings of cooperation and relational signaling in contractual relationships. J. Manage. Governance **4**(1), 11–33 (2000)

[LN10]   Lee, J.-E.R., Nass, C.I.: Trust in computers: the computers-are-social-actors (CASA) paradigm and trustworthiness perception in human-computer communication. In: Trust and Technology in a Ubiquitous Modern Environment: Theoretical and Methodological Perspectives, pp. 1–15. IGI Global (2010)

[Luh79]   Luhmann, N.: Trust and Power. Wiley (1979)

[LW85]   David Lewis, J., Weigert, A.: Trust as a social reality. Soc. Forces **63**(4), 967–985 (1985)

[McP17]   McPhee, M.: Mastering Kali Linux for Web Penetration Testing. Packt Publishing (2017)

[MM14]   Meucci, M., Muller, A.: OWASP testing guide v4.0 (2014). https://www.owasp.org/index.php/OWASP_Testing_Project

[MOD15]   MOD: Allied joint doctrine for psychological operations (jp-3.10.1) (2015)

[Mol06]   Mollering, G.: Trust: Reason, Routine, Reflexivity. Emerald Group Publishing (2006)

[NKR+12] Nickerson, C.: The Penetration Testing Execution Standard (2012). http://www.pentest-standard.org/index.php. Accessed 8 June 2019

[oD14] Department of Defense: Joint Publication 3–13: Information Operations (2014)

[Off14] Offensive Security Ltd.: Penetration testing with Kali Linux, v1.0.1. Course Material (2014)

[Pay06] Payne, S.C.: A guide to security metrics. SANS security essentials: GSEC practical assignment (2006)

[PC12] Pfleeger, S.L., Caputo, D.D.: Leveraging behavioral science to mitigate cyber security risk. Comput. Secur. **31**(4), 597–611 (2012)

[PR10] Prandini, M., Ramilli, M.: Towards a practical and effective security testing methodology. In: Proceedings of the 15th IEEE Symposium on Computers and Communications, pp. 320–325. IEEE Computer Society (2010)

[PS13] Pornel, J.B., Saldaña., G.A.: Four common misuses of the likert scale. Philippine J. Soc. Sci. Hum. Univ. Philippines Visayas **18**(2), 12–19 (2013)

[PSF14] Pfleeger, S.L., Angela Sasse, M., Furnham, A.: From weakest link to security hero: transforming staff security behavior. J. Homel. Secur. Emerg. Manag. **11**(4), 489–510 (2014)

[RBD+06] Rathore, B., et al.: Information Systems Security Assessment Framework (ISSAF) (2006)

[RS08] Rothstein, B., Stolle, D.: The state and social capital: an institutional theory of generalized trust. Comp. Polit. **40**(4), 441–459 (2008)

[RSM03] Riegelsberger, J., Angela Sasse, M., McCarthy, J.D.: The researcher's dilemma: evaluating trust in computer-mediated communication. Int. J. Hum. Comput. Stud. **58**(6), 759–781 (2003)

[RSM05] Riegelsberger, J., Angela Sasse, M., McCarthy, J.D.: The mechanics of trust: a framework for research and design. Int. J. Hum. Comput. Stud. **62**(3), 381–422 (2005)

[RSM07] Riegelsberger, J., Angela Sasse, M., McCarthy, J.D.: Trust in mediated interactions. In: The Oxford Handbook of Internet Psychology, pp. 53–70 (2007)

[Sch09] Schulte, J.: Real time services information assurance test plan. Technical report, Defense Information Systems Agency (2009)

[SF05] Sasse, A.M., Flechais, I.: Usable security: why do we need it? how do we get it? In: Garfinkel, S., Cranor, L. (eds) Security and Usability. O'Reilly (2005)

[Sha14] Shackleford, D.: A penetration testing maturity and scoring model. Talk at RSA Conference 2014 (2014)

[SHH+18] Spring, J.M., Hatleback, E., Householder, A., Manion, A., Shick, D.: Towards improving CVSS. Technical report, Software Engineering Institute, Carnegie Mellon University (2018). https://resources.sei.cmu.edu/library/asset-view.cfm?assetid=538368

[SJ15] Shanley, A., Johnstone, M.: Selection of penetration testing methodologies: a comparison and evaluation. In: 13th Australian Information Security Management Conference (2015)

[SO04] Schultze, U., Orlikowski, W.J.: A practice perspective on technology-mediated network relations: the use of internet-based self-serve technologies. Inf. Syst. Res. **15**(1), 87–106 (2004)

[SP11] Stuttard, D., Pinto, M.: The Web Application Hacker's Handbook: Discovering and Exploiting Security Flaws, 2nd edn. Wiley (2011)

[SSCO08] Scarfone, K., Souppaya, M., Cody, A., Orebaugh, A.: Technical guide to information security testing and assessment. Technical report, National Institute of Standards and Technology (2008)

[Tad10] Taddeo, M.: Trust in technology: a distinctive and a problematic relation. Knowl. Technol. Policy **23**(3–4), 283–286 (2010)

[TFS+18] Tugnarelli, M.D., Fornaroli, M.F., Santana, S.R., Jacobo, E., Díaz, J.: Analysis of methodologies of digital data collection in web servers. Comput. Sci. CACIC 2017, 265–271 (2018)

[Tul08] Tullberg, J.: Trust–the importance of trustfulness versus trustworthiness. J. Soc. Econ. **37**(5), 2059–2071 (2008)

[UKS13] Bank Mellat v Her Majesty's Treasury (No. 2) [2013] UKSC 39, 19 June 2013

[VNVS10] JF Van Niekerk and Rossouw Von Solms: Information security culture: a management perspective. Comput. Secur. **29**(4), 476–486 (2010)

[WC03] Weber, L.R., Carter, A.I.: The Social Construction of Trust. Springer, Boston (2003). https://doi.org/10.1007/978-1-4615-0779-6

[Wil13] Wilhelm, T.: Professional Penetration Testing. Syngress, 2nd edn. (2013)

[Wol17] Woltjer, R.: Workarounds and trade-offs in information security-an exploratory study. Inf. Comput. Secur. (2017)

Vision: A Critique of Immunity Passports and W3C Decentralized Identifiers

Harry Halpin[✉]

K.U. Leuven, ESAT/COSIC, Kasteelpark Arenberg 10, 3001 Leuven, Belgium
harry.halpin@esat.kuleuven.be

Abstract. Due to the widespread COVID-19 pandemic, there has been a push for 'immunity passports' and even technical proposals. Although the debate about the medical and ethical problems of immunity passports has been widespread, there has been less inspection of the technical foundations of immunity passport schemes. These schemes are envisaged to be used for sharing COVID-19 test and vaccination results in general. The most prominent immunity passport schemes have involved a stack of little-known standards, such as Decentralized Identifiers (DIDs) and Verifiable Credentials (VCs) from the World Wide Web Consortium (W3C). Our analysis shows that this group of technical identity standards are based on under-specified and often non-standardized documents that have substantial security and privacy issues, due in part to the questionable use of blockchain technology. One concrete proposal for immunity passports is even susceptible to dictionary attacks. The use of 'cryptography theater' in efforts like immunity passports, where cryptography is used to allay the privacy concerns of users, should be discouraged in standardization. Deployment of these W3C standards for 'self-sovereign identity' in use-cases like immunity passports could just as well lead to a dangerous form identity totalitarianism.

Keywords: Immunity passports · Decentralized identifier · Verifiable credentials · W3C · Security · Privacy · Standardization

1 Introduction

With the outbreak of COVID-19 in 2020, there became a surge of interest in what are called 'immunity passports' and various technical proposals to implement these passports in order to allow people to work and travel. In fact, one academic paper claims that in terms of COVID-19 immunity passports, there's "an app for that" [13]. Indeed, given the scale of the crisis inflicted on the world by COVID-19, it should not be surprising that the vision of a digital application that could allow people to return to work and travel would be appealing to many governments, and some governments such as Chile[1] and El Salvador are

---

[1] https://www.thelancet.com/journals/lancet/article/PIIS0140-6736(20)31096-5/fulltext.

© Springer Nature Switzerland AG 2020
T. van der Merwe et al. (Eds.): SSR 2020, LNCS 12529, pp. 148–168, 2020.
https://doi.org/10.1007/978-3-030-64357-7_7

continuing to propose COVID-19 immunity passports.[2] A vaguely UN-related organization called 'ID2020' has begun to certify digital immunity passports by companies such as BLOCK BioScience as a "good ID" to sell to governments.[3] Therefore, even though there is yet no evidence that a negative test after COVID-19 infection presents long-lived immunity, there appears to be momentum for digital immunity passports. While there has already been considerable medical, ethical, and legal objections to immunity passports [26], there has yet to be a technical analysis of the proposed standards used by immunity passports.

Although the possible social benefits and harms of immunity passports are outside of the scope of a technical analysis and so will only be briefly discussed, it should go without saying that the status of a person's COVID-19 antibody test results are sensitive personal data. Therefore, a technical analysis should provide a comprehensive overview of the privacy and security properties of any given immunity passport system. The particular use-case of immunity passports and the wider context of digital identity is reviewed in Sect. 2. Then each component of the proposed technical architecture of the COVID Credentials Initiative (CCI),[4] which has already gained considerable media coverage[5] and claims over a hundred members, will be inspected. CCI currently has at least fifteen members building on World Wide Web Consortium (W3C) standards, a membership-driven standards bodies known for such standards as XML and early versions of HTML. Note that while we use the term 'immunity passport' (as well as 'immunity credential,' the digital implementation of an 'immunity passport') in this analysis, our usage of the term and analysis also covers antibody test results in general, including vaccination test results.

For each component, we will first present the standard and then a critique. First, the W3C Verifiable Credentials Data Model is analyzed in Sect. 3 and then W3C Decentralized Identifier standards in Sect. 4. This lets us analyze in detail the technical architecture put forward when used in an actual user-facing immunity passport app that is built on these W3C standards in Sect. 5. In conclusion, we'll review the dangers of unscoped and premature optimization in standardization and ways to prevent emergencies such as COVID-19 from leading to the abuse of security standardization in Sect. 6, before concluding with our vision for next steps and future research in Sect. 7.

---

[2] https://www.premiumtimesng.com/coronavirus/408007-el-salvador-to-give-immunity-passport-to-those-who-recovered-from-covid-19.html.

[3] https://www.biometricupdate.com/202008/id2020-certifies-blok-bioscience-immunity-passport-with-self-sovereign-approach-to-digital-id.

[4] https://www.covidcreds.com/.

[5] https://www.coindesk.com/covid-19-immunity-passport-unites-60-firms-on-self-sovereign-id-project.

2   Immunity Passports: The Killer Use-Case of Digital Identity?

2.1   Immunity Passports

An immunity passport can be thought of as a kind of digital *credential* that contains information needed to determine if an individual has contracted a particular disease or not and whether or not they may be immune to future development of the disease. The concept of immunity credentials were inspired by the idea of a digital update to the well-known 'Carte Jeune' paper cards needed to prove yellow fever vaccination and so authorize travel in certain countries. However, it has been noted the development of yellow fever is not analogous to COVID-19, but rather to measles, as measles became widespread in the population and vaccination was mandatory (and so no paper card for travel was needed) [26]. However, a possible future COVID-19 vaccine could be proposed as a kind of 'immunity passport' to allow travel and work.

An immunity credential for COVID-19 would have to contain the measurement of antibodies taken by a particular institution at a particular time. The serological antibody measurements include both Immunoglobulin M (the largest antibody) and Immunoglobulin G (the most common antibody) responses to COVID-19 [29]. There are other tests that are commonly available that include tests for the presence of COVID-19 DNA, such as polymerase chain reaction (PCR) tests and antigen tests, but these tests only detect if COVID-19 is active and so do not detect whether or not a person has been infected or vaccinated in the past.

Critique. There are a large number of critiques of the very concept of immunity credentials and we will only overview a selection. It has been thought that having COVID-19 antibodies would lead to immunity for a period of time, although recently there have been documented cases of reinfection [29]. Of course, the primary critique is that the immunoglobulin tests do not actually provide any level of immunity medically and that, even if they did, the level of false positives and negatives is still too high to be acceptable [26]. The effects of antibodies is to confer some level of immunity for an unknown, but likely very short, period of time [26]. Medical research is still unclear how long antibodies could prevent COVID-19, if at all, and whether the COVID-19 virus itself is mutating such that antibodies are even relevant [29].

Social effects of immunity credentials are possibly dangerous as immunity credential holders could become an 'immunity elite' with increased social stratification from those without certificates, violating existing laws on discrimination in many countries [25]. One dangerous outcome would be people attempting to infect themselves in order to gain the advantages conferred by immunity [26]. Although the term 'immunity passport' has gotten such a bad reputation that it may seem unlikely to be implemented, the push for COVID-19 vaccination could cause the idea of a digital certificate for COVID-19 test results to be revived in the near future. A digital certificate for COVID-19 test results would be subject to the same critique on a social level as an immunity passports.

2.2 Digital Identity

The field of digital identity has long existed in national standards for identity databases, but became a focus of standardization after the tremendous success of the World Wide Web led many people to become interested in the prospects for an internet-enabled digital identity. On the one hand, the Web used an identity system, the domain name system (DNS), which has been wildly successful at providing unique names for web-sites. On the other hand, the internet did not include any provision for providing unique identities for people and organizations that worked across websites, with cookies as a means for implicitly establishing user identities being added later in the development of the Web by browsers.

An augmented social network built on digital identity was theorized as possibly leading to another cycle of innovation and profit as powerful as the original Web [24]. Although obviously limited and ontologically problematic [18], digital identity is usually construed as an unique identifier connected to a set of attributes, such as a name, age, and citizenship. 'Self-sovereign' identity gave the identified individual themselves the ability to control these attributes, as opposed to a centralized government or corporation.[6]

The goal of digital identity is to avoid identifier collision by assigning globally unique identifiers. The first proposed standard that tried to assign humans and organizations permanent identifiers was eXtensible Resource Identifiers (XRIs) at the OASIS standards body.[7] Individuals are given identifiers such as *+david.*[8] Like DNS, XRIs are resolved by XDI (XRI Data Interchange), which would then retrieve an XRDS (Extensible Resource Descriptor Sequence) with the person's attributes such as name and address. Also like DNS, XDI was run by a single organization called *XDI.org* that held a license to patents from the Cordance company.[9] Although XRIs were put into early federated identity versions of OpenID [35], XRIs failed to gain real-world usage, and they were eventually dropped from the more successful federated OpenID Connect system [37], which was instead built instead on the IETF OAuth standard for authorizing accessing to data without globally unique identifiers [19].

In contrast to the standards for digital identity that focus on assigning globally unique identifiers, cryptographic research focused on anonymous credentials that allowed users to directly show to verifiers their claims without revealing their identity, much less using a globally unique identifier [10]. Of particular interest are zero-knowledge proofs for identity [7] that led to attribute-based credential systems such as Microsoft's U-Prove [6] and IBM's Idemix [8] (currently

---

[6] https://www.lifewithalacrity.com/2016/04/the-path-to-self-soverereign-identity.html.

[7] OASIS is the Organization for the Advancement of Structured Information Standards, was mostly known for various XML related standards and allowing, unlike the W3C and IETF, patent licensing fees in standards.

[8] https://www.oasis-open.org/committees/download.php/15376/xri-syntax-V2.0-cs.html.

[9] https://danbri.org/words/2008/01/29/266.

used in Hyperledger Fabric.[10]) These anonymous credential schemes offered a high degree of privacy without trusted third parties. Although some schemes use blockchain technologies to achieve decentralization, these are still too computationally expensive for real-world use [14]. There has even been some initial work like the SecureABC proposal on deploying cryptographic anonymous credentials in the context of immunity passports, although the ethical concerns still remain and there seems to be no move towards widespread implementation of the SecureABC anonymous credential scheme for immunity passports [21].

One of the core problems with digital identity was the requirement for a centralized database of these globally unique identifiers. Blockchain technology appeared to both guarantee the non-collusion of identifiers and not require a centralized database of identifiers while enabling a seemingly infinite number of identifiers to be minted. Thus, the vision of a decentralized database of globally unique identifiers for people seems plausible technically, and many of the efforts and people involved in prior work on digital identity re-emerged in the W3C in order to re-invent standards for a globally unique identity for every person on top of blockchain technology. This effort received relatively little attention until COVID-19 led to a push for immunity passports. While there earlier seemed no real use-case for a cross-border global identity system, immunity passports were seized upon as the 'killer' use-case by groups like CCI. Given the rush to push for immunity passports and vaccination test results to revive travel by various governments, with trials even starting in the United Kingdom[11] and funding for W3C digital identity standards by the Department of US Homeland Security,[12] it would seem that a technical analysis of the W3C standards being pushed into these immunity passports is in order.

3   W3C Verifiable Credentials

Currently, all proposed immunity credential schemes rely on an obscure standard, the W3C Verified Credential Data Model 1.0 standard [38]. A verified credential is defined by the specification as "a tamper-evident credential that has authorship that can be cryptographically verified" [38], or in other words, a cryptographically signed message. However, rather than simply sign a byte-string, W3C Verifiable Credentials present an abstract data model for the idea of *claims*, which are any list of attributes and values pertaining to a *subject*, the "entity about which claims are made" [36]. These claims are created by an *issuer* who then creates a verifiable credential, which in turn are processed by a *verifier*. The issuer is split into the issuer and the holder roles. For example, the issuer could be a medical laboratory that is testing the COVID-19 immune response of a patient, the subject and holder of a verifiable claim about their antibody

---

[10] https://hyperledger-fabric.readthedocs.io/en/release-2.0/idemix.html.

[11] The United Kingdom is testing the closed-source CommonPass by the Commons Project, as announced at https://thecommonsproject.org/newsroom/safer-travel-and-accelerate-border-reopenings.

[12] https://www.sbir.gov/sbirsearch/detail/1302459.

status. While the specification is written to have one assume the holder is the person themselves, there is nothing to prevent the holder being a government database that the patient has no knowledge of.

More importantly, the claims are not a simple list of attribute value pairs or even arithmetic circuits that could be verified in zero-knowledge, but instead a graph build from the nearly forgotten W3C Semantic Web standards [4], which has important ramifications upon processing. Namely, the Verified Credential specification recommends JSON or the Semantic Web serialization that uses JSON, JSON-LD [39]. Cryptographic signatures can either be specified by IETF JSON Web Tokens [23] or the non-standardized "Linked Data Proofs" document [31]. An example of a W3C Verifiable Credential for immunity credentials created by a member of the COVID Credentials Initiative is given in Fig. 1.[13]

```
{
    "@context": [
        "https://www.w3.org/2018/credentials/v1",
        "https://w3c-ccg.github.io/vc-examples/covid-19/v1/v1.jsonld"
    ],
    "id": "http://example.com/credential/123",
    "type": [
        "VerifiableCredential",
        "ImmunoglobulinDetectionTestCard"
    ],
    "issuer": {
        "id": "did:web:vc.transmute.world",
        "location": {
            "@type": "CovidTestingFacility",
            "name": "Stanford Health Care",
            "url": "https://stanfordhealthcare.org/"
        }
    },
    "issuanceDate": "2019-12-11T03:50:55Z",
    "expirationDate": "2020-12-11T03:50:55Z",
    "name": "Immunoglobulin Detection Test Card",
    "description": "Immunoglobulin detection tests are based on the qualitative detection of IgM and IgG...",
    "credentialSubject": {
        "id": "did:key:z6MkjRagNiMu91DduvCvgEsqLZDVzrJzFrwahc4tXLt9DoHd",
        "type": "ImmunoglobulinDetectionTestSubject",
        "givenName": "Louis",
        "familyName": "Pasteur",
        "birthDate": "1958-07-17",
        "IgM": false,
        "IgG": true,
        "image": "data:...''
    }
}
```

Fig. 1. Example W3C Verified Credential for an "Immunity Passport"

As can be seen from this example, Verifiable Credentials essentially offer a number of mandatory properties, such as `type` to determine the kind of credential, an `id` (to refer to a W3C DID [36]), and `issuer` property with a date of issuance (`issuanceData`) and date of expiration (`expirationDate`), as well as information stored about the subject as `credentialSubject`. Following W3C Semantic Web conventions used in the W3C Resource Description Framework (RDF) standard [30], nearly all identifiers are identified either with a standard `https:` URL or a kind of DID [36]. As such a verifiable credential is simply a data format, the role of an application, as illustrated in Fig. 2,[14] will be creating

---

[13] https://github.com/decentralized-identity/c19-vc.com/blob/master/src/
bindingModels/ImmunoglobulinDetectionTestCard.json.

[14] The image is from https://github.com/decentralized-identity/c19-vc.com.

what is termed by the W3C as a *verifiable presentation* that presents some of subset of the attributes for human inspection or further machine processing.

Critique. Note that injectivity of the serialization scheme is necessary for the security of digital signatures. The W3C Verifiable Credentials standard can depend on the problematic Semantic Web RDF format, which lacks standardized bit-serialization necessary for signatures [9]. RDF does not specify a syntax like XML, but 'semantic' graphs of URIs (Uniform Resource Identifiers, such as *http://example.org*) and values where the same graph can be serialized in different manners [30]. Worse, there is no unified way to skolemize 'blank nodes' (i.e. existential variables) across serialization formats. Instead, RDF features a number of ad-hoc canonicalization forms given in non-standard documents, with W3C VC relying on a non-standard algorithm.[15] Also, Semantic Web serialization can depend on the resolution of external documents to URIs to 'link' data, similar in spirit to XML namespaces [30]. The Semantic Web also even has issues with TLS support [17]. Further increasing the likelihood of attacks, implementers are recommended that Linked Data Proofs "are detached from the actual payload."[16] The combination of these problems, where a variable number of signatures can be arbitrarily detached and re-attached to messages combined with the (possibly insecure) retrieving of unknown external documents leads RDF in general, and likely Verifiable Credential implementations that use RDF, to be vulnerable to the same kind of attacks that rendered XML digital signatures insecure in practice [33].

In detail, this leads to *signature exclusion* and *signature replacement* attacks where an adversary can remove the signature of a signed message, perhaps replace it with another signature, and to trick the verifier into falsely accepting the message as valid due to ambiguity in parsing. There exists a mitigation of these canonicalization and serialization issues as VCs can be used without RDF, and instead serialized with the well-specified IETF JSON Web Tokens (JWT) serialization [23]. Yet even in this case, there still exist in some JWT implementations (although the IETF specifications have fixed these issues in the specification) the ability to easily misuse cryptography, which can lead to intentional *cryptographic downgrade* attacks on the cryptography in JWTs [22]. In general, it seems as if all that is needed is to prove a signature of a valid health care provider or hospital on a credential presented by a user; it is unclear why an error-prone data format without a clear byte order that is badly suited for cryptography should be used. A simple signature over a byte-string signifying the result would suffice.

The most likely reason for using Semantic Web standards is that W3C Verifiable Credentials are to be used for data integration rather than privacy. Semantic Web standards are notoriously inefficient due to being stored as labeled graphs with existential variables as well as cycles, making canonicalization difficult [15]. Each blank node must be uniformly given a stable identifier, and different graphs

---

[15] The "RDF Dataset Normalization" document http://json-ld.github.io/normalization/ spec/.
[16] https://www.w3.org/TR/vc-imp-guide/.

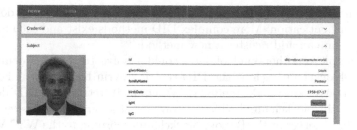

Fig. 2. Verifiable presentation of an 'Immunity Passport'

can be output in different orders. Even if canonicalized and then serialized, the graph isomorphism problem is NP complete so it cannot be determined if two graphs match efficiently. The Semantic Web has found usage in government data integration by the Department of Homeland Security [11] as the goal of the W3C standards is to allow the "linking" of data via the reuse of URIs as labels of nodes in the graph [39]. Linking of user data seems at odds with user privacy, as privacy is typically defined as unlinkability [34]. However, the ability to link patient data may have use cases for the government and medical data.

4   W3C Decentralized Identifiers

Decentralized identity management means that identity is provisioned using a decentralized technical infrastructure such as distributed ledger technology [12], and so there is no single identity provider or key registry. A **Decentralized Identifier (DID)** is a W3C standard under development to provide a uniform naming scheme for what is termed "subjects" to be identified [36]. The scope of subjects has cosmic ambitions: "Anything can be a DID subject: person, group, organization, physical thing, digital thing, logical thing" but the DID document maintains that each DID is unique per subject, so that "a DID has exactly one DID subject" and that somehow "a DID is bound exclusively and permanently to its one and only subject" [36]. In the context of immunity credentials, a DID is an attempt to create one or more universally unique identifiers for every person that includes whether or not they have been infected by COVID-19 or not.

Technically, a DID is simply a URI scheme that specifies a *DID method*, which in turn is used to resolve a DID into a concrete (if possibly unsigned) *DID document*. The *DID document* in turn contains references to key material and routing information to one or more *DID service endpoints* that allow access to yet another document describing the subject of the DID and so including explicitly personally identifiable information (PII) in RDF using VCs. DIDs are represented as an `id` relationship in a DID document. An example DID is shown in Fig. 1 as `did:key:z6MkjRagNiMu91DduvCvgEsqLZDVzrJzFrwahc4tXLt9DoHd`. This method, as defined in yet another non-standardized document,[17] defines a

---

[17] https://w3c-ccg.github.io/did-method-key/.

DID document where a single Ed25519 public key is used for signing documents as well as authentication. More complex DID methods exist and each new DID-enabled system can add register a new method.[18]

For example, another kind of DID could resolve to a DID document via access to a blockchain such as the DID-centric Sovrin blockchain.[19] For example, the DID `did:sov:29wksjcn38djfh47ruqrtcd5` retrieves a DID document from the Sovrin blockchain,[20] which is considered a *verifiable registry* as much as a centralized server or the Bitcoin blockchain according to the W3C Verifiable Credentials standard [38]. Verifiable registries are simply a public key infrastructure for the key discovery needed to verify a W3C VC, and so a blockchain is used in this context merely as a global public database of time-stamped DID documents that contain keys and service end-points. An end-point can retrieve additional personal data about DID subjects like an immunity credential.

Critique. Although the idea of a registry with at least one unique identifier for every possible object that may exist could be considered itself a suspect concept for a standard, W3C DIDs suffer from a number of purely technical weaknesses. The resolution from a DID to a DID document is customized per implementation, and in practice permissioned federations such as Sovrin resolve the DID to the necessary DID document, and so the blockchain is equivalent to using a public database of DID documents (without access control) replicated by a threshold number of trusted authorities. In other words, there seems to be no technical reason outside availability to use a blockchain rather than a trusted public third party database for the verifiable registry containing DIDs [41]. Unlike other blockchain-based systems like Claimchain [28], there is no access control specified and all identifiers are shared in public. The privacy issues are to some extent worse in W3C DIDs than in even centralized or federated identity systems, as correlation attacks may not only be done by a malicious identity provider, but by any actor as typical DIDs are stored in public chains and, if the DID document is public, anyone can search the chain to discover the times of changes not only to DIDs, but to key material if the DID document is public.[21]

Most importantly, there is no way to enforce the privacy of any attributes attached to the Verifiable Credentials produced by service end-points accessed via DID documents and DIDs. As for DID documents themselves, it is only stated that "it is strongly recommended that DID documents contain no PII" [36]. As they are effectively permanent identifiers written to a public blockchain, W3C DIDs may of course be correlated. One-time use DIDs are not enough, as the W3C DID standard notes "the anti-correlation protections of pseudonymous DIDs are easily defeated if the data in the corresponding DID Documents can

---

[18] https://w3c.github.io/did-spec-registries/.
[19] https://sovrin-foundation.github.io/sovrin/spec/did-method-spec-template.html.
[20] https://sovrin.org/library/sovrin-protocol-and-token-white-paper/.
[21] Although the DID standard permits these attacks, these issues could in theory be addressed per implementation in a customized manner, as Microsoft claims is done in their ION identity system: https://techcommunity.microsoft.com/t5/identity-standards-blog/ion-booting-up-the-network/ba-p/1441552.

be correlated" [36]. While it could be claimed that simply storing key material and end-points for services does not compromise user privacy and only identifiers without personal data is stored on the chain, storing identifiers as well as keys and service end-points publically can leak valuable data. For example, the addition of service end-points for COVID-19 testing centers would leak the fact that a person with this key material had been tested for COVID-19, along with the likely approximate physical geolocation as correlated with the hospital and day of the test, as given by the update to the DID document.

Although DIDs claim to support zero-knowledge proofs, there is no advanced cryptography used outside of RSA and elliptic curve Ed25519 signatures in the standards themselves [36]. In other publications, at least one of the authors of the W3C DID standard believes a "trusted witness," i.e. a trusted third party nominated by the user with control over their personal data, is a better paradigm than zero-knowledge proofs due to the lack of trust in the verifier or holder of a credential [1], although the solution of adding yet another trusted third party does not seem to solve the actual problem, but merely displace it. Other DID deployments, like those at Microsoft, claim to that they will use zero-knowledge proofs but end up being anonymous credentials with no special need for the identity machinery of DIDs and VCs.[22]

Another question is whether or not the blockchain is necessary at all. If DIDs are indeed supposed to be for one-time usage, then why use DIDs on a blockchain at all rather than just an anonymous credential scheme without DIDs? The actual Verifiable Credentials are not stored on the blockchain but stored by service end-points, which can be centralized servers rather than some necessarily decentralized actor. Indeed, it appears that in many of these cases, it is assumed the actual party that holds the VC document is a third-party service that functions as an *identity provider*. This identity provider could be relatively benign, such as the hospital that performed the test, but it could be yet another for-profit blockchain-based digital identity startup. Rather than disintermediate identity providers like Facebook or government identity databases, the actual database access simply requires the additional step of contacting yet another third party database, namely the verifiable registry, before communicating with their actual personal data pointed to from the verifiable registry. The blockchains used as verifiable registries can be decentralized but can also be federated permissioned blockchains using "proof of authority" where a quorum, or sometimes any member, can simply add a block with a new DID identifier. So not only is there no gain in terms of privacy, but no gain in terms of decentralization if decentralization is to be defined as the absence of a trusted component in a system [40]. A system would leak far less data if the holder of a VC simply included a method to directly contact the issuer with the VC itself rather than use excessive redirection based on a public blockchain for key management.

---

[22] https://github.com/decentralized-identity/snark-credentials/blob/master/whitepaper.pdf.

5   Immunity Credential Systems: A Case Study

Although there are many systems for immunity credentials being built (currently over fifteen) in countries ranging from Hong Kong to Italy according to the COVID-19 Credential Initiative Implementation Workstream Homepage,[23] most of the published proposals are high-level sketc.hes [2]. As of late 2020, only one academically published immunity credential system has a detailed specification called "COVID-19 Antibody Test/Vaccination Certification: There's an App For That," by Eisenstadt et al. [13]. Like the CCI work, this app uses the DID and VC W3C standards. The paper puts forward the technical design goals that an immunity credential is meant to address in addition to the non-technical requirements of being "cost-effective" and "easy to administer" [13]:

- **Privacy-preserving**
- **Un-forgeable**
- **Scalable**: "to millions of users"
- **Easily verifiable**: "while still preserving privacy"

The overall motivation for using digital certificates for immunity passports is that, not only are they more cost-effective and more scalable but that they can be secure as "a paper version is too vulnerable to alteration or forgery" [13]. It seems as if the primary security argument of Eisenstadt et al. is that digital signatures are unforgable, and so could prevent both a hospital from forging a credential or a person from using a false credential. They also seemingly narrowly conceive of privacy as only the explicit prevention of the release of personal identifying information such as a patient's name and social security number, while traditionally it would be considered that linking usages of a credential would violate privacy. There is no explicit threat model given, but it does seem like the authors are aiming for a weak local passive adversary, rather than an active adversary that can observe changes of state in the blockchain used by DIDs in order to re-identify subjects or one that can carry out replay attacks with credentials.

The minimal PII needed by each actor in the immunity credential system is not detailed. The privacy and security properties are claimed to be fulfilled by the use of W3C DIDs in tandem with the actual VCs containing the immunity results stored using a Semantic Web architecture known as 'Solid,' designed by W3C director and inventor of the Web, Berners-Lee [32]. This architecture is composed of *pods* which store RDF data like VCs using HTTP access points. The core concept is that personal data can be stored locally on a device like a mobile phone or even a "favorite cloud server" [13]. The claim of Eisendstat et al. is that "the provider's access to the data is limited by the user's preference," although currently it appears no cryptographic techniques are used to encrypt the data in Solid [13]. There is an unformalized access control language used by

---

[23] https://docs.google.com/document/d/1dbWvs1m8uziTsbhUQv_nPofTXAyDSkxI5 CZtoo1SlRY.

pods.[24] Currently backed by a startup called Inrupt,[25] the platform is build in Javascript.

The app uses a distributed ledger called OpenEthereum, a fork of Ethereum by the Open University and ran by a consortium (and so is call a "Consortium blockchain"). In contrast to Ethereum but similar to other DID-based chains like Sovrin, it is based on "proof of authority" (i.e. a permissioned blockchain where any validator or quorum of validators may write to the chain, but not other actors like users). It is then argued that while DIDs allow pseudonyms and Solid pods give an user "a choice regarding whether and where to host personal information" (which would include the results of the COVID-19 tests), "a hash of the Verifiable Credential is stored on the Consortium blockchain"so that the immunity credential itself can be verified [13].

The information flow of the application is given below and illustrated in Fig. 3, where information is assumed to shared using QR codes:

- **Step 1.** The patient (the holder, also the "subject" of a DID) and the hospital doing the immunoglobulin tests (the issuer) are assigned DIDs (A) that can be resolved on the permissioned blockchain (B). After an identity check (C), the patient gives their DID and required personal information for an immunity credential to the hospital.
- **Step 2.** The hospital gives antibody test (D) and sends its DID with the test results signed by its public key to the patient (E), which then receives it and uploads a hash of the signed immunity credential to the blockchain.
- **Steps 3.** The patient can then show their employer (the verifier) the immunity credential (F) with associated DID (G), who can then check the hash of the credential by looking up the DID and verifying if the signature of the test results in the immunity credential are correctly attributed to the hospital by retrieving the hospital's DID and retrieving the hash of immunity credential from the blockchain to compare it to the immunity credential shown by the patient (H), and then approve or deny the patient some action.

Critique: As Solid is being backed by the inventor of the Web, one would hope it would offer privacy or security properties. Yet Solid offers no security properties or privacy properties, currently having only the aforementioned access control language but usage of kernel security modules or other ways of providing assurance are missing. There are draft ideas on authentication.[26] It seems that giving a user the choice of where to store their COVID-19 antibody test results will likely not lead to more security, as users may store their test results on a mobile phone whose operating system needs updating, a insecure personal server, or in some other location that is highly unlikely to be secure in terms of systems administration. While Solid democratizes storage and avoids creating a centralized honey-pot of test results, does it make sense to allow people to be given a technical choice over where to store their data rather than embedded

---

[24] https://github.com/solid/web-access-control-spec.
[25] https://inrupt.com/.
[26] https://solid.github.io/authentication-panel/solid-oidc/.

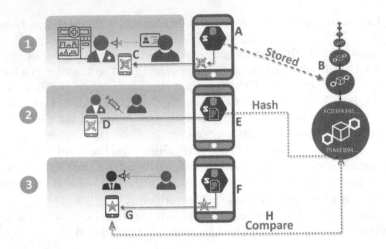

Fig. 3. Information Flow of an W3C Verified Credential and DID for an "immunity passport" as given in Eisenstadt et al. [13]

in the operating system or using secure enclaves? The use of RDF, due to the underlying graph model, has poor scalability compared to traditional relational databases or key-value stores [15]. The main purpose of VCs using RDF in Solid appears to be to integrate data using unique identifiers based on URIs like DIDs.

The use of Semantic Web technologies appears to be designed to make medical data more amendable to fusion and analytics by hospitals or governments, given there is a dearth of user-centric services that consume or produce Semantic Web data. This makes it difficult to believe that "pairwise-unique DIDs and public keys" will be used in practice, as that would eliminate any benefits of using Semantic Web techniques [13]. If a DID was used just once, then why have an identifier at all? Another core idea is that "user preference" can also eliminate the capture of data by servers, as Eisenstadt et al. claim that "Everything in this app is decentralized. Anyone wishing to abandon involvement in this kind of certification can just delete the Verifiable Credentials stored on their Solid Pods. There will be no records whatsoever, as if they had never been on the system" [13]. Yet there is no serious proposal to prevent the operating system of a mobile phone or a server from copying the immunity certificate for the purposes of sharing, and deletion cannot be guaranteed to have actually happened.

The authors of the paper also seem to have misconceptions about cryptography, leading to insecure uses of hashes for storing immunity credential information in a publicly accessible blockchain. In particular, the authors hold that storing the hash of their immunity certificate on the blockchain allows "individuals who have been tested to change their minds and quit the scheme, knowing that even cryptographically encoded data will be 'orphaned' (no data pointing to it), rendering it meaningless" [13]. The authors seem not to be aware of dictionary attacks and how the storage of sensitive data using hashes can be securely implemented. Although it is true that for arbitrary data, a hash is a one-way function that can not be reversed per se and maps this data to fixed size values, by itself a hash function is typically deterministic and the possible claims embedded in the credential are finite. For example, the number of unique birth-dates of living individuals is on the order of fifty thousand, and so if one wishes one to discover a hashed birthdate, one simply iterates through the birthday values (as in a 'dictionary') with the hash function until a match is discovered. This would be even simpler for test results that are either positive or negative, and continues to holds true even when "deleting data on the Solid Pods" although the authors claim that this "will also turn the hashes on the blockchain into 'orphans' (no data pointing to the hash), i.e. the hashes will become meaningless: it is not possible to recover the original data from a hash" [13]. If an adversary knows some fairly basic personal data about a person such as their name and birthday, as per the example in Fig. 1, and one wished to discover their test results, an adversary could simply iterate through the possible results of an immunity test to determine the results of a patient's immunity test from only the hash on the blockchain.

The storage of even hashed immunity certificates on a public blockchain also is a poorly thought out idea for avoiding leaking sensitive data on a public blockchain. Using a hash would only make sense if appropriate salting could be done, but the salt would have to be somehow shared to verify the hash. Simply using a seemingly 'random' string of bytes in the VC like a photo would not be enough to secure the hash, as the photo would be revealed and remain the same over usages of the credential and so would not be a salt, as an adversary could capture it. Alternatively, publishing the ciphertext of the results encrypted under an ephemeral asymmetric public key on the blockchain, where the corresponding decryption key could be given on an as needed basis, would be a better design. Nonetheless, having such sensitive data permanently available on a public blockchain, even if encrypted, would be a risk. W3C DIDs attempt to do the right thing by publishing only a reference to a key on chain. Even in the case where only a public key is published on the blockchain, it would be better to use encryption than hashing to preserve privacy, as has been explored in work with well-defined privacy and security properties for decentralized key management [28].

Given these earlier problems, it should not come as a surprise that this immunity credential architecture does not address the fundamental problem of digital immunity passports: Having this information in digital form by nature increases the ability for this data to be copied and altered. Although the use of cryptography can prevent some of these attacks, this is not the case in the proposed architecture. For example, the verifier could not copy the passport and do a replay attack with the credential. This is easily possible, as no private key material operations are required for usage of the immunity credential that require the holder having any secret key material such as decryption of or selectively disclosing the credential.

Surprisingly, the only cryptographic operation the verifier has to do is retrieve the public key of the issuer from the blockchain. Despite various claims that "the app allows the user selectively to present only the specific test result," no details on zero-knowledge proofs are given by Eisenstadt et al. [13]. It is recommended by Eisenstadt et al. that when using digital credentials an identity check with a physical photographic identity card is done, although this methodology would also argue in favor of simply using physical paper certificates as immunity credentials [13]. Eisenstadt et al. propose that it should be possible to have "burned" the photographic identity into the credential, i.e. have a copy of a valid visual identity as part of the credential so that physical national identity paperwork should not have to be checked when showing an immunity credential [13], although this increases the amount of sensitive data used in the credential. In terms of W3C standardization, methods for verifying a credential holder's identity is left outside of the scope of the document. There is a mention of a challenge-response protocol to prevent replay attacks given in the non-normative Verifiable Credentials Implementation Guidelines but the protocol, as outlined, uses an unsigned nonce and so is vulnerable to replay attacks.[27]

The privacy properties of the immunity passport scheme proposed are claimed to result primarily from the supposed virtues of the underlying W3C standards "the concepts underlying Verifiable Credentials and the Decentralized Verification of Data with Confidentiality are diametrically opposed to any kind of central data storage or Big Brother-style snooping and data collection, and indeed provide excellent and agreed standards for avoiding such snooping and data collection" [13]. As shown earlier, these claims over the privay and security of the W3C DID and VC standards are dubious. The immunity passport design put forward by Eisenstadt et al. seems aimed at those with a background in the "Semantic Web" (a cluster of W3C standards for data management [20]) and are missing cryptographic security assumptions as well as a realistic privacy impact assessment. However, there may be other immunity credential schemes that address these concerns in the future that may be attempted to be rolled out in the future. The problem is both the idea of immunity credentials and the standards used to implement, and these are separable if interlinked problems. Trying to move the paradigm from the ill-conceived idea of immunity passports to the newer but very similar idea of vaccination test certification, Eisenstadt et al. (whose earlier versions[28] envisioned deployment to the whole population) now state that credentials "should only be applied to workers in healthcare and other comparable key sectors" and added the term "vaccination" to their title [13]. Yet the design still has the same problems. The other problem is that there is a more structural issue regarding how these W3C standards like VCs and DIDs came to become standardized and therefore assumed to be suitable for high assurance use-cases like immunity credentials.

---

[27] https://www.w3.org/TR/vc-imp-guide/.
[28] https://arxiv.org/abs/2004.07376.

6   The Abuse of Security Standardization

The goal of security standardization should be both to guarantee the security and privacy properties of a particular technology and then promote their widest deployment. The technical proposals for immunity passports have almost all entirely been based on the World Wide Web Consortium's Decentralized Identifier (W3C DID) and Verifiable Credentials (W3C VC) standards, and these standards are currently being proposed for widespread usage by groups like the COVID-19 Credentials Initiative. The problem is two-fold: 1) a lack of clarity on what is a standard at the W3C and 2) the lack of review by the wider security and privacy community despite being standardized, in the case of W3C VC, or "standards-track" like W3C DID. A diagnosis of the underlying issues is required in order to assure the high quality of future security standardization.

First, what makes a standard? In the case of the W3C, a standard is a standard by virtue of a guarantee of royalty-free licensing of the underlying technology. In the case of the growth of the Web, the importance of the W3C is that it is in effect a patent pool for the World Wide Web that allowed many developers and companies to build on the Web in a permission-less fashion.[29] W3C standards are explicitly licensed by W3C members under a royalty-free license.[30] In contrast, the IETF "Note Well" policy simply requires disclosure of known patents by individuals.[31] The much stronger W3C policy creates a kind of 'patent war-chest' composed of all W3C standards, from XML to HTML5. This patent pool is then enforced by a 'balance of terror' so that any member that makes a patent claim on a W3C standard triggers their loss of royalty-free licensing for *all* W3C standards. The W3C patent pool was created precisely as an attempt to prevent patents from becoming part of standards at the W3C. The membership requirement of the W3C, as opposed to the more informal IETF, is due in part to the licensing requirements of patents. This protection against patents is one of the primary features of standards as a common good.

The problem is that the line between what is a standard and what is not a standard at the W3C has blurred. Over the years the relative importance of patents declined and the importance of communities based on open standards and protocols increased, first due to the development of HTML as a 'living standard' by WHATWG outside of the W3C,[32] and then as shown by the explosion of interest in blockchain technologies since 2017. This led to the formation at the W3C of Community Groups, which are open to all and have no review from the rest of the W3C but can produce documents that appear to have the imprimcater of the W3C without review, with patent licensing being only to contributions and only opt-in to the entire specification.

In the case of W3C's digital identity efforts around W3C VCs and DIDs, there is a larger extended group of documents, ranging from the nascent DID

---

[29] Note that a patent holder can still claim patent infringement even if an idea is embodied in a standard (such as an IETF RFC) and in open source code.
[30] https://www.w3.org/Consortium/Patent-Policy-20040205/.
[31] http://www.rfc-editor.org/rfc/rfc3979.txt.
[32] https://html.spec.whatwg.org/.

Authentication to Linked Data Proofs, that it appears are also crucial to immunity passports and DID usage in general. These documents originate in either a W3C Community Group or the newly created Decentralized Identity Foundation,[33] but are considered as "standards" by proponents of W3C Verifiable Credentials and DIDs. This could confuse anyone, including a government interested in immunity passports, into thinking the underlying technology was both unburdened of intellectual property and of a high standard in terms of security and privacy. Furthermore, this development of an endless multitude of non-standards (mostly by the same small editorial group as the W3C VC and DID standards) makes implementation by developers an error-prone work of endless exegesis and seems to serve primarily to deflect criticism from the actual problems with the existing W3C standards for digital identity. Every privacy and security issue with DIDs and VCs can be claimed to be 'solved' by yet another half-baked non-standard document or a product that has some yet-to-be-released non-standardized feature. Therefore, standards bodies should clearly separate standards from non-standards, scope standardization efforts to a finite number of documents, and reduce the dependency of the former on the latter.

Second, the purpose of security standardization can be construed as wide review and analysis of the security properties of standards. It is unclear how Verifiable Credentials and DIDs became W3C standards without review by security and privacy experts. One reason could be the influx of dues-paying blockchain companies as W3C members and a lack of attention from browser-oriented companies. As Verifiable Credentials were relatively unsuccessful in a large number of fields, ranging from internet of things [3] to educational credentials [27], the work did not attract the attention of the security research community. Also, as the standardization effort has no clear boundaries, it is unclear where to begin or end such a security and privacy review. With the growing interest from governments in immunity passport schemes, the security community should focus on these global identity schemes. Yet these identity standards have crucial dependencies on non-standardized documents that are in a state of flux.

The W3C and other standards bodies should impose more stringent guidelines for security and privacy review on their future work. Overall, although the group of documents needed for W3C VC-based immunity passports is vast, these documents do not possess the technical (and in particular, cryptographic) detail needed for a security and privacy analysis, much less formal verification. Our thesis is that the underlying effort around immunity passports and associated W3C efforts are examples of *cryptography theater*, which we define as the appeal to cryptography without a concrete specification or protocol in order to claim to be secure without necessarily being so. While the designers of W3C DIDs and VCs may have designed the technology to the best of their ability, every standard should have a rigorous security review. A state of emergency caused by COVID-19 should require more, not less, review in terms of security and privacy for immunity passports given the possibility of widespread usage and abuse.

---

[33] https://identity.foundation.

7   Conclusion

Our vision of security standardization is that it should either provide wide review of proposed standards in order to correct security and privacy flaws, or prevent their standardization in the first place. The fact that specifications like W3C Verifiable Credentials even became standards is problematic without security and privacy review by experts, and it would be better if future standards that touched upon security and privacy were done at the IETF and follow a more rigorous multi-stakeholder process that involves academics and verification of the claims of security properties of the standards, as was done in TLS 1.3 [5]. The unnecessary complexity and lack of review of these standards can lead to concrete privacy and security harms for users, who are naturally confused by claims of privacy and security dependent on cryptography.

The use of W3C standards to legitimize immunity passports is a prime example of how a security standardization process, without an actual functional standards body that achieves wide review by experts, can be hijacked by self-interested government or business interests without providing any protection for users. It simply is dangerous to build on standards that are not well-understood, and standards bodies like the W3C that 'rubber stamp' such standards should be held to account by the security research community.

As shown, there may be concrete steps that can help the W3C. For example, all RDF related formats can be dropped from VCs until bit-serialization is standardized. Work on DIDs at the W3C can simply be halted as global identity on a blockchain cannot be done in a secure and privacy-preserving manner without advanced cryptography, which DIDs lack. For the use-cases of identity management, there are many well-known cryptographic techniques that offer strong and rigorous guarantees of privacy and security, although they are not used as the foundation of the W3C standards for digital identity, but merely included as an optional afterthought. One somewhat surprising aspect of immunity passport proposals is their reliance on blockchain technology. Blockchain technology has uses, but these uses should be justified in terms of concrete security and availability properties given by design goals.

The most concrete immunity passport proposal dangerously puts the hash of personal data on the blockchain [13]. Even the use of blockchain technology by specifying resolution of an on-chain mapping of an identifier to a key in systems like Sovrin ends up being a redirect to centralized servers, undermining a claim of the blockchain promoting decentralization. As the use of blockchain technology does not seem necessary for the goals of the immunity passports and likely hinders rather than helps privacy, immunity passports – and more widely both W3C DIDs and VCs – use blockchain for blockchain's sake.[34]

The problem is not just one of broken standards and an off-the-rails standardization process at the W3C. The conflict over DRM at the W3C demon-

---

[34] One plausible reason for a blockchain would be censorship-resistance via peer-to-peer gossip networks, but this seems to be an implausible goal for immunity credentials. Lastly, a decentralized PKI in of itself does not require a blockchain even for censorship resistance of key material [28].

strated already the W3C standards process was prone for corporate capture and capable of being abused [16]. The underlying problem is the cultish desire for a "self-sovereign" global identity system runs counter to privacy. Standards bodies should avoid cults. The technical proposal for immunity passports based on W3C DIDs could allow the COVID-19 crisis to be a driver for a larger vision of a global digital identity system where every single human has a permanent and globally unique identifier. This form of digital identity runs counter to privacy, opening the door for a new form of *identity totalitarianism* where every person must be identified in a database – of which a blockchain is merely a fashionable new form – in order to be part of society.

The question should not be whether or not immunity passports can be technically secure and private, but whether or not they should be built at all. Due to the state of emergency caused by COVID-19, fundamental rights – such as the freedom of movement – could be taken away based on data connected to persistent digital identity. Yet temporary measures meant for a purpose as seemingly harmless as reviving tourism could become normalized as the blockchain-based identity databases are by design permanent and are difficult to disassemble once the crisis has past. Blockchain technology could just as easily allow automated discrimination based on personal data as it could enable travel during COVID-19, and form the technical basis for a 'social credit' system that crosses borders.

Digital identity has many use-cases outside of immunity passports, from the relatively benign domain of education to the critical infrastructure of medical data, but also many dangers. For example, the use of blockchain identities for refugees could be useful in allowing them access to bank accounts, but could also be easily used for surveillance.[35] Identity systems exist to help large institutions manage and control populations. The promotion of digital immunity passports using the rhetoric of decentralization and self-sovereignty may be appealing and done with the best of intentions, but the COVID-19 crisis should not be treated as an excuse to push out standards or software that may harm users.

References

1. Arnold, R., Longley, D.: Zero-knowledge proofs do not solve the privacy-trust problem of attribute-based credentials: what if Alice is evil? IEEE Commun. Stand. Mag. **3**(4), 26–31 (2019)
2. Bansal, A., Garg, C., Padappayil, R.P.: Optimizing the implementation of COVID-19 Immunity Certificates using blockchain. J. Med. Syst. **44**(9), 1–2 (2020)
3. Bartolomeu, P.C., Vieira, E., Hosseini, S.M., Ferreira, J.: Self-sovereign identity: use-cases, technologies, and challenges for industrial IoT. In: 2019 24th IEEE International Conference on Emerging Technologies and Factory Automation (ETFA), pp. 1173–1180. IEEE (2019)
4. Berners-Lee, T., Hendler, J., Lassila, O.: The semantic web. Sci. Am. **284**(5), 34–43 (2001)

---

[35] https://www.qeh.ox.ac.uk/content/blockchain-refugees-great-hopes-deep-concerns.

5. Bhargavan, K., Blanchet, B., Kobeissi, N.: Verified models and reference implementations for the TLS 1.3 standard candidate. In: 2017 IEEE Symposium on Security and Privacy (SP), pp. 483–502. IEEE (2017)
6. Brands, S., Paquin., C.: U-Prove cryptographic specification v1.0 (2010)
7. Camenisch, J., Krenn, S., Shoup, V.: A framework for practical universally composable zero-knowledge protocols. In: Lee, D.H., Wang, X. (eds.) ASIACRYPT 2011. LNCS, vol. 7073, pp. 449–467. Springer, Heidelberg (2011). https://doi.org/10.1007/978-3-642-25385-0_24
8. Camenisch, J., Van Herreweghen, E.: Design and implementation of the Idemix anonymous credential system. In: Proceedings of the 9th ACM Conference on Computer and Communications Security, pp. 21–30 (2002)
9. Carroll, J.J.: Signing RDF graphs. In: Fensel, D., Sycara, K., Mylopoulos, J. (eds.) ISWC 2003. LNCS, vol. 2870, pp. 369–384. Springer, Heidelberg (2003). https://doi.org/10.1007/978-3-540-39718-2_24
10. Chaum, D.: Security without identification: transaction systems to make Big Brother obsolete. Commun. ACM **28**(10), 1030–1044 (1985)
11. Ding, L., Kolari, P., Finin, T., Joshi, A., Peng, Y., Yesha, Y., et al.: On homeland security and the Semantic Web: a provenance and trust aware inference framework. In: Proceedings of the AAAI Spring Symposium on AI Technologies for Homeland Security (2005)
12. Dunphy, P., Petitcolas, F.A.P.: A first look at identity management schemes on the blockchain. IEEE Secur. Priv. **16**(4), 20–29 (2018)
13. Eisenstadt, M., Ramachandran, M., Chowdhury, N., Third, A., Domingue, J.: COVID-19 antibody test certification: There's an app for that. IEEE Open J. Eng. Med. Biol. **1**, 148–155 (2020)
14. Garman, C., Green, M., Miers, I.: Decentralized anonymous credentials. In: Proceedings of the Network and Distributed System Security Symposium - NDSS 2014. Internet Society, February 2014
15. Groppe, S.: Data Management and Query Processing in Semantic Web Databases. Springer Science & Business Media, New York (2011)
16. Halpin, H.: The crisis of standardizing DRM: the case of W3C encrypted media extensions. In: Ali, S.S., Danger, J.-L., Eisenbarth, T. (eds.) SPACE 2017. LNCS, vol. 10662, pp. 10–29. Springer, Cham (2017). https://doi.org/10.1007/978-3-319-71501-8_2
17. Halpin, H.: Semantic Insecurity: Security and the Semantic Web, p. 2017. In Society, Privacy and the Semantic Web-Policy and Technology (PrivOn (2017)
18. Halpin, H.: Decentralizing the social web. In: Bodrunova, S.S., et al. (eds.) INSCI 2018. LNCS, vol. 11551, pp. 187–202. Springer, Cham (2019). https://doi.org/10.1007/978-3-030-17705-8_16
19. Hardt, D.: The OAuth 2.0 authorization framework. IETF RFC 6749 (2012). https://tools.ietf.org/html/rfc6749
20. Hepp, M., Leymann, F., Domingue, J., Wahler, A., Fensel, D.: Semantic business process management: a vision towards using Semantic Web Services for business process management. In: IEEE International Conference on e-Business Engineering (ICEBE 2005), pp. 535–540. IEEE (2005)
21. Hicks, C., Butler, D., Maple, C., Crowcroft, J.: SecureABC: Secure AntiBody Certificates for COVID-19. arXiv preprint arXiv:2005.11833 (2020)
22. Jager, T., Paterson, K.G., Somorovsky, J.: Backwards compatibility attacks on state-of-the-art cryptography. In: NDSS, One bad apple (2013)
23. Jones, M., Bradley, J., Sakimura, N.: JSON Web Token (JWT). IETF RFC 7519 (2015)

24. Jordan, K., Hauser, J., Foster, S.: The augmented social network: building identity and trust into the next-generation Internet. First Monday **8**(8) (2003)
25. Kaminer, D.: Discrimination against employees without COVID-19 antibodies. New York Law Journal (2020)
26. Kofler , N., Baylis, F.: Ten reasons why immunity passports are a bad idea (2020)
27. Kontzinos, C., Kokkinakos, P., Skalidakis, S., Markaki, O., Karakolis, V., Psarras, J.: Decentralised qualifications' verification and management for learner empowerment, education reengineering and public sector transformation: The QualiChain Project. Mobile, Hybrid, and On-line Learning (eLmL 2020), p. 51 (2020)
28. Kulynych, B., Lueks, W., Isaakidis, M., Danezis, G., Troncoso, C.: Claimchain: improving the security and privacy of in-band key distribution for messaging. In: Proceedings of the 2018 Workshop on Privacy in the Electronic Society, pp. 86–103 (2018)
29. Larremore, D.B., Bubar, K.M., Grad, Y.H.: Implications of test characteristics and population seroprevalence on immune passport strategies. Clinical Infectious Diseases (2020)
30. Lassila, O., Swick., R.R.: Resource Description Framework (RDF) model and syntax specification. W3C Recommendation (1999)
31. Longley, D., Sporny, M.: Linked Data Proofs. W3C Draft Community Group Report (2020). https://w3c-ccg.github.io/ld-proofs/
32. Mansour, E.: A demonstration of the Solid platform for social web applications. In: Proceedings of the 25th International Conference Companion on World Wide Web, pp. 223–226. International World Wide Web Conferences Steering Committee (2016)
33. McIntosh, M., Austel, P.: XML signature element wrapping attacks and countermeasures. In: Proceedings of the 2005 Workshop on Secure Web Services, pp. 20–27. ACM (2005)
34. Pfitzmann, A., Hansen, M.: A terminology for talking about privacy by data minimization: anonymity, unlinkability, undetectability, unobservability, pseudonymity, and identity management (2010)
35. Recordon, D., Reed, D.: OpenID 2.0: a platform for user-centric identity management. In: Proceedings of the Second ACM Workshop on Digital Identity Management, pp. 11–16. ACM (2006)
36. Reed, D., Sporny, M., Sabadello, M.: Decentralized Identifiers (DIDs) v1.0. W3C Working Draft (2020). https://www.w3.org/TR/did-core/
37. Sakimura, N., Bradley, J., Jones, M., de Medeiros, B., Mortimore, C.: OpenID Connect Core 1.0 incorporating errata set 1 (2014). http://openid.net/specs/openid-connect-core-1_0.html
38. Sporny, M., Longley, D., Chadwick, D.: Verifiable Credentials. W3C Recommendation (2019). https://www.w3.org/TR/verifiable-claims-data-model/
39. Sporny, M., Longley, D., Lanthaler, M., Champin, P.-A., Lindstrom, N.: JSON-LD 1.1: a JSON serialization for Linked Data. W3C Recommendation (2020). https://www.w3.org/TR/json-ld11/
40. Troncoso, C., Isaakidis, M., Danezis, G., Halpin, H.: Systematizing decentralization and privacy: lessons from 15 years of research and deployments. Proc. Privacy Enhancing Technol. **2017**(4), 404–426 (2017)
41. Wüst, K., Gervais, A.: Do you need a blockchain? In: 2018 Crypto Valley Conference on Blockchain Technology (CVCBT), pp. 45–54. IEEE (2018)

Author Index

Printed in the United States
By Bookmasters